# Cash, Color, and Colonialism

## DATE DUE

# CASH, COLOR, AND COLONIALISM
## The Politics of Tribal Acknowledgment

Renée Ann Cramer

University of Oklahoma Press : Norman

Library of Congress Cataloging-in-Publication Data

Cramer, Renée Ann.
  Cash, color, and colonialism / the politics of tribal acknowledgment /
Renée Ann Cramer.
    p.   cm.
  Includes bibliographical references and index.
  ISBN 978-0-8061-3671-4 (cloth)
  ISBN 978-0-8061-3987-6 (paper)
    1. Federally recognized Indian tribes. 2. Indians of North America—
Legal status, laws, etc. 3. Gambling on Indian reservations—Law and
legislation—United States. I. Title.

  KF8210.R42.C73 2005
  342.7308'72—dc22
                                                              2004058011

The paper in this book meets the guidelines for permanence and durability
of the Committee on Production Guidelines for Book Longevity of the
Council on Library Resources, Inc. ∞

2 3 4 5 6 7 8 9 10

*In loving memory of*
*Carl and Esther Cramer,*
*and for Aaron*

# Contents

# Tables

# Preface

I was born in South Dakota and raised in Dell Rapids, a small town in the southeastern corner of the state. My first political memory is of skipping school in the tenth grade to watch presidential candidate Jesse Jackson speak to a regional meeting of the National Congress of American Indians (NCAI). I graduated from high school the year that Kevin Costner's *Dances with Wolves* was released, and I can recall that its filming was an enormous event for the state and, for some, for raising consciousness about Indian issues.

As a teenager, when I drove the back way to my grandparents' house, the route took me past the Flandreau Sioux Tribal Offices and school. And, after 1988, my grandparents would often take me to the Royal River Casino, run by the Tribe, for the Sunday buffet. When our high school teams met the Flandreau Indian School in sports competitions, I remember the intensity of the rivalry and the tendency of folks to make a racist remark or two about the Indian School team.

After college, whenever I went home, I'd try to fit in a trip "west river," which is what South Dakotans call any place in the state west of Chamberlain. I'd take camping trips in the Black Hills and would include visits to the Wounded Knee Memorial on the Pine Ridge Reservation, as well as stops to view the progress on the Crazy Horse Memorial and into the town of Deadwood to check out the non-Indian casinos that lined the streets.

Most of all, I recall being aware of the extreme beauty of the state, and how at odds that beauty was with the racial divide in its population, the extreme poverty on the reservations, and its ugly history of genocide.

Certainly, my views on the topics of Indian identity, tribal economic development, and the appropriateness of gaming grow directly from what I experienced and observed as a non-Indian South Dakotan. However, I did not go to graduate school with a deep desire to study American Indian issues.

Rather, as a political scientist and public law scholar, I wanted to research topics that stood at the intersection of law and politics. I wanted to learn to tease out the "political" from the "legal" and show how the two interacted. I place my scholarly work within that of a group of scholars who term their research "sociolegal," and who have argued that law has too long been studied divorced from the social, economic, and political contexts that lend texture and comprehension to legal regimes and legal practices. These scholars have called for "bottom-up" approaches to law, for studies that move analysis away from consolidated legal power (courts) and toward the myriad ways in which law and society interact with and affect one another. This type of academic work takes legal regimes away from the center of the study of law and focuses instead on contexts of, and contestations between, the formal (conventionally known as legal) and informal (conventionally known as social) sites of sociolegal practices.

Although I was not looking for a research topic related to American Indian issues, I became incredibly interested in federal acknowledgment after reading a law review article that described the process. I literally got goose bumps when I read that there is a government agency that determines tribal status, and that more than 260 groups are currently seeking such recognition. Even though federal recognition does not seek to certify racial, or Indian, identity, it seemed to me, when I read about the Branch of Acknowledgment and Research (BAR), that legitimating some people's identity, while taking away the legitimacy of others', was a necessary outcome of such a government endeavor. In the BAR, and other federal acknowledgment processes, there is an immediate and visceral intersection of law and politics.

Newly recognized tribes, and those seeking acknowledgment, are a diverse group. They come from every geographic region of the country (with the exception of Alaska and Hawaii); some have been very small (with fewer than ninety members), others quite large (with more than three thousand members). Statistics and verbal snapshots of recognized tribes, denied tribes, and still-hopeful groups raise a number of questions about acknowledgment. Some of these questions focus on resources: knowing that acknowledgment is expensive and time consuming, are some groups automatically dissuaded from seeking acknowledgment? Are some more likely to attempt recognition in particular forums, for instance, because of the resources available to them—if they have a good relationship with their senator, are they more likely to seek legislation than to go through the BAR? Are some groups more likely to achieve acknowledgement in a particular forum, because of resources they can bring to bear on the process?

Other questions about acknowledgment focus on context: there are many states in which one tribe has achieved recognition through the BAR while others have failed—does regionalism matter in tribal acknowledgment? There has been a tremendous slowdown in BAR decisions since 1988. What could be the cause of this, and how has it affected petitioning groups? Have new elements of Indian law, such as the Indian Gaming Regulatory Act, made a difference in recognition decisions? Do local homeowners and legislators have influence in acknowledgment through the comment period and interested party communications with the Bureau of Indian Affairs? Does the media play a role in acknowledgment claims?

I began searching for answers to these questions by reading everything I could get my hands on. For the most part, scholarly attention to federal acknowledgment processes (FAPs) comes from historians and anthropologists. Most of that work focuses on a particular tribe's struggle for recognition and on what happened after recognition. Very few political scientists write on the subject, but the work of David Wilkins and Anne McCulloch helped form my approach: their article on Catawba and Lumbee recognition claims showed me that a comparative and regional view of federal acknowledgment was possible and desirable.

I began to understand that federal acknowledgment does not happen in a vacuum, but in response to regional and national events; acknowledgment outcomes do not only reverberate in formal, legal settings—federal acknowledgment has repercussions in informal, social settings like powwows and bingo halls. Federal acknowledgment does not only involve the tribe that achieves it—it affects unrecognized groups in the region; non-Indian communities local to it; and pan-Indian, state, and national politics.

I developed a comparative research design that focused on two geographic regions—the Deep South and the Northeast. Because I believed that state politics was a factor in federal acknowledgment, and because I was interested in groups that did not achieve acknowledgment as well as those that did, I looked for states that had recently recognized tribes, groups that had been denied recognition, and groups that were midway through the recognition process. In order to examine the interaction between legislative and administrative attempts at acknowledgment, I wanted to conduct research in states that had legislatively, as well as administratively, recognized tribes. I also wanted to study the recognition process in states where the non-Indian population had little awareness of Indian issues outside of recognition; therefore, I sought out states in which the Indian population was minimal and in which there were no longstanding recognized tribes.

For a very long time, I resisted including a study of Indian gaming in my research design. I believed at the outset of this project, and still feel strongly today, that to focus on the success some tribes have had in gaming enterprises makes the impoverished tribes of the United States even more invisible to the public and likely to be overlooked by policymakers. If gaming were not such a large part of the debate over acknowledgment, and were not such an effective means toward self-government for a great number of tribes, I would leave it to others to write this part of the story.

Once I admitted that gaming is a huge factor in acknowledgment practices, however, it became clear that Connecticut and Alabama were ideal locations for this research.

Throughout my graduate education, I lived and studied in New York City, a stone's throw away from Connecticut, home of the recently recognized Mohegan Tribe and Mashantucket Pequot Tribe, as well as the Mohegan Sun and Mashantucket Pequot Foxwoods Casinos. The BAR recognized the Mohegan Tribe in 1994; the Mashantucket Pequot Tribe had achieved legislative recognition in 1983. In addition to these two federally recognized tribes, Connecticut is home to the Eastern Pequot Tribe (recognized by the BAR in 2000), the Schaghticoke Tribe (recognized by the BAR in 2004), and the Golden Hill Paugussett Tribe, which is state-recognized only.

Alabama has seven state-recognized tribes: the Poarch Band of Creeks, the Mowa Choctaws, the Echota Cherokee Tribe, the Cherokee Tribe of Northeastern Alabama, the MaChis Lower Creek Tribe, the Star Clan of Lower Muscogee Creek Indians, and the Cherokees of Southeast Alabama. Only the Poarch Band of Creeks is federally recognized, having achieved recognition from the BAR in 1984. The others have all sought federal recognition, but none so aggressively as the Mowa Choctaws, who have been denied by the BAR and have had several acknowledgment bills fail in the U.S. Congress.

As I began interviewing tribal leaders and members in both regions and conducting archival research, it became clear to me that similar issues were at stake in these states. Within the context of a history of colonization, Indian gaming and Indian racial identity are the two points of crystallization around which debates about federal acknowledgment occur. The similarities in the history and goals of the Poarch Creek and Mashantucket Pequots, as well as the obstacles faced by the Mowa Choctaws, Eastern Pequots, and Golden Hill Paugussetts became the focus of my research.

Previous scholarship on acknowledgment has taken resource dependency and racial identity as two components of the "structural positions" within colonialism from which tribes pursue acknowledgment. Through my research it became clear to me that critics of the acknowledgment process are right—race and resources affect acknowledgment claims. I argue, though, that they do not determine acknowledgment outcomes. In a purely structuralist view, groups that are poor are doomed to failure in the expensive process; groups that have intermarried with African Americans are destined to remain unrecognized. I interpret race and resources differently; rather than determining outcome, they constitute elements of the process, and they add to the richness and complexity of acknowledgment law as it is practiced today. While I retain colonialism as a key aspect of federal acknowledgment law, I have renamed the structural positions "cash" and "color" to signify that public perceptions (as seen in the non-Indian media, for instance) focus less on complex issues of class and identity and more on the hot-button, readily identifiable, and hugely divisive questions: How much money does a tribe make? And who proved that they were really Indians?

In short, I find that gaming has forever changed public perceptions of acknowledgment as well as tribal experiences of the process.

Much of the public outcry over gaming that has bled into acknowledgment discourse and practice has, in turn, its roots in public perceptions of American Indian racial identity.

There are limitations to this work that I want to be up front about.
First, it is not an ethnographic account of recognition in the Northeast and the Deep South. Though I lived in the Northeast for nearly
twelve years (during six of which I conducted this research) and in
Alabama for two month-long periods, and for six months in 2001, I
did not in any way attempt to immerse myself in tribal life. Rather, I
interviewed a select number of tribal elites and had conversations
with tribal members; I observed cultural events that were open to the
public, such as powwows and conferences; and I was a frequent visitor
at tribal museums and research centers.

Second, as a regional study, there are limitations on its ability to
generalize. Recognition politics in the Midwest and West (in states
like Michigan, Washington, Texas, and California) play out differently.
Though I believe that Indian gaming and perceived racial identity
are the overwhelming factors in public discussion about recognition,
there are other issues at stake in these regions that were not as dominant in the Deep South and the Northeast.

Third, this manuscript does not present a causal model of acknowledgment. The methodologies I undertook in accessing and analyzing
the data I collected during field research (interviewing, participant-
observation, and informal conversation) and document analysis
(archival studies of State Indian Affairs Offices, Bureau of Indian
Affairs [BIA] documents, and local and national journalistic accounts
of acknowledgment) are interpretive, hermeneutic methods. These
methods challenge positivism in social science. As such, when using
these methods, I do not frame causal hypotheses to be tested; I do
not argue that certain events *caused* particular outcomes. In this
research, there were no variables to operationalize and nothing to
falsify.

Finally, and perhaps this is not a severe limitation, I do not make
judgments about which tribes "should" have been recognized or not.
I am not a genealogist; nor am I a historian, nor an anthropologist.
My expertise does not lie in untangling the claims of groups to
Indian ancestry. It may become clear where my sympathies lie, but
these sympathies are not learned evaluations and are not to be taken
as such.

What then, is the value of this book?

In an article on acknowledgment published in 1985, anthropologist Susan Greenbaum argued that researchers could produce useful work in applied anthropology by helping tribes document their claims; she heeded her own advice by working for the Mowa Choctaws. Her work makes clear that there is much that scholars can do to help the tribes and the BAR to more quickly determine outcomes in acknowledgment proceedings.

Studies of the various contexts of acknowledgment law, of the racial, political, and economic issues in play, may shed light on how to improve the processes themselves. This particular study of the political contexts and public perceptions of acknowledgment has been part of my contribution to Greenbaum's call. I have shown that the contexts within which acknowledgment law plays out matter to participants. Though such contexts may or may not affect acknowledgment outcomes, they certainly influence tribal, bureaucratic, and legislative actions. Neither the resources a tribe has, nor whether or not it seeks gaming, nor the perceived racial composition of the members *should* affect acknowledgment decisions. These considerations have no real place even entering the public discourse; however, they clearly do.

Once scholars, activists, and administrators are aware of this, once the patina of legal neutrality has been rubbed from federal acknowledgment processes, perhaps all involved will more readily interrogate biases in evaluating and reporting on acknowledgment claims. It is my hope that this study will contribute to a shift in public perceptions surrounding tribal recognition and to greater fairness in the acknowledgment process.

# *Acknowledgments*

It was not until I sat down to write these words of gratitude that I realized the irony of beginning a book on tribal acknowledgment with a section called Acknowledgments. Though these are words of thanks and gratitude, they are also, perhaps more appropriately, words of recognition for the help, guidance, and encouragement I've received from so many people and organizations. I appreciate the opportunity to personalize this work, to thank and recognize those who have formed it.

I offer my sincere thanks to those who let me into their lives and tribal offices—members and leaders of the Poarch Band of Creeks, Mowa Choctaws, and Golden Hill Paugussetts who spoke to me for hours about their recognition claims, gave me tours of tribal facilities, and accompanied me to powwows as well as congressional hearings. I appreciate the public candor of the leadership of Eastern Pequot and Mashantucket Pequot Tribes, whose words I was privileged to hear at BIA technical assistance meetings, at conferences, and in the Mashantucket Pequot Museum and Research Center.

The staff and librarians at the Branch of Acknowledgment and Research, the Department of the Interior Library, the Alabama State Archives, the Connecticut State Archives, and the Mashantucket Pequot Museum and Research Center all made my life easier, helping me access their extensive holdings regarding federal acknowledgment. The staff of the *Atmore Advance,* a local paper in Alabama, were kind enough to give me my own room for weeks on end while I read every issue of the paper ever printed. Similar thanks are due to the staff at the Washington County, Alabama, courthouse, who gave me a table for similar purposes with the *Call-News Dispatch*.

This project was begun while I was a graduate student and McCracken Fellow at New York University; preliminary fieldwork was funded by a College of Arts and Science summer grant (1998), and the final year of dissertation writing was funded by the Bradley Foundation. Without this funding, the work may never have been done. I am exceptionally grateful for the ability to write the dissertation full time.

I am truly grateful for the several years of guidance, support, and enthusiasm for this project from my scholarly advisor, Professor Christine Harrington, and for the example she has set for me. I feel a similar gratitude to Professor Karen Blu, who warmly welcomed a political scientist into her anthropologist's office and classroom, and to Professor Russel Barsh, who helped me consider a variety of perspectives, voices, and ideas.

I have presented papers based on this work in numerous forums and have always appreciated the feedback I have gotten. For this, I am thankful to faculty and students in New York University's Political Science and Anthropology Departments and to the Institute for Law and Society. I offer special thanks to Michael Nest, for his friendship and encouragement, and to Stephanie McNulty, for her hospitality in D.C., help with defining dependant variables, and long phone calls.

I am grateful, as well, to my colleagues and friends on faculty at California State University, Long Beach, to the discussants and audience members at the American Political Science Association Meeting (2000); Law, Culture, and Humanities Working Group (2000); Western Political Science Association Meetings (2001 and 2002); and Law and Society Meetings (2000–03). Participants in the 1999 Law and Society graduate student workshops were ideal sounding boards at the preliminary stages.

The two anonymous readers provided by University of Oklahoma Press were instrumental in shaping the project as it is presented today. I cannot express enough how grateful I am for their generous and thorough reading of the text, their meticulous attention to detail, and their willingness to correct my several errors. This manuscript is much better for their suggestions; any failures remaining are mine alone.

Though this project was begun as a graduate student, and has roots in my childhood in South Dakota, it would never have come to fruition without my college education. I was fortunate to attend Bard College, and to have a truly invigorating educational experience. The professors, administration, and students at Bard fed my intellectual curiosity, showed me the joy in learning and thinking, and taught me the skills I would need to complete this work. I am grateful for the full scholarship that allowed me to attend Bard, and I credit my four years there with shaping the person I am today.

During my college and graduate schooling, my family has gamely kept track of my traveling and writing and sent tons of appropriate newspaper clippings. Thank you, Mom, Denny, and Tami. Thank you, Dad and Paula. Thanks also to Mike and Nancy Harpold, and to Dauna and Dale Hawkins, for noticing and noting the exciting moments in my life and career.

Though it might seem odd to thank them, my cats—Al, Mouffe, and PJ—were tremendous writing companions at the first stages of this project. And Daisy Dog has been a joy—she sits staring up at me whenever I work, tempting me with a long walk in the park.

Most of all, I am grateful to my husband, Aaron. You're patient and calm where I tend toward the opposites. You cheerfully understand work that takes longer than expected and the fabulous energy created by completion. I appreciate the balance you bring to my work and life and the love you bring to our home.

# CASH, COLOR, AND COLONIALISM

## CHAPTER ONE

# Contexts of Federal Acknowledgment

In early March 1999, *Time* magazine ran a short article on tribal acknowledgment.[1] The article was based on an interview of Chief Quiet Hawk, of the Golden Hill Paugussett Tribe. It opens under a picture of him standing in front of the Connecticut State Supreme Court.

The picture shows that Chief Quiet Hawk looks nothing like a stereotypical Indian; he is not "red-skinned"; his hair is not long and braided; he is not tall; his posture is not particularly erect. Rather, his appearance is that of an African American businessman. Below his picture, the caption reads, "Intermarriage with blacks has been an obstacle in winning recognition."

The text of the article begins with a quote from Quiet Hawk. "I'm trying," he says, "to get the best possible deal for the tribe to live out its culture and heritage." And what, the authors ask, would he and "his followers" do if they won "Washington's seal of approval"? They would seek the return of some of their ancestral lands, on which they would establish a museum and model village.

But that's not the end of Quiet Hawk's goals.

"We're talking," he adds, "about having the largest casino in the world."

The quoted conversation, accompanied by the photo of Chief Quiet Hawk on the state supreme court steps, insinuates a couple of things. First, claims to Indian identity may be suspect; blacks have intermarried with Indians, and now they may simply be claiming the

more politically palatable and viable group identity. Second, such
identity claims may be motivated solely by a desire for casinos. A second *Time* article, this one a featured cover story in December 2002,
is even more accusatory.[2] With the incendiary tag line, "Looks Who's
Cashing In at Indian Casinos. Hint: It's Not the People Who Are
Supposed to Benefit," the cover juxtaposes scenes of indigenous fishermen, in photos provided by the Mashantucket Pequot Museum
and Research Center, with the interior of the opulent Mohegan Sun
Casino. Other pictures show the impoverished reservations of nongaming tribes, with captions that indicate that "white backers" of
Indian gaming are "raking in the millions." The ensuing article
makes a point of questioning the Indian identities and indigenous
traits of many gaming tribes.

By highlighting the recently recognized Mashantucket Pequot
and Mohegan Tribes, the article places an unflattering spotlight on
issues inherent within federal acknowledgment. It juxtaposes casinos,
federal recognition, and suspect tribal identities and motives.

Clearly, issues of Indian racial identity and casino ownership provide the contemporary contexts within which tribal acknowledgment claims are decided and are the lenses through which federal
acknowledgment processes (FAPs) must be studied. However, mainstream journalism like the *Time* magazine articles has been the most
prevalent source of public information about acknowledgment, and
such journalism has been nearly the only source of widely available
information and open discussion on gaming and racial identity.

Existing scholarship on federal acknowledgment has focused on
the barriers to acknowledgment encountered by hopeful tribal groups.
Specifically, the literature has argued that the process of achieving
acknowledgment is overly resource dependent, that acknowledgment
reifies Western notions of "Indian," "tribe," and "state," and that
acknowledgment focuses energy on racial considerations rather
than kinship ties and social and political cohesion.[3] As such, current scholarship has usually examined either racial considerations
or resource dimensions of the process; it has done so, quite appropriately, from the perspective of groups seeking acknowledgment. Existing scholarship has also tended to focus, in the form of ethnographic
or historical study, exclusively on one or two groups' experiences
with acknowledgment, or with one aspect of the acknowledgment

regime—the bureaucracy—in isolation from other routes.[4] This
book departs from that previous work in three important ways.

First, I examine resource constraints and racial stereotypes within
the process as they operate in concert and postulate that the intersections of race and resources, embodied specifically in the Indian
Gaming Regulatory Act (IGRA) and public responses to successful
casino operations, provide the most important context within which
acknowledgment law operates and by which acknowledgment
processes must be understood. Second, although groups nationwide
go through the acknowledgment process, I focused on groups in the
Deep South and on the eastern seaboard. I traveled to those regions
to interview tribal leaders and state politicians, observe tribal governance and practices, and examine the available archival records.
Finally, I accept the scholarly claim that, as a part of U.S. Indian law,
acknowledgment is indeed tied to a colonial past; however, I examine the possibility that acknowledgment is being used by tribal
groups in their quest for a more independent relationship to the
federal government. In distinction to those scholars who focus on
the dependency of tribes seeking and achieving acknowledgment,
this work seriously investigates the claim of some tribal officials that
acknowledgment is a route to sovereignty.

Before going further, however, an overview of federal acknowledgment processes is in order.

## What is Federal Acknowledgment?

The legal term "federal acknowledgment" is used interchangeably
with the folk term "federal recognition."[5] Both signify the same thing:
a trust relationship between the federal government and an Indian
tribe that is acknowledged, or recognized, by both parties.[6] The U.S.
government currently recognizes such a relationship with the more
than 560 tribes administered by the Bureau of Indian Affairs.[7] These
relationships were established by individual treaties with several tribal
nations, constitutional provisions detailing federal responsibility for
negotiating treaties with the tribes, legislative acts appropriating
federal funds to administer Indian policies, and the Indian Reorganization Act. The trust relationship entails the acknowledgment of the

federal government's responsibilities toward tribal peoples. These responsibilities have grown to include the BIA's administration of tribal trust funds and lands,[8] the provision of law enforcement and health care,[9] and loan opportunities for Indian businesses, education, home improvements, and the leasing of land. Even though the Bureau has severely mismanaged its fiduciary duties, especially regarding tribal trust monies,[10] these services are considered necessary to the survival of reservations and to the survival of the tribes themselves.[11]

Federally recognized Indian tribes benefit from tax-exempt status (though federal income tax is deducted from tribal members' paychecks earned from tribal enterprises). Income that Indians receive from trust resources, or as part of a treaty agreement, is also untaxed. Members of federally recognized tribes are entitled, as well, to hiring preferences within the BIA.

Recognized Indian tribes may assert reclamation rights to archaeological burial findings under the Native American Graves Protection and Repatriation Act (NAGPRA).[12] They may also seek artistic protection under the Indian Arts and Crafts Act of 1990 (IACA).[13] No such arrangements or protections are available to the more than two hundred federally unrecognized Indian groups in the United States. In fact, in order to sue in federal courts for the return of land or to rectify treaty violations, a tribe must first be federally recognized.

Though some of the unrecognized groups are acknowledged by the states in which they are located, the acknowledgment of a relationship between state and tribal governments does not guarantee, nor even recommend, federal recognition. In many cases, the Indian heritage of state-recognized tribal members is unquestioned, but their tribal status and political history are contentious. Members of unrecognized tribes, even those widely known as Indians by dominant society, do not have access to the federal trust relationship nor to federal programs that often define "Indianness" differently from the state entities.

These tribes became and remain unrecognized for several possible reasons, all having to do with varying Indian responses to U.S. colonialism. Many of the tribes located in the Northeast and along the eastern seaboard, for example, never made treaties with the federal government. Rather, the colonial governments of the present-day states shared responsibility for making treaties with, and warring on, the tribes they encountered. Heavily decimated by such wars, the tribes were often removed to state-administered reservations and remained unacknowledged by the federal government.[14]

In the Deep South, a number of the groups currently seeking acknowledgment claim to be constituted by the descendants of those Cherokee, Choctaw, and Creek peoples who successfully resisted removal to what became the state of Oklahoma. Present-day members of these groups, sometimes called remnant tribes, proudly claim a common heritage with those who avoided leaving their homeland by hiding and living in relative isolation or by assimilating into the larger, non-Indian population around them.[15] Their members cannot trace descent to membership lists of removed groups, however, so it is difficult to prove their ties to the historic tribe, and they often remain unrecognized.

Finally, many of the treaties signed in the northwestern forests of present-day Washington and Oregon and on the California coasts never made it back to Washington, D.C., for ratification. As treaties were being horse ridden across the nation for delivery to Congress, it was common for the messenger either to defect from the service or to be killed somewhere in the middle of the nation. Although some of the treaties that were returned to the capital remained unratified, more still went unenforced. Both a lack of ratification and a lack of enforcement can result in a lack of acknowledgment for a tribe. In the state of Washington, though several groups participated in the Stevens Treaties, ratified in 1854 and 1855, many of the Indian tribes were unthinkingly consolidated on reservations, with and without benefit of treaties, and lost their land as a result.[16]

An additional cohort of tribes was "terminated" by governmental policy in the 1950s and 1960s. The goal of Termination policy, literally, to terminate the trust relationship, was accomplished by encouraging Indians to move from reservations into urban areas, where, it was hoped, they would become further assimilated into dominant society and less dependent on the federal government. Termination was also accomplished by several laws meant to increase federal jurisdiction over Indian lands and reduce the power of tribal government. More than fifty tribal governments were dissolved by Termination, and vast amounts of Indian land left tribal hands. Under the Nixon

Administration, Congress reversed the trend of Termination; since the repeal of that policy, most Terminated tribes have been successful in getting Congress to reinstate the trust relationship, through a legislative process known as restoration of tribal status.

As a result of the increased politicization of Indian identity in the 1960s and 1970s, Indians began to make demands upon the federal government in myriad ways. They organized sit-ins and land takeovers, testified at congressional hearings, and used the legal system to bring land, water, and identity claims in federal district courts throughout the nation. This activism, and some of the benefits won by Indians, contributed to a renaissance in Indian identity and led to questions about who had the right to claim tribal status. Some case law had addressed the issue of tribal status and Indian identity, but the federal government had no coherent policy regarding unrecognized groups. Tribes without federal recognition began to demand it. Although many unrecognized tribes had been demanding recognition and clarification of their status *long* before the 1970s, the activism of the 1960s and 1970s led an increased number of Indian groups to agitate for federal recognition. Certainly, the activism of that period is what compelled the BIA to establish the Branch of Acknowledgment and Research, rather than continue to evaluate recognition requests on an ad hoc basis.

Some tribes approached the judiciary, asking for resolution of their tribal status and land claims; others lobbied their legislators, requesting bills of acknowledgment and congressional support at the BIA. Many made a concerted effort to convince BIA officials that established recognition criteria were necessary. Responding to Indian demands, administrators at the BIA developed the Branch of Acknowledgment and Research, in 1978, to adjudicate the claims of unrecognized tribes and provide them with a means for economic development and cultural viability.[17] Between 1978 and 2000, fifteen tribes were recognized through this process. Since the passage of the IGRA, this process has been incredibly politicized and increasingly placed in the public eye. The enormous success of gaming operations run by some newly recognized tribes has brought more attention to the acknowledgment process, as non-Indians seek to limit tribes' ability to run casinos, by limiting their access to acknowledgment.

## Contextualizing Federal Acknowledgment Processes

This book began from an understanding that legal decision making is not a neutral endeavor that can be studied apart from what we commonly call "society." Rather, law and legal decisions are historically contingent, geographically and temporally bounded, and in constant interaction with society. It is only with an understanding of the broader, more general contexts of specific legal regimes that we can comprehend and articulate their specificity.

BAR regulations themselves recognize the importance of placing in context the history, community, and politics of the groups whose claims they evaluate. The regulations provide that tribal political processes are "to be understood in the context of the history, culture, and social organization of the group."[18] This understanding is deepened in the work of Karen Blu, who offers a version of this contextualization of unrecognized Indian groups as a process of "reading back" from contemporary communities in order to better place and evaluate historical documents.[19]

Such a need is recognized, as well, by anthropologist Jack Campisi. Campisi has had extensive experience with federal acknowledgment processes; he served as an expert witness on behalf of the Tribe in the Mashpee trial, wrote amicus briefs on behalf of the Gay Head Wampanoag, and is now working for the Mashantucket Pequot, at their Museum and Research Center. In an article published in 1985, Campisi argued that the different routes hopeful groups take to acknowledgment are "based upon the level of involvement of the states, the intensity of local opposition, and the nature of internal tribal politics."[20] Nonlegal aspects of acknowledgment—how hard a town fights against it, the cohesiveness of tribal leadership—influence the formal, legal choices tribes and bureaucrats make about acknowledgment, and, perhaps, impact formal, legal acknowledgment outcomes. The need for a deep context is clear: we must place BAR processes themselves in the contexts of history, culture, and social organization; we must do so by "reading back" into the history of the regulations' development while reading the present. We must see the BAR situated within the two contexts of gaming and race, because they so influence federal acknowledgment processes.

# U.S. Governmental Policies, Indian Activism, and the Politicization of Indian Identity

Once contact between colonial governments and tribal nations was made, colonial dominance was eventually instituted militarily and governmentally through a variety of means. Though each colonial government was different, and each tribal nation had varying goals for the relationship, the overwhelming focus of non-Indian government policy became the goal of removing Indians from their land and opening that land for white settlement. Removal was accomplished by military force, by treaty, by trickery, and by the inadvertent extermination of Indians through disease. Though this chapter offers a brief history of all major federal Indian programs, readers are cautioned that these comments are generalizations made about federal programs and Indian responses, and that several excellent works exist that discuss particular programs and particular tribal nations and regions. Attention to these particular tribal nations, regions, and programs is vitally important but outside the scope of this chapter.

One of the roles of law in North American society has been to define spaces and peoples, to offer boundaries to territories and identities. In this role, law often acts as a mythmaker; it creates and legitimates stories to justify the categories of peoples and places it creates. The myths constructed in and by law unify a fragmented story of the "nation" by resolving inconsistencies and oppositions of social life.[1]

The joint legal myths of discovery and dependency, which were constructed by Chief Justice John Marshall in *Cherokee Nation v. Georgia* and *Worcester v. Georgia,* defined Indian populations both as "domestic dependent nations" (in *Cherokee Nation*) and "distinct and independent political communities" (in *Worcester*).[2] In the earlier of these two cases, Chief Justice Marshall determined that Indian tribes in the United States constituted domestic dependent nations within the United States. They were not technically foreign, in the sense that they were located within the boundaries of this nation (thus, domestic); yet they were still nations, as they were neither colonies nor states. "Dependent," then, became the operative term in defining the trust relationship—Indian tribes were said to be in a state of pupilage, requiring the guidance and aid of the nation's leaders. Yet the Marshall Court's decision one year later, in *Worcester,* also maintained that tribal nations had some measures of autonomy, in particular as against state incursions into tribal land. Marshall found it difficult to reconcile ideas of tribal sovereignty, U.S. authority, and the trust relationship.

Several authors have noted the continued impact of Marshall's interpretation of the doctrines of discovery and dependence. They argue that his interpretations constitute myths—a myth of an entire nation newly "discovered" by European settlers and a myth of tribal peoples as unable to cope with the changing conditions brought by those settlers. These scholars further argue that these myths of discovery and dependence have facilitated the assimilation, genocide, and domination of American Indians.[3] U.S. definitional policies, flowing from these myths, have had a similar impact on Indian and tribal life.[4] Together, these myths and policies form the basis of American Indian law as it is practiced and administered today, including the creation of the Branch of Acknowledgment and Research.

## Constitutional Interpretation and Definition in the Early Founding Period

The federal nature of U.S.-Indian relations was defined through the treaty-making process, as authorized in the Constitution by Article I, Section 10 and Article VI, Section 2. From 1778 until 1871, the United States and Indian tribes made more than 370 treaties.[5] Vine Deloria and Raymond DeMallie's compilation and analysis of these diplomatic documents show that treaties accomplished a variety of things. Some established peaceful relations between the tribes and white settlers; others provided for continued Indian hunting, fishing, and spiritual rights. Some treaties ceded Indian lands, others protected Indian lands. Whereas some treaties established white government control over Indian lives and created a mechanism for reinforcing Indian dependency, other treaties established beneficial systems of trade and exchange as well as systems for mutual protection. Treaties established jurisdictional boundaries, created opportunities and imperatives for education, and offered opportunities for maintenance of diplomatic relationships.

During this early period of the country's founding, the Supreme Court further refined the constitutional status of the tribes. Chief Justice John Marshall wrote a series of opinions that created doctrines to govern the relationship between the tribes and the federal government, and, as noted by legal scholar Robert Williams, cloaked both parties in masks that seemed to determine that relationship.[6] In the joint myths of discovery and dependence, tribal nations' role in the relationship was that of needy pupil; the federal government was cast as the benevolent caregiver and tutor.[7] In *Johnson v. M'Intosh* (1823)[8] Marshall began to develop the "doctrine of discovery," which he had articulated previously in *Fletcher v. Peck* (1810).[9] Though "discovery" has several meanings in international law, and has been used in a variety of ways by U.S. lawmakers, according to Marshall's interpretation in *M'Intosh*, the doctrine of discovery gave the discovering power (the U.S. colonial government) exclusive rights to discovered territory against other colonizing nations. In fact, the Illinois and Piankeshaw Tribes, the original inhabitants of the land at issue in this case, had lost their land through purchase, not the military action of "conquest."[10] Even so, Marshall rested his decision in *M'Intosh* on a theory of discovery rooted in conquest; in this conceptualization, the doctrine of discovery also extended to the United States a full right to "appropriate the lands occupied by the Indians." This legal principle allowed the United States to claim fee, or simple, title to Indian lands, extinguish Indian claims to possession, and limit tribes to mere occupancy.

According to Marshall's decision in *M'Intosh*, Indians still held title to their land; they held, in fact, "original title." Original title was to be "consummated by possession," wherein the "original inhabitants'" rights to the land were "impaired" but not "entirely disregarded." Marshall acknowledged that the Indians were the original occupants of the soil, with a legal as well as a just moral claim to retain possession of it, and to use it according to their own discretion. However, as Mario Gonzalez and Elizabeth Cook-Lynn note, "their rights to complete sovereignty, as independent nations, were necessarily diminished and their power to dispose of the soil at their own will, to whomsoever they pleased, was denied by the original fundamental principle, that discovery gave exclusive title to those who made it."[11] This right of occupancy granted by a conquering power is clearly far different from a right of possession and a far cry from an acknowledgment of territorial sovereignty.

Marshall's decision is, in large part, apologetic; Professor Jo Carrillo believes that Marshall saw the settlers as "ambitious, innocent, [and] at worst pretentious"—certainly not cold-blooded.[12] Apologia aside, the mythic construction of the doctrine of discovery makes the easily anticipated outcome—the dispossession of Indian lands and a reduction in territorial and political sovereignty—inevitable. Because Marshall's decisions construed them as destined to be dispossessed, Indians appeared destined to become dependent. Marshall's later decisions recognized this.

## The Myth of Dependency:
## The Construction of the Trust Relationship

Chief Justice Marshall asserted that by virtue of discovery the United States had gained title to Indian lands; according to these decisions, Indians could continue to occupy their land, and even achieve some measure of success, assuming that they entered positions of "wardship" and "tutelage" under the federal government. Jill Norgren argues that these doctrines articulated by Marshall form the foundation of a mythical and harmful understanding of the federal trust relationship, typified by extreme dependence of Indians upon the federal government.[13]

The basis for the federal government's trust responsibility, articulated by Marshall in *M'Intosh,* and reread by Mario Gonzalez (attorney for the Sioux Nation in its landmark claim against the U.S. government), is found in the moral imperatives imposed on the United States by its supposed conquest of the Indians.

> The title by conquest is acquired and maintained by force. The conqueror prescribes the limits. Humanity, however, acting on public opinion, has established, as a general rule, that the conquered shall not be wantonly oppressed, and that their condition shall remain as eligible as is compatible with the objects of the conquest. . . . [A] wise policy requires that the right of the conquered to property should remain unimpaired.[14]

The concept of a trust relationship founded in conquest constituted the legality of the continuing occupation of Indian land. The trust relationship formed, as well, from the plenary (or, exclusive) power over Indian affairs exercised by the federal legislature. It also constituted the doctrinal and moral imperative to achieve at least a patina of legislative caretaking and concern for justice.

Yet it is important not to conflate the trust relationship with a position of wardship and dependency. The ward-guardian relationship is different from the trust relationship constructed by treaties that comprehended both parties as relative equals and that have been reaffirmed by numerous court cases and acts of Congress.

## Removal

With congressional authorization, the Department of War housed the nation's Indian Office from 1824 until 1849. An act of July 9, 1832, granted the authority to manage Indian Affairs to the commissioner of Indian Affairs, still within the war department; a further act, on June 30, 1834, granted all remaining powers to the president. These acts, combined with the resources of the Department of War, the mandate of the Removal Act of 1830, and a willingness to flout Supreme Court rulings, made Andrew Jackson's brutal policies of Indian Removal possible. Arguing that moving Indians from Georgia and other southeastern states was actually done for their protection, Jackson had campaigned on a platform of the removal of Indian nations to the west of the Mississippi River and the consolidation of tribal peoples on reservations on undesirable land in what became Oklahoma. Though this policy violated numerous treaty agreements, existed primarily by virtue of a specious states' rights argument, and was fought by the tribes subjected to it, Removal was couched in a language of caretaking that recognized the moral obligation of the federal government to protect Indians from white incursion. It was "accomplished" swiftly under Jackson's military. More than seventy thousand Indians were eventually relocated to Oklahoma or died on the long march to that destination.[15]

After the executive branch reorganized in 1849, the nation's Indian Office moved from the war department to the Department of the Interior, and was renamed the Bureau of Indian Affairs. There, officials at Interior instituted a system of "Indian agents" who would treat with, and translate for, the Indians, while providing information to the government on the activities of the various tribes. Within a few years, Congress decided that the Indian agent system was too expensive and too decentralized to efficiently govern federal-tribal relations; congressmen felt constrained by the system and by the treaty-making process. They refused to appropriate any more money to Indian Affairs, unless they could have more power over them, and passed the Appropriations Act of 1871, which officially ended the era of treaty making.

Though treaty making had ended, the legislature still required means of communicating with, controlling, and making exchange with tribal governments. The federal government configured a system of "Indian Agreements" to take the place of treaties. These agreements were similar to treaties in tone, content, and purpose; only their ratification requirements were different. Some agreements, like the actions of the agents during treaty making, focused on assimilating the Indians, prohibiting their cultural and religious activities, and keeping Indian lands separate from white lands. Others formed peaceful relationships and set up mutually beneficial relationships of trade and land tenure. Indian Agreements were vitally important to tribes and the federal government; more than seventy-four of them were penned between 1872 and 1902.[16]

Up until this time—from the earliest treaties to Removal and into the era of Indian Agreements—federal policy was predominantly motivated by the belief that Indians and whites should be kept separate.[17] Though some early acts of Congress sought more assimilative goals, most policymakers perceived separation as the most advantageous route for both groups and saw separation, in part, as the most moral approach to take with the new colonial subjects.

By the late 1880s, however, the politics of Indian-white relations became one that advocated the assimilation of the Indians into "American" life. This was not an entirely new idea at all. In fact, Chief Justice Marshall had previously stated in *Cherokee Nation v. Georgia* (1831) that tribes were "domestic dependent nations . . . in a state of pupilage . . . [in a relationship much like that of] a ward to his guardian" and capable of learning from interaction with whites. Marshall's construction of American Indians by law, the myth of dependency, casts Indians as hopelessly savage and backward and in desperate need of government help, protection, and guidance. In part through the advocacy of missionary societies and progressive, self-named Friends of the Indian such as those who met in upstate New York and held a series of conferences known collectively as the Lake Mohonk Conference, federal policy toward Indian tribes shifted from Removal and separation to assimilation and integration.

The Dawes Act of 1887 (or General Allotment Act) exemplifies the new understanding of the moral imperative indicated by the trust relationship and the tensions those imperatives created as they conflicted with the growing needs of an expansionist nation.[18] With the Dawes Act, U.S. Indian policy changed from forced removal of Indians tribes onto consolidated reservation lands to one of assimilation, population shifting, and detribalization. The primary sections of the act attempted to accomplish this by authorizing the subdivision of tribal lands into private plots to be owned by individual Indians. Indian heads of household were allotted 160-acre plots; each minor child was allotted 40 acres. The allotted land remained in federal trust for twenty-five years; such land could not be sold into private hands.

These provisions were intended to maintain Indian possession of the land. As administered by the local Dawes commissions, however, the General Allotment Act facilitated the rapid and unjust diminishment of tribal acreage. With the advent of the Burke Act, the local commissioners could grant exemptions from trust status to land held by Indians they considered "competent" to make a sale. These competency exceptions encouraged needy Indians to sell their land prior to the end of the twenty-five-year waiting period, often far below market value. In addition, all the land that remained "surplus" after the allotments were made was opened to white purchase and settlement at extremely low prices. Between 1887 and 1905, Allotment reduced tribal lands from 138 million acres to 52 million acres. A full 86 million acres of tribal land, or two-thirds of all tribal territory, went into white hands as a result of the Dawes Act.[19]

In addition to decimating tribal lands, the Dawes Act dramatically reduced the power of tribal governments. Francis Prucha notes that, under Allotment, it no longer mattered what tribal governments wanted to do with reservation lands; it mattered only what individual Indians planned.[20] A key provision of the act granted male Indians U.S. citizenship once they took out a patent on their land.[21] The citizenship provision urged individual Indians to respect the federal government over traditional or tribal regimes. The secretary of the interior also transferred his Allotment law powers over Indian territory to the BIA, firmly establishing that agency as the first and primary institution of control over Indian land. Charles Wilkinson argues, and history bears the claim, that this limitation of tribal authority "weakened Indian culture, sapped the vitality of tribal legislative and judicial processes, and opened most Indian reservations for settlement by non-Indians . . . dashing any remaining hopes that traditional Indian societies might remain truly separate."[22] What resulted, instead, was a measured separatism in which Indian tribes struggled to remain autonomous and powerful while relying on support from the federal government.

In this period of American history, officials within the federal government considered Indianness—signified by a lack of mixed parentage and by ties to the land and traditional ways of life—to be an undesirable trait. Indianness was to be lost by assimilation, Christianization, and intermarriage with whites. Certainly, through the General Allotment Act and other assimilationist policies, American Indians were meant to lose their separate ethnic identities and become *citizens;* as one Indian commissioner put it, "The American Indian is to become the Indian American."[23]

At this time, the net cast to define eligibility for these programs was broad—any tribal member was eligible for programs seeking to assimilate the Indians. However, in order to measure the progress of assimilation, and to ensure that only "real" Indians were allotted lands, this broad definition would soon change. It would become increasingly important for the federal government to restrict access to Indian identity and tribal status.

## Indian Reorganization Act of 1934

Largely content with the progress made toward assimilation and detribalization achieved by the Dawes Act, lawmakers during the early 1900s neglected to enact legislation in aid of the impoverished Indian population.[24] This neglect ended as a result of a report on federal Indian policy that was considered under Franklin Roosevelt's New Deal programs. This report was known as the Meriam Report on Indian Policy of the Allotment Period; it was written under the auspices of the Brookings Institution. The Meriam Report criticized the government for "inadequate appropriations, excessive centralization, and a lack of planning."[25] It recommended increased appropriations to the BIA and called for reform to federal Indian policy.

Under the direction of Commissioner of Indian Affairs John Collier, an FDR appointee, attorney Felix Cohen and Solicitor General Nathan Margold created the Indian Reorganization Act (IRA), also known as the Indian New Deal, which Congress enacted on June 18, 1934.[26] The IRA ended the Dawes-era Allotment policies, extended the federal trust period indefinitely, and gave tribes increased autonomy, subject to approval by the secretary of the interior, to manage their own affairs. With the IRA, Congress affirmed Indian preference in BIA hiring and halted the sale of so-called surplus land to non-Indians.

Collier decreed that those Indian tribes that incorporated and adopted constitutions under the IRA would be granted all powers not inconsistent with the U.S. Constitution. Tribal governments would become responsible, in conjunction with the BIA, for managing all tribal lands; they were authorized to purchase property for landless Indians in order to consolidate tribal territory and were given a new legal status. Under the IRA, tribes became partners within a government-to-government relationship.

Central to the New Deal legislation were provisions for holding IRA elections to establish tribal constitutions modeled on U.S. representative government and subject to approval by the secretary of the interior and the commissioner of Indian Affairs. In referenda, tribes could choose to adopt tribal constitutions to govern political aspects of tribal life (Section 16); they could also choose to adopt a tribal charter of incorporation, which gave the corporate tribal entity the power to own, hold, and dispose of all manner of property (Section 17). Most tribes that approved IRA governments also approved charters of incorporation; they thus created a business arm of the tribe to match its powers of self-government.

Section 19 of the IRA involves government definitions of Indians for the purposes of IRA elections. It reads, in part:

> The term "Indian" as used in this Act shall include all persons of Indian descent who are members of any recognized Indian tribe now under Federal jurisdiction, and all persons who are descendants of such members who were, on June 1, 1934, residing within the present boundaries of any reservation, and shall further include all other persons of one-half or more Indian blood.

Progressives championed the IRA as furthering Indian self-government. They hailed the hearings on the IRA as a "consultative process" meant to further democracy in Indian Country.[27]

However, due in part to its architects' romanticized and stereotyped views of Indians and tribal communities, the IRA was not an unmitigated success. Though many tribes did benefit from forming a government under the IRA, Tom Biolsi argues that in some areas and in some regards, the Indian New Deal actually further disempowered tribal governments and hindered the creation of efficacious tribal politics.[28]

Operating under the misguided assumption that traditional communal "ownership" of Indian lands was an organic version of state Socialism, and hoping to foster its development in the United States, Felix Cohen had been convinced that tribal communities would welcome the opportunity to use constitutional and corporate law to create modern Socialist democracies.[29] He had envisioned a transitional period of indirect colonial rule, during which time tribes would settle land claims with the federal government and develop constitutions and charters for self-government based on Western models.[30] Most tribal governments, however, were uninterested in creating miniature Socialist democracies.[31]

A further problem with the IRA was that indigenous models of self-government were not incorporated into all of the IRA constitutions. In fact, some of these constitutions actually institutionalized a separation of religion and politics that was foreign to many traditional Indian governmental organizations.

Yet the IRA was an important turning point in federal policy. It marked a desire to recognize tribal autonomy and afforded tribal people the opportunity to vote whether or not to incorporate. Ultimately, 250 IRA elections were held, and all but seventy-seven of the tribes voting agreed to develop an IRA constitution. By 1950 a majority of tribes (180) had IRA constitutions, and 157 of those were also incorporated.[32] Though some large tribes voted to reject the IRA constitution, more than half of all recognized Indians are members of tribes with IRA governments.

## Termination Policy of the 1950s

As early as 1944, when tribes were just beginning to incorporate under the IRA, some influential members of Congress began to advocate for less federal responsibility for, and control over, Indian affairs. The ranking members in favor of tribal Termination were Senator Wayne Morse (R-Ore.)—who introduced numerous resolutions proposing the Termination of the Klamath Tribe, geographically encompassed by Oregon's boundaries—and Senator Arthur Watkins (R-Utah). [33] Watkins, as chair of the Senate Committee on Indian Affairs, made several public speeches equating Termination policy to the Emancipation Proclamation.[34] He argued that Termination would "free" Indians from "wardship status."[35] Morse, Watkins, and likeminded senators also claimed that the continued existence of Indian tribes was intolerably expensive for the federal government. Preferring that states shoulder fiscal responsibility for tribes, they offered increased state criminal and civil jurisdiction over tribes in return.

With the change in presidential administrations, the new secretary of the interior, Harold Ickes, appointed Dillon S. Myer to replace John Collier as the head of the BIA. Myer's essential position was that treaties, case law, and legislation had only perpetuated Indian dependency and poverty, that tribal economies had continued to be in deep crisis, and that federal paternalism was retarding Indian economic and cultural advancement.[36] Tribal leaders lobbied vociferously against Myer's appointment as assistant secretary of Indian Affairs; Ickes appointed him against Indian wishes.[37] His appointment to the bureau paved the way for the legislation sought by Morse and Watkins; early Termination bills being debated in Congress had newfound support at the BIA.

The goal of federal Termination policy was to dissolve the government-to-government relationship developed during the colonial and New Deal periods. Legislators and BIA administrators took a three-pronged approach to Termination. First, the government adopted policies that officially encouraged Indians to continue their trend toward urbanization begun during World Wars I and II.[38] The BIA established job placement centers in Chicago, Los Angeles, and Salt Lake City to facilitate this push. Second, Congress passed Public Law 280,[39] which ceded complete criminal and some civil jurisdiction over tribal land to particular states with large Indian populations— California, Nevada, Minnesota, Oregon, and Wisconsin; and partial criminal and civil jurisdiction to eight other states. Third, Congress passed House Concurrent Resolution 108 in August of 1953; HCR-108 set forth timetables and guidelines for the cessation of the federal trust responsibility for a great number of the nation's tribes. It promised that Termination would be completely voluntary and eased by a transitional period estimated to be between one and seven years long. During the transition period, land would be transferred from tribal trust status to private Indian ownership, and tribal assets would be sold, with the profits distributed to tribal members on a per capita basis. Stephen Cornell notes that Termination was, essentially, modern-era Allotment without the limits on land transfer or the social programs provided for by the Dawes Act.[40]

Donald Fixico reports that "between 1945 and 1960 the government processed 109 cases of termination affecting 1,369,000 acres of Indian land and an estimated 12,000 Indians."[41] Although American Indians who were members of Terminated tribes retained their "Indian" identity, they were no longer considered tribal peoples for the purposes of federal law and the administration of the trust relationship. Congress had separated the ethnic identity "Indian" from the legal protection and political identity offered by "tribe."

*Anti-Termination Activism and the*
*Continued Growth of Pan-Indian Politics*

It soon became clear to tribes that Termination was neither voluntary nor as gradual as Congress had claimed, and Indian opposition to Termination became more vocal. Pan-Indian opposition was one of several factors that led President Nixon to halt Termination,[42] but such opposition was not powerful enough to get him or his administration to automatically reinstate relationships with Terminated tribes.

As a consequence, some tribes lobbied Congress for reinstatement of their tribal status. Others were compelled to sue for such reinstatement. In these suits, a 1913 Supreme Court decision, *United States v. Sandoval,* controlled access to the government-to-government relationship. In *Sandoval,* Justice Van Devanter writes:

> Of course, it is not meant . . . that Congress may bring a . . . body of people within the range of [regulatory] power by arbitrarily calling them an Indian Tribe, but only that in respect of distinctly Indian communities the questions whether, to what extent, and for what time they shall be recognized and dealt with as dependent Tribes requiring the guardianship and protection of the United States are *to be determined by Congress, and not by the courts.* [emphasis mine][43]

Two aspects of this decision came to be important in anti-Termination litigation and activism. First, Van Devanter asserted that Congress, and not the judiciary, was responsible for decisions regarding tribal status. Second, he suggested that there might be a time at which Congress decides a tribe no longer requires the guardianship and protection of the United States. The latter had been the juridical justification behind the Termination legislation of the 1950s; the former, then, became the justification for deference to congressional action in the realm of Indian Affairs, including the reinstatement of tribal status.

Congress had terminated the Menominee Tribe of Wisconsin in 1954. With the dissolution of the trust relationship, all tribal lands became known as Menominee County rather than the Menominee Reservation. Menominee Enterprises, Inc., an Indian-run entity, held that land, but the holding company soon went bankrupt. According to tribal history, Termination "led to a drastic decline in tribal employment, increased poverty, and brought about devastating reductions in basic services and health care," including the closing of the only hospital within the reservation/county.[44] In 1967, the tribe approached the Second Circuit bench, asking that court to interpret *Sandoval* as it related to the treaty rights of Terminated tribes.[45] The Menominee argued that Termination of their tribal status should not negatively affect their treaty-granted hunting and fishing rights. The state of Wisconsin argued that Termination had caused the Menominee Tribe to cease to exist, and, as such, had invalidated all of their treaty rights, including those protecting hunting and fishing.

In a novel interpretation of both Termination legislation and the precedent set by *Sandoval*, the Supreme Court, under the well-consolidated leadership of Chief Justice Earl Warren, held on appeal that though Congress had terminated the government-to-government relationship with the Menominee, *the tribe itself had not been terminated*. Since the tribe still existed, all treaty rights continued to exist. The Court further advised, however, that it would not reinstate congressionally Terminated tribes; under *Sandoval*, the Menominee only had recourse to legislation if they desired reinstatement of their federal status.

Already mobilized by litigation, the Menominee Tribal Council sprung into action. Individual Menominee tribal members used a combination of political and social activism; some lobbied their congressional delegation while others occupied an abandoned Alexian Brothers' novitiate on what had been their reservation. Within five years of the Supreme Court decision, the *Menominee Restoration Act* was passed, and the tribe's devastating period of Termination ended.[46]

Ten years after *Menominee*, the Mississippi Choctaw brought a related suit with *United States v. John* (1977).[47] This case questioned the role of the *Sandoval* precedent in the absence of explicit congressional Termination. The Mississippi Choctaw Tribe, though federally recognized, was considered a "remnant group"—a group of Indians that had successfully resisted removal from their homelands in the 1830s and had continued to live by Indian and tribal ways in isolation in Mississippi, doing so without many of the federal benefits that should have attended their status. Particularly problematic was the determination of jurisdiction over tribal land. The Mississippi Choctaw argued that they constituted a tribe in the fullest meaning of the term, and that the land they inhabited was indeed "Indian Territory." Mississippi disagreed and sought regulatory and police powers. The tribe asked the Supreme Court to clarify and reaffirm its recognition status. The Court held that even though government policy had removed the Choctaw Tribe, in the absence of congressional action dissolving the tribe, the Mississippi Band of the Choctaw Nation had not ceased to exist. Accordingly, all land inhabited by the Mississippi Choctaw, and taken into trust status for the tribe, was Indian Country for purposes of federal law.[48]

Up to this point in Indian-white relations, the various branches of the federal government had resisted standardized definitions of Indian identity or attributions of tribal status. Indians were thought to be easily identifiable: they were red-skinned people living on reservations, greatly unassimilated, though in contact with white society.

To be considered Indian by the dominant society meant continued racial marginalization and economic depression and dependency on tribal homelands. Sweeping Indian rights legislation, the Red Power movement, and stunning land claims victories in the Northeast combined to increase reasons to celebrate, and claim, Indian identity. Nevertheless, Indians had long sought full recognition of their tribal status and Indian identity. Though tribal governments knew that the trust relationship entitled them to the protection of their land and offered possibilities for education and health services, many unrecognized Indian communities lacked the high levels of awareness and efficacy necessary to make successful applications for tribal status and increased federal aid. Neither the value of federal recognition nor the value of litigation strategies had ever been as apparent as they would become in the 1960s and 1970s. However, a revolution in Indian law and politics was changing this.

Sociologist Stephen Cornell, who categorized Indian political organization and activism into four axes/groups, undertook what is perhaps the most authoritative scholarly examination of Indian activism in this period, titled *The Return of the Native*. From 1960 until 1985, Cornell notes, American Indian political organization and activism had been oriented toward both pan-Indian and specific, tribally based goals. Both orientations, pan-Indian and tribal, can be distinguished on two additional axes of "activist orientation." The first axis distinguishes between the "transformative" and "reformative" goals of Indian politics. Transformative goals are those that aspire to change the entire structure of Indian-white relations; an example of a transformative goal would be the reopening of treaty relationships between tribes and the federal government. Cornell identifies reformative goals as those that seek the redistribution of political, economic, and social power within the existing structure of

Indian-white relations. IRA constitution making is an example of a reformative tribal goal.

The second axis distinguishes between "segregative" and "integrative" goals. Segregative Indian politics sees dominant society as inherently unresponsive to Indian needs. An example of segregative politics is the occupation of "surplus" lands and the creation of Indian cultural centers in those sites. Integrative Indian politics, on the other hand, believes that U.S. institutions *can* be used by Indians to maximize Indian welfare; integrationist Indian activists have lobbied Congress to achieve legislative gains such as the Indian Child Welfare Act of 1978.[49]

Cornell neglects a vital portion of Indian activism, however—the use of courts by tribal and pan-tribal Indians in order to achieve far-reaching social change. Cornell's neglect of Indian legal activism is ill advised, as it is precisely that form of action that has come to dominate Indian activism in the contemporary period.

## Pan-Indian Legislative Victories

The roots of pan-Indian politics can be traced to Denver, in 1944, and the founding meeting of the National Congress of American Indians (NCAI),[50] the "largest and most powerful of the federally recognized tribes' political and lobbying organizations."[51] In its early years, NCAI platforms opposed Termination policies, supported pan-Indian activism in the legislative arena, and "asked all Americans to respect Indian cultural values and treaty rights, support reservation economic development, and put an end to stereotypes."[52] The NCAI sought to achieve these goals primarily by lobbying Congress for statutory changes to federal Indian law.

Following the NCAI's lead, and using that organization's political clout, a number of tribes were able to make use of the legislature to redress problems such as land takings and the ravages of Termination policies. Among the fruits of the successful alliances between American Indians and state politicians was the Alaskan Native Claims Settlement Act, which recognized Alaskan Native land rights; provided for mineral royalties, land payments, and land transfer for Alaskan Native Villages; and returned contested lands to tribes in Oregon and Arizona.[53] Following shortly on the heels of the Alaskan settlement came Public Law 91-550, which, in 1970, returned Blue Lake and forty-eight thousand acres of land to the Taos Pueblo.[54] Anti-Termination mobilization had been a crucial part of these politics. Beside the success of the Menominee, the following tribes were legislatively restored: Confederated Tribes of Siletz in Oregon (1977), Ottawa in Oklahoma (1978), Paiute in Utah (1980), four Rancherias in California (1980), and the Klamath of Oregon (1988). Each of these restorations was the direct result of tribally based activism and the successful bid for local legislators' cooperation.

The increased attention given to Indian issues as a part of President Lyndon Johnson's Great Society Program (1965), which was itself a response to the successes of the civil rights movement, was also important for changing conditions in Indian Country. The outcome of this presidential attention included the Indian Self-Determination and Education Act, which encouraged Indians to take over from the BIA and administer their own cultural and educational programs, and greatly restricted the power of BIA officials to control tribal finances.[55] These programs were the direct result of Indian lobbying efforts in Washington, and the preamble to the Self-Determination and Education Act states that it was adopted in response to "the strong expression of the Indian people."[56] It is important to note, however, that legislation of this sort addressed the *impoverished* condition of Indians rather than their tribal status or indigenous identity—their *Indian* condition.[57] This result blurred the distinction between American Indians and other ethnic minorities, which could have ultimately harmed claims to sovereign status made by tribes. "Red Power" refocused attention on the particular, *Indian* needs of tribal peoples.

## Red Power

While some Indians were developing legislatively targeted pan-Indian politics, young urban Indians and reservation elders living in traditional lifestyles were forming unique alliances and creating a pan-Indian politics that supported a return to reservations, a revitalization of reservations as "homelands," and, in some cases, radical action against the United States to enforce previously established treaty rights.[58] The period of Termination had made these two sets of activists more suspicious than ever before of the federal government, and the rapidly expanding Indian press served well to carry a radical politics to thousands of American Indians.[59] Government repression of the growing Native American Church and revitalized traditional tribal religions among both urban and reservation Indians led activists to advocate segregationist stances in the protection of the free exercise of their religions.[60]

The American Indian Chicago Conference in 1961 and the National Indian Youth Council's American Indian Capitol Conference on Poverty in 1964 were turning points in the solidification of this type of Indian politics. At these two events, Red Power was born.[61] Based on the Black Power and Back to Africa ideals articulated by black nationalists in the 1960s, Red Power activists asked the U.S. government to recognize tribes as sovereign nations, to respect the integrity of tribal territory, and to enter into new treaty negotiations with tribal nations.

The primary organization behind these demands was the American Indian Movement (AIM). In Minneapolis, Minnesota, in July 1968, a group of urban Indians including Dennis Banks, Russell Means, George Miller, John Trudell, and Clyde Bellecourt formed AIM.[62] The structure of the organization was based on that of the Black Panther Party (BPP), and AIM and the BPP worked together in Minneapolis to monitor police brutality against people of color in the inner city, and they consolidated to provide resources for child-care needs within the community.[63] As a result of AIM activism, for nearly ten years during the Red Power movement, Indian Country erupted in protests, occupations, and caravans, all expressing a radical, segregationist, pan-Indian politics.

The primary method of protest during these years was the technique of occupation. The first of those occupations took place on Alcatraz Island, an unused prison site in San Francisco Bay that nearly one hundred "Indians of All Tribes" held for a period of nineteen months (from 1969 to 1972). During the occupation, Indians of All Tribes established classes in traditional living, hosted press conferences, and met with visiting tribal dignitaries from across the continent.

Alcatraz served as a point of crystallization for the movement and as a model for nearly all of the other occupations, most of which were staged on unused military installations, including Ellis Island (prior to the development of the museum there), the Twin Cities Naval Air Station, former missile sites on Lake Michigan and in Beverly Hills, and an unused Army communications center in Davis, California. Indian activists argued for a reversal of Dawes-era policy; they wanted "surplus" white land returned to Indians. Regional offices of the BIA were occupied in San Diego, San Francisco, Missoula, Billings, Phoenix, Cleveland, Denver, Spokane, and Seattle. A small group of Indians occupied the national offices of the BIA in 1971, but that action received little media attention.

On the eve of the presidential election in 1972, a caravan of cars from across the nation came to Washington, D.C., on what Indian participants termed the "Trail of Broken Treaties." This was a double reference—first to the "Trail of Tears" caused by forced removal of Indians from the South in the 1830s, and second to the unenforced and abrogated treaties signed by the United States with the various tribes. Unable to get an audience with high-level BIA officials, frustrated Indians took control of the bureau. They occupied its offices and destroyed and took possession of records. This occupation did get the national media's attention, as well as the attention of BIA officials. The federal government eventually offered amnesty to the protestors and paid for their return trips home.

The perceived immaturity of the action, however, did not endear tribal activists to the BIA, or to the American public. Lack of widespread support from dominant society guaranteed that their demands—called the Twenty Points, and which called first and foremost for a return to treaty making—were never considered.[64] Though the demands were not met, the 1972 occupation of the BIA did help to radicalize an entire generation of Indian activists. Many of those at the BIA protest had not been on Alcatraz Island; they had not occupied a regional office and had not been part of the protests at Mount Rushmore or the Badlands National Park. They were joining comrades and friends on the trip to D.C. and were getting their first taste of radical pan-Indian politics. Many of them were Indians who had left their rural reservations for the first time; they returned home with a new perspective on Indian affairs and a renewed sense of political efficacy and energy.

In March 1973, traditionalists and elders protesting a corrupt and brutal tribal government on the Pine Ridge Reservation in South Dakota called upon AIM to help keep peace in their community.

The result was "Wounded Knee II," named in remembrance of the hundreds of Minniconjou Sioux men, women, children, and elders massacred at Wounded Knee by the 7th U.S. Cavalry in 1890, in what would prove to be the last major military conflict between whites and Indians in the United States. The occupation known as Wounded Knee II was a seventy-one-day armed standoff between AIM members and Sioux traditionalists against the FBI, which was supplemented by the personal police force (known by the uncomplimentary term "the goon squad") of tribal chair Dick Wilson. The protest camp at Wounded Knee, though not lacking in controversy, was successful in setting up a functioning government and revitalizing the practice of traditional religion; the camp was supported with food and moral support by many members of the reservation community at large. The occupation ended when the federal government used military force and FBI operatives to engage in battle with the protestors; two FBI agents were shot dead, and the camp was dissolved.

### INDIAN LEGAL ACTIVISM: FISHING RIGHTS

During the period of Red Power, Indians on the West Coast effectively mobilized to access their treaty-granted fishing rights. Specifically, the Puyallup Tribe mobilized, for the right to trap and fish the steelhead trout and salmon native to the Puget Sound and Puyallup River, against attacks on those rights by the state of Washington. Indians from across the nation came to support Puyallup efforts to fish by indigenous methods in their ancestral, though nonreservation, territory. They organized and held "fish-ins," in which Native peoples from any tribe fished side by side with Puyallup, on all waters of the river and sound. They did so in defiance of Washington State policy, which had become discredited by a Supreme Court decision rendered in *Puyallup v. Washington*.[65]

*Puyallup I,* as the decision became known, had held that the Treaty of Medicine Creek, made in 1854 with the Puyallup and Nisqually Tribes, effectively prohibited the state of Washington from regulating tribal fishing in the Puget Sound area. Though this was seen as a victory for the tribes, the ruling also caused heated dissension in Indian Country and created problems for the numerous landless and unrecognized tribes in Washington. The Court held that the right to fish according to native methods on the waters of the Puget Sound and Puyallup River was a *tribal* right. Such a right did not apply to individual Indians fishing without explicit tribal knowledge or consent, it did not apply to any Indians not of the Puyallup or Nisqually Tribes, and neither tribe could transfer that right to any individual members of other tribal nations.

In a further blow, the Court wrote, "Regardless of tribal sovereign immunity, individual defendant-members of the Puyallup Tribe remain amenable to the process of the Washington Courts in connection with fishing activities occurring off of their reservation." In other words, individual Puyallup and Nisqually Indians who allowed nontribal Indians to fish with them outside reservation boundaries would be subject to prosecution. The decision limited the rights of pan-Indian activists in the fish-in movement, and their continued activism was rendered illegal.

This was not the end of litigation on the issue, however. The Supreme Court heard a claim brought by non-Indian sport fishermen from Washington in *Puyallup II* (1973).[66] In *Puyallup II,* the Court demanded that Washington state courts devise a formula, adherence to which would ensure that the steelhead trout and salmon catch could be fairly apportioned between Indian net fishers and non-Indian sport fishers.

The apportionment made by the Washington court was also appealed, and, as fish-ins increased and became violent confrontations, with celebrities such as Marlon Brando in attendance, the Supreme Court heard *Puyallup III* under expedited review in 1977.[67] In *Puyallup III,* Justice Stevens's majority opinion acknowledged that the creation of such a fair apportionment scheme was impossible without disturbing tribal (treaty) fishing rights on reservation lands.

The Puyallup Reservation encompassed some seven miles of steelhead spawning waters within the Puyallup River. If those seven miles could be culled in unlimited fashion by tribal members, very few fish would ever make it out of reservation waters, leaving less than the "fair" share for non-Indian fishermen downriver. Significantly, Stevens noted that the Puyallup were a "federally recognized" tribe and could not be regulated by the state. However, he argued that the state of Washington could extend its jurisdiction over individual tribal members on reservation land, in the service of fair apportionment of fish, and that, additionally, members of federally unrecognized Indian tribes had no fishing rights at all in Puget Sound or on the Puyallup River as it left reservation land.

Justice Brennan and Justice Marshall offered a dissent. They would have extended the fishing rights of Washington Indians to any place that the Indians chose to fish. They also argued strenuously against the claims made by Washington State that the Puyallup Tribe had ceased to exist due to assimilation. Brennan and Marshall argued that the continued existence of the tribe and reservation should be the sole factor in deciding the case and that tribal sovereign immunity should hold supreme.

The issue of whether or not tribes could cease to exist because of their assimilation, brought previously in *John* and now indirectly in *Puyallup III*, continued to be brought before the courts during this period. The question resonated particularly in the Northeast, where a legal revolution was underway.

## INDIAN LEGAL ACTIVISM: LAND CLAIMS

Across the country from the Puget Sound two young lawyers in Maine were developing a new litigation strategy that would allow standing for some unrecognized Indian groups. Thomas Tureen and Barry Margolin pioneered the creative deployment of a seldom-used construct of Indian law, the *Trade and Intercourse Acts* of 1790 and 1834.[68] Often called the Non-Intercourse Acts, these federal statutes invalidated any contractual agreement between Indians and whites that were not approved by Congress—including those between tribes and state or colonial governments.

Congress had established an Indian Claims Commission (ICC) in 1946, in part as a response to the Sioux Nation's continued struggles to retrieve their land in the Black Hills of South Dakota.[69] At the ICC, tribes were able to argue that treaties had not been enforced and that land takings had occurred for which they had not been compensated, though such compensation was mandated by the Fifth Amendment. For reasons explained in chapter 1, most East Coast tribes had no treaty claims to bring to the ICC.

But, under the direction of Tureen and Margolin, tribal groups did begin to bring Non-Intercourse claims to that body, as well as in federal court, contending that the numerous transactions made

between tribes (and individual Indians) and colonial governments
in the Northeast were invalid. In addition, they argued that since
tribes had continued to use as much of their ancestral lands as was
possible for hunting, fishing, and ceremonial purposes, their rights
to the land had not been extinguished.

Tureen and Margolin went to the Department of the Interior in
1972, representing the Penobscot and Passamaquoddy Tribes of
Maine.[70] The tribes requested that the United States, through Interior,
litigate against the state of Maine for Non-Intercourse Act violations;
the stated goal of their suit was to secure the return of tribal land equal
to two-thirds of the state of Maine. Interior resisted bringing the claim,
and ultimately the Passamaquoddy sued the department to bring the
land claims litigation against Maine. A First Circuit Court ruling favorable to the tribe brought about a series of high-level negotiations at
Interior,[71] which culminated in the Maine Indian Claims Settlement
Act of 1980.[72] The act provided a significant cash settlement and set up
reservations for the tribes on three hundred thousand acres of land in
northern Maine.[73] In response to this success, tribes throughout the
region filed suit, bringing eleven major Non-Intercourse claims in the
next fifteen years.[74]

MASHPEE: PAN-INDIAN POLITICS, LAND CLAIMS
LITIGATION, AND RED POWER MEET

A land claim brought to the Massachusetts District Court by the
Mashpee Wampanoags against the town of Mashpee and the corpo-
ration of New Seabury, Inc., became an important instance of Non-
Intercourse Act litigation. It also had immense importance for the
debate over the legal status of tribal identity. In hearing that case,
Judge Walter Skinner ruled that the Non-Intercourse Act land claim
could not be decided until a jury established whether or not the
Mashpee Wampanoags were even a tribe at all.[75]

The town of Mashpee, Massachusetts, on the southwestern portion
of Cape Cod, was incorporated in 1870. From that date on, the Indians of Mashpee, who in 1870 held the majority of the town's territory
(over twelve thousand acres), lost control of their land, their political
power, and their means of subsistence as affluent white settlers
moved onto the Cape. By 1976, the tribe held title to a mere fifty-five

acres. In August 1976, the Mashpee Wampanoag Tribal Council, using the techniques developed by Tureen and Margolin, brought suit in federal court alleging violations of the Non-Intercourse Act. The tribe claimed ownership of sixteen thousand acres of land in southern Mashpee proper under development by a local business named the New Seabury Corporation.

Participants and observers alike found the resulting trial to be incredibly confusing.[76] Since the trial turned on whether or not the Mashpees had assimilated so much as to cease to exist as a tribe, New Seabury's attorney refused to even utter the word "tribe" and instead used the terms "group" and "community." Counsel and witnesses for the Mashpee Indians used only "tribe" in their testimony. However, none of the expert (academic) witnesses on either side agreed on what, exactly, a "tribe" was.[77]

Racial stereotypes also complicated the Mashpee trial. Basing their expectations on commonly held images of Indian identity, the Boston jurors and national media may have been disappointed when the Mashpees were not red-skinned people with high cheekbones.[78] Anglo and African American–looking Indians compensated for a lack of Indian physiognomy by wearing clothes that marked them as Indian; they donned feathers, beads, and headgear.

The trial was also confusing because it was apparent that, for many purposes, the federal government was already interacting with the Mashpees as Indians, if not as a tribe. There was a federally funded Indian education program in the Mashpee schools (the Indian Parent Education Committee), which had been set up prior to 1974.[79] The Mashpee Wampanoag Tribal Council president, Russell Peters, had worked for the Coalition of Eastern Native Americans (CENA), which, though made up primarily of unrecognized tribes, had much of its operating and administrative costs covered by federal monies.The Mashpee Tribal Council itself operated on a federal grant, even during the trial.

Judge Skinner required the Mashpees to show that they had existed, as a tribe, during six distinct time periods. He instructed the jury to evaluate whether there was a tribe in Mashpee on six dates that he felt were important to tribal history, such as the date of first-recorded contact and the date of the incorporation of the town of Mashpee. The dates to be examined were as follows:

July 22, 1790
March 31, 1834
March 3, 1842
June 23, 1869
May 28, 1870
August 26, 1976

Skinner's instructions were: "If at any time [the jury] found tribal status in Mashpee to have been voluntarily abandoned, then it could not be revived. Once lost, it [tribal status] was lost for good."[80]

Skinner then instructed the jury to apply a definition of "tribe" found in legal precedent, not in scholarly writings. He defined "tribe" by standards set in *Montoya v. United States* (1901),[81] which stated that a tribe was "a body of Indians of the same or similar race united in a community under one leadership or government and inhabiting a particular, though sometimes ill-defined territory." Race, territory, community, and leadership all had to be continuously present in order for the jury to recognize the Mashpee Wampanoags as a tribe.

Many commentators at the time thought that the standard set by Skinner worked to the favor of the Mashpee Wampanoags. However, *Montoya* was actually one of a line of cases in the early twentieth century that managed to profoundly confuse the issue of what a tribe was, and for what purposes. *Montoya* relied on *United States v. Joseph* (1876),[82] which had found that the Pueblos of New Mexico were not tribes, for purposes of Non-Intercourse regulations. The Court, in *Joseph*, held that land sales and takings from Indians by the state and private parties were valid, arguing that federal restrictions of such transactions did not apply to Pueblos, since Pueblos were *communities*, not tribes. However, in speaking about the same Pueblos in *Montoya*, thirty-seven years later, the Supreme Court held that they *were* tribes for purposes of state and federal liquor laws. While whites and the state could purchase Indian land without regard for Non-Intercourse restrictions, Indians could not purchase alcohol for themselves on Pueblo (tribal) land.[83] Based on *Joseph* and *Montoya*, *United States v. Candelaria*[84] held that Pueblos were, again, not tribes; *Candelaria* granted the state of New Mexico unlimited criminal jurisdiction over Pueblo lands, based on their community, as opposed to tribal, status.

After twenty-one hours of deliberation, undoubtedly some time of which was spent in confusion over the *Joseph-Montoya-Candelaria* progeny, the jury returned its verdict: the Mashpees *were not* a tribe on July 22, 1970; they *were* a tribe on March 31, 1834; they *were* a tribe on March 3, 1842; and they *were not* a tribe during any of the other periods evaluated, including August 26, 1976. Since there were periods during which the Mashpee Tribe ceased to visibly exist, the jury, of necessity, found that they were no longer a tribe at all. All land claims brought by the Mashpee Tribe were thus invalidated. This verdict was upheld on appeal; the Mashpees are still awaiting administrative review of their recognition claim.[85]


*Tying Together the Various Strands of*
*Indian Litigation and Activism*

Both mainstream pan-tribal organizations and radical Indian activists had supported the claimants at Mashpee. Tribal drummers, medicine men, and spiritual leaders were present in the courtroom, as were leaders of the CENA, the NCAI, and the Native American Rights Fund (NARF). Indian poverty, white racism, and the peripheral existence of tribes were all highlighted by the trial and by the Red Power movement in general. By this time, though, the increased interaction with courts and lawyers, as well as the influence of the civil rights and antiwar movements, gave Indian people new tools to fight the system.[86] Indian identity in this period became politicized, and access to the federal trust relationship became exceedingly important.[87]

The Mashpee trial, the fishing rights cases, and the land claims all helped to galvanize unrecognized Indians to fight for the realization of their needs. Decisions like *John* and *Mashpee* also showed officials in Washington, D.C., that changes regarding unrecognized tribes were both necessary and imminent.

## CHAPTER THREE

# Roadblocks on the Paths to Acknowledgment

Sociologist Stephen Cornell argues that the federal government responded to the Indian activism of the 1960s and 1970s in three ways.[1] First, the most radical Indian activists were suppressed through a variety of means. Second, presidential administrations under Johnson, Nixon, and Ford offered sweeping accomodationist reform through the Indian Civil Rights Act of 1968, the Indian Self-Determination and Education Assistance Act of 1975, and the Indian Child Welfare Act of 1978,[2] as well as a strengthened commitment to Indian preference hiring policies at the BIA, which withstood legal challenges culminating in *Morton v. Mancari* (1974). Finally, government officials sought to strengthen the institutional structure of Indian-white relations, particularly at its weakest link: the Bureau of Indian Affairs.

The BIA was already under attack on Capitol Hill for its lackadaisical mishandling of tribal trust lands and funds when a 1976 American Indian Policy Review Commission (AIPRC) report faulted the bureau for its treatment of unrecognized groups. AIPRC noted with disdain that the BIA did not even publish a list of which tribes were federally recognized; the status of the relationship was privy only to those tribes party to it.[3] Recognition of new tribes occurred on a purely ad hoc basis.[4] Occasionally, the BIA would extend services to a tribe previously unable to access them or denied them through Termination. However, although the BIA exerted far-reaching control over most aspects of Indian-U.S. relationships and was the primary agency that tribal leaders interacted with, it was not the only place unrecognized tribes could go for recognition. Congress occasionally extended recognition to groups upon recommendation of the Senate Committee on Indian Affairs and the federal judiciary was also responsible for allowing a small number of tribes into the government-to-government relationship. Congress made no statutory or appropriations distinctions between those tribes that were administratively, legislatively, or judicially recognized.

Recognition practices in the three branches were far from uniform and continued unregulated until the BIA responded to the 1976 AIPRC recommendations, at which point the bureau moved quickly to assert its monopoly over the acknowledgment process. Aware that Congress was considering bills on the matter, some of which threatened to divest Interior of its power to acknowledge tribes, and unwilling to be bound by congressional rules for acknowledgment, officials at Interior urged legislative restraint and reassured members of the Senate Committee on Indian Affairs that the BIA would take care of recognition issues.[5]

It did so rather quickly, with the creation, in 1978, of mandatory criteria for acknowledgment and the development of an adjudicatory staff now known as the Branch of Acknowledgment and Research. Reasoning that its long history of administering Indian Affairs made the BIA the agency best suited to the job, officials at the bureau treated the process as a normal administrative rulemaking—they developed rules, sought input from interested parties through a comment period, and published the written regulations in the *Federal Register.* Congress never passed authorizing legislation for the BAR, nor did Congress ever approve the mandatory criteria.

BAR staff members wrote the criteria to reflect the legal definition of tribe as it was laid out in an early U.S. Supreme Court decision, *Montoya v United States,*[6] and in accordance with the so-called Cohen Criteria, in use informally since Felix Cohen's tenure at the BIA. The BAR's criteria were adopted in 1978; as a result of congressional hearings, they changed slightly in 1988 and more substantially in 1994. Currently, in order to be recognized through the BAR, an Indian tribe must do the following:

a. Establish that the group has been identified as an American Indian entity on a substantially continuous basis since 1900.

b. Establish that a predominant portion of the petitioning group comprises a distinct community and has existed as a community from historical times until the present.

c. Establish maintenance of their political influence and authority over its members as an autonomous entity from historical times until the present.

d. Furnish a copy of current tribal governing documents, including membership criteria.

e. Furnish a membership list, and establish that the petitioner's membership consists of individuals who descend from a historical Indian tribe or from historical Indian tribes which combined and functioned as a single autonomous political entity.

f. Establish that their membership is not substantially composed of members of other tribes.

g. Establish that Congress has not barred them from achieving recognition as an Indian tribe, and that they have not been Terminated.[7]

As a result of the 1994 Senate hearings, the BAR's criteria (known as 25 CFR 83) were amended to the form seen above. The primary change was in the second criterion, in which a former requirement of geographic cohesion was replaced with social cohesion, which can be interpreted to mean maintenance of geographic proximity. Additionally, the BAR sought to "reduce the burden of proof imposed upon petitioners"[8] by changing criterion 83.7(a) in such a way that external identification of the group as an Indian entity was no longer required from earliest historical times to the present, but only from 1900 to the present.[9] Similar thresholds were changed for 83.7(b) and 83.7(c). The amended criteria also reduced the burden of proof for previously acknowledged tribes and added a list of facts or circumstances that demonstrate community and political authority, to give the tribes a better sense of what they needed to provide BAR evaluators. Finally, the 1994 changes included a provision for "expedited review" of petitioners' claims when they clearly do not, and cannot, meet the criteria in 83.7(e). If a tribe cannot prove in early review that its members descend from more than one ancestor who was a member of a historic tribe, the BAR issues a proposed negative determination without addressing the other criteria.

## *The Mechanics of Bar Processes*

The first step on the road to acknowledgment by the BAR is for a group to file a letter of intent to petition. The group then researches and compiles evidence addressing all seven criteria, which is submitted as a petition to the BAR. A BAR team then reviews the petition, and sends, if necessary, a "letter of obvious deficiency" to the group, highlighting potential problems with the petition. The BAR allows time for the group to respond to the so-called OD letter, and may engage the group in formal (on the record) and informal (off the record) technical assistance meetings.

Ideally, BAR staff numbers at ten; however, the branch is often shorthanded. BAR staff members are primarily scholars trained in the fields of history, genealogy, and/or anthropology. Most are career public servants. At the May 2000 technical assistance meetings on the Eastern Pequot and Paucatuck Eastern Pequot petitions for acknowledgment, BAR staff member George Roth stated that he had been with the bureau for twenty-two years, Virginia DeMarce for seven years, and Lee Flemming for three years. There is extensive crossover between the BAR workforce and scholars hired by the petitioning groups. For example, Steve Austin, an anthropologist working for one of the tribes whose recognition was in question at that meeting, had previously had a rather long career at the BAR.

Once the petition is completed and the problems outlined in the OD letter have been addressed, the BAR makes a recommendation on the petition to the assistant secretary of Indian Affairs (AS-IA), who issues a proposed finding, published in the *Federal Register.* A 120-day comment period commences—interested parties such as state Senators, Indian rights groups, other tribes, and local businesses may offer comment on the group's petition. After the comment period, which can legally be extended indefinitely, a Final Judgment, also known as the Final Determination, is issued by the BIA and printed in the *Federal Register.* The Final Determination, which either extends or denies acknowledgement, is signed by the AS-IA, who usually, but not always, follows the recommendations of the BAR staff. Four recent proposed positive findings signed by AS-IA Kevin Gover went to him from the BAR staff as proposed negative determinations. These were the findings for the Nipmuc Nation, Chinook, Eastern

Pequot, and Paucatuck Eastern Pequot Tribes. The BIA does occasionally change its mind, issuing a Final Determination different from its proposed finding; however, only two groups that have received proposed negative findings at the BAR have managed to resubmit evidence and achieve a positive Final Determination: the Gay Head Wampanoag (1987) and the Mohegan Tribe (1994). The Gay Head proposed finding, in particular, brought an avalanche of criticism down on the BAR staff; critics of the negative proposed finding charged that racism and historical inaccuracy had colored the process.

Indian groups that feel they have been unfairly denied recognition at the BAR must exhaust the appeals process provided by the Department of the Interior before moving a claim to a judicial setting. These dissatisfied parties take their appeals to the Interior Board of Indian Appeals (IBIA).[10] If accepted for review at the IBIA, an administrative law judge reviews the procedural aspects of the decision and may remand it back to the BAR for reconsideration. Several tribes have attempted to gain a hearing at the IBIA; two in particular—the Mowa Choctaws (Alabama) and the Golden Hill Paugussetts (Connecticut)— have challenged the expedited finding against their recognition under the new provisions of 1994.

The Mowa Choctaws' case against the BAR was recently invalidated at the IBIA; its proposed finding against recognition was finalized in the winter of 2000. The BAR found that the state-recognized Mowas were unable to prove that their claimed ancestors had any ties to the historic Choctaw Tribe. The BAR made a similar finding on the Golden Hill Paugussett (GHP) petition—the GHP are recognized by the state of Connecticut but were unable to prove that their claimed ancestor, William Sherman, was a Golden Hill Indian. The GHP have had two successful hearings at the IBIA; both times their petition was remanded back to the BAR with procedural instructions. As of fall 2002, they remained waiting for a reconsidered finding from the BAR.

Since its inception, the BAR has received 250 letters of intent to petition. Fifty-five petitions have been completed and filed by hopeful groups. From 1978 until 2000, the BAR completed the adjudication of thirty-three claims through administrative processes.[11] Fifteen of the petitioning groups were recognized in Final Determinations; two more had proposed findings in favor of acknowledgment on record in 2000. Fifteen additional tribes were denied recognition

## TABLE 3.1
*Tribes Recognized by the BAR*

| Name | State | Year Recognized |
|---|---|---|
| Grand Traverse Band of Ottawa and Chippewa | Mich. | 1979 |
| Jamestown Klallam Tribe | Wash. | 1980 |
| Tunica-Biloxi Indian Tribe | La. | 1981 |
| Death Valley Timbi-Sha Shoshone Band | Calif. | 1982 |
| Narragansett Indian Tribe | R.I. | 1983 |
| Poarch Band of Creek Indians | Ala. | 1983 |
| Wampanoag Tribe of Gay Head (Aquinnah) | Mass. | 1984 |
| San Juan Southern Paiute Tribe | Ariz. | 1989 |
| Mohegan Indian Tribe | Conn. | 1994 |
| Jena Choctaw Band of Indians | La. | 1994 |
| Huron Potawatomi, Inc. | Mich. | 1995 |
| Samish Indian Tribe | Wash. | 1996 |
| Match-e-be-nash-she-wish Band of Potawatomi Indians | Mich. | 1996 |
| Snoqualmie Indian Tribe | Wash. | 1999 |
| Cowlitz Indian Tribe | Wash. | 2000 (proposed) |
| Eastern Pequot Tribe/Paucatuck Eastern Pequot | Conn. | 2000 (proposed) |
| Little Shell Tribe of Chippewa Indians | Mont. | 2000 (proposed) |

SOURCE: U.S. General Accounting Office, *Indian Issues: Improvements Needed in Tribal Recognition Process.*

between 1978 and 2000, and one group had a proposed Final Determination against recognition pending in 2000 (see tables 3.1 and 3.2). A determination is "final" once it has been signed by the AS-IA and been published in the *Federal Register;* prior to that, a finding is considered "proposed." The publication of a proposed finding initiates a 120-day comment period, which can be extended indefinitely,

### TABLE 3.2
*Groups Declined Recognition by the BAR*

| Name | State | Year Denied |
|---|---|---|
| Lower Muskogee Creek Tribe East of the Mississippi | Ga. | 1981 |
| Creeks East of the Mississippi | Fla. | 1981 |
| Munsee-Thames River Delaware | Colo. | 1983 |
| Principal Creek Indian Nation | Ala. | 1985 |
| Kaweah Indian Nation | Calif. | 1985 |
| United Lumbee Nation of North Carolina and America | Calif. | 1985 |
| South East Cherokee Confederacy (American Cherokee Confederacy) | Ga. | 1985 |
| Northwest Cherokee Wolf Band of South East Cherokee Confederacy | Ore. | 1985 |
| Red Clay Inter-Tribal Indian Band, SECC | Tenn. | 1985 |
| Tchinouk Indians | Ore. | 1986 |
| MaChis Lower Alabama Creek Indian Tribe | Ala. | 1988 |
| Miami Nation of Indians of Indiana, Inc. | Ind. | 1992 |
| Ramapough Mountain Indians, Inc. | N.J. | 1998 |
| Mowa Band of Choctaws | Ala. | 1999 |
| Yuchi Tribal Organization | Okla. | 2000 |
| Steilacoom Tribe of Indians | Wash. | 2000 (proposed) |

Source: Compiled by author

and decisions in the proposed finding stage can be repealed or revoked at will of the BAR. Recent BIA changes have resulted in a review of several acknowledgment decisions accomplished in the Clinton administration's second term as well as the litigation of several others.

Acknowledgment by the BAR is "pass/fail," and one missing criterion is enough to deny acknowledgment. An examination of BAR documents shows that most groups failed to earn acknowledgment because they lacked the same four criteria: 83.7(a), 83.7(b), 83.7(c), and 83.7(e). The majority of the groups were unable to show that they had been "identified by reliable external sources as an Indian entity since 1900" (a); that they had "maintained a continuous community from 1900 to the present day" (b); and that their leadership had "exhibited substantially continuous political authority or influence since 1900" (c). In addition, most of these groups failed to show that their members descended from a historic tribe (e).

Noted exceptions to these general trends are the Principal Creek (Alabama) and Tchinouk (Oregon) Tribes, which were able to show that their members were descendants from the historic tribes, but failed the other criteria, and the Miami Nation (Indiana), which was able to show descent, and that outsiders had identified it as an Indian entity since 1900, but could not establish maintenance of social cohesion. The Duwamish (Washington) were denied recognition by the BAR in 1996; the BIA agreed to reconsider that decision in 1996, and granted the Tribe recognition in 2001. However, the incoming Bush administration reversed that grant, so the Duwamish, though they have met all the criteria, remain unrecognized.

All of the petitioning groups have been able to provide the BAR with copies of recent membership and governing documents and have proven that they had not been forbidden, by Termination legislation, from seeking acknowledgment through the BAR processes. However, the Kaweah and United Lumbee, both from California, failed to show that their membership was not made up substantially of members of other recognized tribes; overlapping tribal membership is forbidden by the criteria.

## Recognition through Legislation

Indian tribes frequently approach acknowledgment through several overlapping paths.[12] Though the BAR appears to have an effective monopoly over the recognition process and criteria, it is actually within the authority of Congress, and not the executive branch, to recognize relationships with tribes. Article 1, Section 8, Clause 3 of the U.S. Constitution, sometimes referred to as the Indian Commerce Clause, grants *Congress* the authority to regulate Indian affairs and recognize tribes. The BIA's rulemaking on the acknowledgment process did not seek, or gain, official congressional approval, yet acknowledgment processes are primarily handled by the BAR.

## TABLE 3.3
*Tribes Recognized by Congress*

| Name | State | Year Recognized |
|------|-------|-----------------|
| Pascua Yaqui Tribe | Ariz. | 1978 |
| Houlton Band of Maliseet Indians | Maine | 1980 |
| Cow Creek Band of Umpqua Indians | Ore. | 1982 |
| Western (Mashantucket) Pequot Tribe | Conn. | 1983 |
| Kickapoo Traditional Tribe (as part of Kickapoo Tribe of Oklahoma; recognized as a separate tribe in 1989) | Tex. | 1983 |
| Ysleta Del Sur Pueblo | Tex. | 1987 |
| Lac Vieux Desert Band of Lake Superior Chippewa Indians | Mich. | 1987 |
| Coquille Tribe | Ore. | 1988 |
| Aroostook Band of Micmacs | Maine | 1991 |
| Pokagon Potawatomi Indians of Indiana and Michigan | Ind. | 1994 |
| Little Traverse Bay Band of Odawa Indians | Mich. | 1994 |
| Little River Band of Ottawa Indians | Mich. | 1994 |
| Central Council of the Tlingit and Haida Indian Tribes | Alaska | 1994 |
| Loyal Shawnee Tribe | Okla. | 2000 |

SOURCE: U.S. General Accounting Office, *Indian Issues: Improvements Needed in Tribal Recognition Process.*

However, hopeful Indian groups can and do seek, as an alternative to the BAR, acknowledgment legislation. Since the BAR's creation, Congress has recognized fourteen tribes and has restored thirty-seven from Terminated status (see table 3.3 for a list of congressionally recognized [not restored] tribes). Some of these bills have been passed at the request of the BIA, in order to rectify previous congressional wrongs in the form of Termination or improper takings of land. In no case has the legislative recognition occurred after a BAR finding against the tribe; however, some groups have halted their petition's progress at BAR in order to pursue, and achieve, legislative recognition. In the Mashantucket Pequot case, in particular, Congress recognized the tribe against the advice of Interior, which was concerned that the tribe could not credibly complete the BAR process.

Congress does not have to provide reasons for rejecting tribal acknowledgment claims;[13] the congressional process has no substantive requirements for or specialty in determining who qualifies as an Indian tribe. Accordingly, some instances of Congressional acknowledgement have been controversial in the halls of the BIA, as well as on the reservations of Indian Country.

Many groups view legislative acknowledgment as particularly fraught with danger; one person I interviewed for this project was particularly clear on this subject. She told me, "Sometimes our representatives make decisions, or they do it for the wrong reason, and they're not knowledgeable about what the history is, or the genealogy." Once, she asked a congressman sponsoring a bill for another group's federal acknowledgment the following question: "I said, 'Why are you supporting this bill for recognition through the legislative process?' And his answer to me was, 'Because they asked me to.' So, see, to me, that's a danger. . . . I didn't feel that that was a good enough reason, just 'Because they asked me to.'"

This person also pointed out that congressional recognition appeared to be an unsafe option.

> Congress can make laws and they can change them. And what if Congress recognizes you as an Indian tribe, these politicians, you know you got somebody, you know, and they are sensitive to you, and they understand you and maybe they're from your district, and maybe they get the bill passed and they recognize you as an Indian tribe and that's well and good. . . . Ok, well in the next four years, say like you get Democrats and the next year the Republicans come along. This other politician, he's in there, and he don't like you, or he don't like your tribal leader. [He says,] "Them people aren't Indians," . . . and he gets his clique together and then that year they say, well, "We're gonna withdraw your recognition." They can. They make laws and they can change them. What are you going to do? So for us the safest and securest way was to do it through the [BIA's] process. Its not that there's anything wrong with the legislative process. Its just that it's politics, it's political, and politics change.[14]

Indeed, the process of securing congressional acknowledgment is risky; it is also expensive and time consuming. Hopeful groups must hire lobbyists, finance trips to Washington, and wage a media campaign in their home state. For some, this raises the uncomfortable specter that wealthier or more well-connected Indian groups could buy federal recognition with lobbying money or promises of votes.

However, the idea that tribes may be successful at purchasing federal recognition seems an overblown fear. Congress has been reticent to recognize tribes without BIA approval. As the chief of staff for one Alabama congressman told me about bills to recognize the Mowa Choctaws,

> [the] congressman did introduce [recognition] legislation in the House. It did not go very far. As I recall, it may have died because we ran out of time in that session. But the Committee met it with stiff opposition. I don't think they were picking on [the congressman] or on our particular case as much as the fact that they had only had six legislative recognitions since 1982, I believe. And, so, it's not something that Congress is anxious to do; number one, it oversteps the role of BIA, and number two, it conceivably sets a dangerous precedent.[15]

Certainly, congressional reticence accounts for a significant failure rate for tribes approaching Congress. The executive branch has a further check on congressional activity with presidential veto power. In one case, that of the Jena Choctaw Band of Indians, the tribe was successful in its *fifth* attempt at legislative acknowledgment, only to have President Bush (Sr.) veto the bill in 1992 because it bypassed the BIA. Bush's deference to the BIA's monopoly on the process was especially frustrating to the tribe, as the BAR recognized the tribe two years later, after it concluded administrative proceedings and the BAR staff reached a positive Final Determination.

Although only eleven tribes have failed at acknowledgment in the legislative setting, this number requires special attention; it represents only the number of tribes that have been successful in getting their bill to the floor for a vote. An even greater number of potential acknowledgment bills remain dormant in committee or in their senator's offices. Many tribes are repeat players in legislative acknowledgment—the number of failed bills in the last twenty-five years is nearly five times the number of failed tribes. By their sheer volume, these bills represent a significant proportion of the business of the Senate's Indian Affairs Committee.

## Proposed Changes to the BAR

Federal acknowledgment processes (FAPs) in general, and the BAR's operations in particular, have been exceedingly controversial and there is great debate over where acknowledgment processes should be housed. In past congressional hearings on changes to acknowledgment, three voices have been heard most prominently. BAR staff and BIA officials, as well as representatives from some recognized tribes and unrecognized groups, have argued that FAPs belong in the BIA;[16] they have urged reform intended to simplify and shorten the processes. On the other hand, some scholars and activists have argued that the BAR, and all recognition processes, should be abolished. Somewhere in the middle are representatives from several Indian tribes and unrecognized groups, who, though they disagree on whether or not the current criteria are appropriate, advocate the end of the BAR and the creation of an independent commission to adjudicate acknowledgment claims.

### THE BAR PERSPECTIVE

Aside from keeping the process within the BIA, and receiving increased appropriations, the BAR staff also supports a "sunset" provision, whereby no new letters of intent to petition would be accepted after a given date. The BAR staff recognizes that its processes are too slow, but offers some reasons in its defense and suggestions for change. First, staff members argue that recognition is so important a topic that its research and determinations should be meticulously conducted. Few would dispute that claim; most would agree that FAPs are necessary to guard against imposter tribes.

However, the BAR staff also desires an end to acrimonious acknowledgment proceedings and an end to legal challenges of its decisions. Staff members say that the heavy workload caused by litigation—in the form of brief preparation and Freedom of Information Act requests—slows the process. The BAR's official guidelines, provided to petitioning groups, spell out agency preferences quite clearly.

> To move the evaluation and review of your petition faster, you should focus on explaining how your group meets the regulations (which will get you acknowledged through the process the way it exists now). Arguing against the regulations (if you or your lawyers don't agree with them, philosophically or legally) may not matter in the end and will often take valuable energy, time and resources away from advancing your goal of acknowledgment.[17]

They add, "prepare the petition in a factual, businesslike way so that these people [*sic*] who work for these government agencies [*sic*] can understand it. Experimental or overly sentimental writing may only end up lowering the overall credibility of your petition."

To staff members' dismay and frustration, even procedural matters at the BAR get misinterpreted; the staff's best intentions are often misrepresented. The "letter of obvious deficiencies," provided by the BAR "to comment on areas of the petition that seem likely to be problematic in the subsequent full review, in order to provide an opportunity to amend the petition before the formal review begins" is an example of this miscommunication. Gerald Sider writes, "The idea, which on the BIA's part is regarded as friendly and helpful [is seen by many Native people] as harsh, unreasonable, and designed to chase them away."[18] BAR staff members see their job as neutrally applying the criteria and ask that petitioners give them the benefit of the doubt. Given most groups' natural suspicion of the BAR, in part a residual effect of the BIA's mishandling of tribal issues, particularly tribal trust funds, this seems a tall order.

### THE A-BAR-LITIONIST PERSPECTIVE

I affectionately refer to a particular group of scholars as the "a-BAR-litionists."[19] They represent the anti-colonial viewpoint, and their strongest voice is Ward Churchill's. Churchill advocates a return to treaty making, with that process's recognition of the inherent sovereignty of Indian tribes.[20] The implications of understanding the inherent, rather than delegated, sovereignty of Indian tribes include his conclusions that the territory of American Indian Nations is entitled to the same integrity as Canada's or Mexico's; that since governance must be self-determined, Indian Reorganization Act (IRA) constitutions are imposed, and are thus illegal; that tribes should have complete criminal jurisdiction; and that the Citizenship Act of 1924 was an imposition by the United States on American Indians, in violation of their right to exist without external interference.[21] Attempts by the U.S. government to identify Indians, to quantify them, or to regulate access to Indian identity are colonial remnants that, further, are unconstitutional and "fly in the face of international conventions," even when sanctioned by tribal governments. Ultimately, such efforts at recognition, or acknowledgment, are genocidal.

Anthropologist and lawyer Russel Barsh agrees. He writes that, in processes of recognition, we can see

> the emergence of a new legal standard of "Indianness" which gives the administration a loaded gun to point at recalcitrant tribal leaders. While in limited respects the federal government is relinquishing its traditional day-to-day control over Indians' lives and lands, and boasting of its commitment to "self-determination," it has claimed instead a far more powerful disciplinary weapon: the authority to decree tribes nonexistent.[22]

Other Indian scholars stress a different aspect of the BAR. Vine Deloria has long advocated self-recognition; he argues strenuously that Indians know "who we are." Annette Jaimes agrees that self-identification is key to a "true process of decolonization and reestablishment of [tribes] as national entities."[23] From this position, tribal self-determination of the boundaries of Indian Country is mandatory.

However, some who find this analysis persuasive also find the federal government's power in this realm hegemonic. Castile has argued that self-identification is ideal but impossible in the continuing context of colonialism. What *may* be possible, though, may be the creation of an independent commission, separate from the BIA, to oversee acknowledgment claims. Such an independent commission may be the hybrid position—it takes the idea of self-determination seriously, and removes the process from the BIA, yet still requires criteria and standards quite similar to those in place at the BAR.

The push to create an independent, presidentially appointed commission to adjudicate acknowledgment claims is not new. The AIPRC's 1976 report, out of which the BAR ultimately grew, recommended just such an independent body. However, the majority of reform-minded proposals in the last ten years have latched onto the commission idea as a new, and novel, approach to the federal acknowledgment process. Those in favor of such a commission recognize the necessity of continued classificatory schemes for the maintenance of tribal powers and boundaries, but also recognize the conflict of interest the BIA staff might have in the recognition process. Proponents of an independent regime also argue that it will be speedier for the tribes and cheaper in operations for the federal government.

Senate Bill 611 (S 611) is the most recent bill related to recognition processes to be heard by the Indian Affairs Committee; it proposed the creation of an independent commission. Had it passed, it would have created a three-member commission, with an eight-year deadline for the introduction of new petitions and a twelve-year "sunset" provision. The criteria for acknowledgment would not have substantially changed; however, S 611 would have required the petitioners to establish identification as an Indian entity on a substantially continuous basis since 1871, rather than the BAR's current 1900 threshold.

Although it is uncertain if such a commission will come to fruition, it does seem likely that, if it did, it would avoid some of the problems encountered by the BIA where the bureau has "political and financial interests in minimizing the number of tribes the government acknowledges."[24] However, it certainly could not insulate the process from the resource, race, and political considerations that the BAR has similarly been unable to avoid. Even Senator Daniel K. Inouye (D-Hawaii), a sponsor of the bill, acknowledged as much when he asked a hearing participant, tongue-in-cheek, "Wouldn't that [a commission] make the process *political?*"[25]

In addition, the staffing of such a commission raises even more complicated questions—who would be eligible and appropriate to serve? Most agree that Indians should be on the commission, but that raises the very question that the committee would purport to answer: who is an authorized Indian? Inouye questioned Arlinda Locklear, an attorney representing a number of unrecognized groups (and herself a member of the Lumbee Tribe): "What if we had

Indian Country give twelve names" and then let Indian Country sort out the appointments to the committee? Locklear responded that that would be a favorable move, but cautioned that "Indian Country" must be defined to include both recognized and unrecognized groups.

## Scholarly Critiques

The positions taken in senate hearings on the topic reflect the scholarly critiques of acknowledgment offered by a small but vocal group of anthropologists, historians, lawyers, and political scientists who have studied federal acknowledgment, particularly as it is practiced by the BAR and by the courts prior to the BAR. This literature presents structural and institutional reasons for the problems with federal acknowledgment.

The predictions and explanations generated by these critiques rely on an understanding of the structural determinants in operation that place Indians in a subordinated role in U.S. society. Critiques within the structuralist perspective oppose current acknowledgment proceedings and practices because those practices are comprehended as operating to reproduce class, racial, and colonial subordination.

Other scholars offer a primarily procedural critique. Procedural critics of the BAR express their dismay at long time delays, the expense of petitioning, and the ambiguity of both the rules and the process; they do not always develop a detailed structural or colonial analysis. When taken together, the procedural and substantive critiques of BAR processes are quite powerful.

### CASH: ECONOMIC CONSTRAINTS ON ACKNOWLEDGMENT

Participation in the BAR involves a substantial commitment of time and resources on the part of the petitioning groups. On average, a petitioner spends six to ten years collecting and transcribing oral histories, drawing maps, and researching county records as it documents its claim.[26] The BAR staff spends another six to ten years, on average, evaluating a petition and moving it through bureaucratic channels. In hearings before the House Subcommittee on Native American Affairs, some charged that the BAR staff routinely ignores its own deadlines while holding petitioners accountable to rigid timetables; others argued that BAR criteria are highly subjective and that contention within the agency about what standards to apply lengthens and overburdens the process.[27] Jack Campisi, an anthropologist who has worked on several acknowledgment claims, calls the BAR a "bureaucratic mill that makes the continental drift look like a speedy process."[28] Such lengthy delays and opportunities for review within the administrative process exacerbate the serious economic constraints on the often impoverished groups seeking acknowledgment.

It is widely acknowledged that recognized Indian tribes have populations that live in desolate conditions and poverty. Reservations are typically located in the most impoverished areas of the states in which they are located, and reservations are overwhelmingly located in the poorer states, such as New Mexico, South Dakota, Idaho, and Oklahoma.[29] According to the 1990 national census, one-third of all Native Americans and Alaskan Natives lived below the poverty level. This situation was not improved by the 2000 census, which reports that American Indians have the highest rates of poverty of any ethnic group—24.5 percent of all Indians live below the poverty line (the national poverty rate is 11.6 percent; the poverty rate for African Americans is 22.9 percent; the poverty rate for non-Hispanic white Americans is 7.6 percent).

American Indians have the highest rates of unemployment of any ethnic group. The *Indian Labor Force Reporter,* published by the Department of Labor, notes that in 1997, 50 percent of American Indians in the labor force were unemployed, as compared to 17 percent of blacks, 14 percent of Hispanics, and 10 percent of whites.[30] In part thanks to the success of gaming enterprises, these numbers had turned around a bit by 2000.[31] By then, only 12.4 percent of all American Indians and Alaskan Natives were unemployed (compared to 5.8 percent unemployment for the United States as a whole). Though the outlook is better, Gary Sandefur notes that high rates of unemployment have historical antecedents: "Among all U.S. racial and ethnic groups, American Indians were those least likely to be employed the full year throughout the 1959–1979 period."[32]

In addition, though unemployment rates are down, wages have not risen dramatically. Fully employed American Indians and Alaskan Natives earned an average of $12,893 in 2000 (compared to $21,587 for the United States as a whole). American Indian households had a median income, according to the 2000 census, of $30,599; though higher than in past years, this dollar amount is still eleven thousand less than the average U.S. household income.

As could be expected from their rates of poverty, American Indians receive more pubic assistance than any other ethnic group in America. Poor economic indicators are also accompanied by disproportion-ately high rates of many social ills. A 1999 Justice Department report notes that American Indians experience crime at a rate of 124 violent crimes per one thousand people over the age of twelve—double the national rate. Though they make up 0.6 percent of the American population, American Indians experience 1.4 percent of the nation's violent crime.[33] American Indians have disproportionately lower rates of literacy and educational attainment and suffer low mortality rates among reservation residents.[34] Diabetes has become epidemic on reservations, as has high blood pressure. Indian youth suicide deaths, in those areas monitored by Indian Health Services, are nearly 19 percent higher than the U.S. average,[35] and youth alcoholism deaths are nearly 5 percent higher than the U.S. average.[36] In 1999, the drug-related death rate for American Indians was 18 percent higher than for all other races; the death rate for American Indian men in motor vehicle accidents was 3.2 percent higher than for all other races (for American Indian women, the death rate is 3.7 per-cent higher). The Justice Department reported in 1999 that American Indians have an arrest rate for nonviolent alcohol violations (2,545 violations per 100,000 Indians) that is more than double the national arrest rate (1,079 violations per 100,000 of all other ethnic groups).[37]

The picture is often even bleaker for members of unrecognized tribal groups; they fare even more poorly than reservation and urban-dwelling members of recognized tribes. Individual Indians from unrecognized groups may be eligible to receive government funds earmarked for Indian programs, but the tribes have limited access to federal funds earmarked for tribal concerns, and they are not eligible for Bureau of Indian Affairs programs. Most are without a substantial land base that they could use for economic develop-ment. These groups are made up of poor people of color living in individual (not reservation) settlements, in primarily rural areas, with few tribal resources at their disposal and with limited access to federal money spent on Indian populations. It was not until the 2000 census that they were even counted as a distinct population.

The 2000 census shows that unrecognized Mowa Choctaws, for example, had an average household income of $6,250, and that 80 percent of their members live below the poverty level.

Congressional testimony in 1994 revealed that the research necessary for a petition could be exorbitantly expensive for such an impoverished population. The production of an acknowledgment petition is increasingly professionalized. In what could be termed a "cottage industry," tribes contract with outside scholars, who complete a good deal of the research and petition preparation. The BAR's guidelines for petitioners include three pages on how to manage the scholar-tribe relationship, with advice to clarify, early and in writing, who owns the research and documents produced in recognition efforts. Even when volunteers prepare the entire petition, the tribe incurs travel, photocopying, and equipment costs.

The BIA does not provide funds to groups for the purpose of pursuing their acknowledgment claim. An informational brochure provided by the BIA does, however, provide the names and addresses of various groups that provide financial support to groups seeking acknowledgment. These groups include the Indian Rights Association, Legal Services Corporation, National Indian Lutheran Board, Native American Rights Fund, and Americans for Indian Opportunity. Many unrecognized tribes will also qualify for need-based legal assistance from legal services organizations.

Despite their likely poverty, unrecognized groups must spend substantial amounts of money to attain acknowledgment. From 1978 to 1990, sixteen hopeful groups spent roughly $8 million researching their petitions.[38] The price tag for recognition consideration at the BAR has suffered gross inflation since 1994; the cost since then has been nearly $1 million per petition. Surely these expenditures are not easy for groups whose people live in conditions of extreme poverty. Even at the lowest estimated rates, $50,000 to $100,000 for a petition, costs are prohibitive for tribes that cannot meet the basic needs of their people.

A second economic constraint on federal recognition is that American Indians' marginal position in the political landscape ensures that Indians and the bureaucratic agencies meant to serve them lack access to power in Washington. Consequently, though the BIA serves a large and needy population, it is severely underfunded and lacks power in Washington.[39]

In particular, the BAR lacks necessary financing. The former head of the BAR, John "Bud" Shapard, estimated that, in its first twelve years, the BAR spent roughly $285,000 evaluating each petition; from 1990 to 1994, when the BAR completely reviewed only three petitions, the cost for reviewing them rose to nearly $1 million each.[40] Although this represents less than 1 percent of the $2 billion-operating budget of the BIA during this time, it far outspends the average annual appropriation of $900,000 specifically made to the BAR.[41] The sheer cost to the federal government of operating the BAR leads to its own institutional precariousness, which, in turn, makes it institutionally difficult to acknowledge new tribes.

More so, the cost to the government of acknowledging tribes increases after acknowledgment, since recognition entitles tribes to a variety of federal Indian services and monies, including medical and dental care, education funds and support, housing, eligibility for certain loans, and legal aid.[42] The BIA allocates $160,000 in start-up money to fund tribes with 1,500 or fewer members and $300,000 for tribes with 1,501 to 3,000 members (acknowledged groups with more than 3,000 members are funded on a case-by-case determination).[43] Since acknowledgment of new tribes represents a reduction in the Indians' piece of the economic pie distributed by the BIA, the BIA has an apparent conflict of interest—by acknowledging more groups, it increases its service population without having the wherewithal to increase its funding. In fact, other tribes have put incredible pressure on BIA officials to deny recognition to large petitioners, such as the Lumbee Tribe of North Carolina (which, as reported in the 2000 federal census, numbers 51,913 people).

Political scientist David E. Wilkins (Lumbee) and others have argued that it is in part due to the economic marginality of Indian affairs that the Lumbee have not achieved full recognition.[44] BIA officials have admitted that the agency finds it financially "impractical" to recognize groups like the Lumbee.[45] The Lumbee and Houma have bills that have failed numerous times in Congress.

The February 2000 directive issued by then-assistant secretary of Indian Affairs Kevin Gover, which forbade BAR staff members from completing technical reports or engaging in extended fieldwork to research pending acknowledgment petitions, was intended as both a time- and money-saving effort.[46] The directive also included instructions intended as a response to the racial controversy engendered by

BAR decisions. Scholars and activists have argued since its inception that, as an authenticator of tribal (and, therefore, Indian) identity, the BAR perpetuates a racial hierarchy that essentializes and marginalizes Indian people.

## COLOR: RACIAL STEREOTYPING OF AMERICAN INDIANS

Steven Leuthold examines stereotypes of Native peoples and constructions of dominant society's power in his collection on indigenous aesthetics; he writes that typical stereotypes of American Indians are both "iconic" and "reductionist." Stereotypes are chosen for their emotional, representational values (and are therefore iconic), but represent only "the essential or core elements of the outsiders' perception of the subculture" (and are therefore reductionist). Stereotypes, he notes, are "images that tend to fix a certain meaning about the subculture in the minds of the audience."[47]

Racializing stereotypes need not invoke biological determinism; their use is not always born of hate. Often, though, racializing language—totalizing and stereotyping characterizations based on perceived or imagined racial traits of a person or a people—is racist. At its core, all racism is a matter of power—the power to include or exclude, the power to stereotype and set apart, and the lack of power to resist the separation and stereotyping.[48] American Indians are subjected to racism in the form of essentializing, reductionist stereotypes that, whether casting them as heathens or healers, deny their authenticity, humanity, and diversity.[49] These denials also attempt to disempower.

There is a long colonial legacy of racism from the Dutch, Spanish, French, and British settlers in what became the United States.[50] Colonial stereotypes of Indians served to justify and allow the dispossession of Indians from their land. As Thomas Gossett notes in his classic work on race, "hatred and contempt for the Indians were strong among those who stood most to gain from appropriation of Indian lands."[51] This hatred and contempt found root in the ideas that Indians are lazy, unwilling to properly work the land, drunken, and lacking productivity as measured by Western standards. Such racism also hinged on Christian biases against indigenous religious practices. Indians' supposed savagery was articulated in terms that described them as "bestial" and "heathen"; it was captured by photographs of the era, which highlighted "dark skin, long hair, odd costumes, and a variety of weapons" and "images of bare-breasted women and armed men," all confirming that Indians are "Others"—"counter to all that had come to mark civilized life."[52]

Most contemporary stereotypes of American Indians are rooted in these colonial encounters and constructions. The twenty-first century view of Indians reiterates the negative stereotypes of laziness and drunkenness and adds the modern characteristics of impoverished and welfare dependent. This view of American Indians, as poor, lazy, and primitive, and the countervailing belief that affluent and successful individuals cannot be "real" Indians, is what anthropologist Kate Spilde calls "Rich Indian Racism."[53] It forms the basis of much of the resentment toward tribes such as the Mashantucket Pequots in Connecticut.

Against the claims of those who find racism on the wane in America, there is a multitude of stunning evidence of the virulence of current anti-Indian sentiment. In the state of Washington, the Republican Party adopted a year-2000 platform that originally contained provisions calling for the military occupation of Indian lands and forced assimilation and removal of reservation inhabitants. In Alabama, in 1997, a state legislature debate regarding Indian police forces degenerated into name-calling, "war whooping," and references to scalping and tomahawks. A 1999 paid advertisement in a South Dakota newspaper declared "open season" on Indians in the state, urging hunters to "thin out" the Indian population, or, as the ad writer put it, "Worthless Red Bastards, Dog Eaters, Gut Eaters, Prairie Niggers, and F—— Indians." While advocating the use of "bloodthirsty, rabid hunting dogs," the advertisement recommended finding Indians in bars and liquor stores (caution is urged, since "bullets may ricochet and hit civilized white people"), in lines for welfare services and government food distribution, and in city alleys littered with "trails of empty wine bottles," "disposable diapers," and "empty books of food stamps."[54]

The writers of this calumny manage to hit all of the stereotypes: Indians are portrayed as poor, drunk, and lazy; nevertheless, they are also seen as wildly procreative savages. They are distinct from the brave whites exhorted not to "hunt" in groups of more than 150 and to obtain a special license for "road kill Indians." A final insult is offered in the context of the advertisement's placement—it announces "Open

Season" on Indians to rectify real shortages of wild game, such as deer, turkey, elk, and antelope. The supposed shortage of this game is not overhunting by white sport shooters, but restricted boundaries, meant to protect reservations against white encroachment and hunting, and treaty-based provisions for unreserved game limits for Indian hunters. The subtext is that Indians, supposedly protectors of the earth and keepers of game, have failed in managing wildlife for the benefit of white sport and subsistence hunters. This subtext makes concrete the abstract idea that even so-called positive stereotypes are racially biased and harmful to the groups subjected to them.

The most common positive stereotyped views of Indians are the "noble savage" and "wise medicine man" images. The idea of the noble savage, also cast as the "ecological Indian," is that Indians are uniquely able to care for the environment, adept at wildlife management, excellent fishermen, always in harmony with nature, and, most important for acknowledgment cases, tied to the land.[55] The Noble Savage-Ecological Indian is best remembered as the "Crying Indian" of the 1970s antipollution campaign, which featured Indian actor Iron Eyes Cody moved to tears by the indignities his white brothers brought onto Mother Earth. This Indian has most often been portrayed in Hollywood movies as a plains Native, usually Sioux, "with [a] galloping pony and flowing headdress."[56] It must not be forgotten, either, that this version of the Indian embodies the tragic myth of the Vanishing American, the myth that posits the eventual extinction of the Indian.[57]

The medicine man image, perpetuated by New Age spiritualist movements, is the "positive," or flip side, of earlier images of the Indian as heathen or pagan. The medicine man is portrayed as a wizened old Indian who speaks only in his indigenous language,[58] is fully in touch with and in control of his masculinity, and is able to be both a warrior and a shamanic healer. Ward Churchill quotes an excerpt from a speech by Men's Movement leader Robert Blye that captures the heart of this mythical Indian: "We [men] must get in touch with our true selves, recapturing the Wild Man, the animal, the primitive warrior being which exists in the core of every man. We must rediscover the meaning of maleness, the art of being male, the way of the warrior priest."[59] Blye, who is not an American Indian, advises his non-Indian followers to participate in Native sweat lodges, drumming circles, and vision quests.[60]

Critics of FAPs argue that they are predicated on cultural reproduction and legal codification of stereotyped views of Indian identity, and that FAPs help to maintain the racialized place of American Indians in the structure of U.S. society. Most analysts of acknowledgment processes argue quite persuasively that white-Western stereotypes of American Indians are mobilized in acknowledgment, and that they significantly affect acknowledgment outcomes. Identities become politicized at the BAR (and elsewhere) in the seemingly benign assumptions that the criteria make about what it means to have an Indian culture, or to be an Indian tribe.

Certainly this is true in the case of landless groups—since the ecological Indian is tied to the land, and is unwilling to give land up, even in the face of potential genocide, an Indian group without access to land ceases, in the eyes of many, to be a tribe at all. Unfortunately, most landless groups became that way through white greed and government actions; these groups are doubly punished.

The image of shamanic leadership also betrays many unrecognized groups; for instance, some tribes have governing structures and leadership invisible to those looking for sachems, shamans, or chiefs. Other tribal norms may prohibit petitioners from showing BAR officials their culture, religion, or governing structures. In testimony before the Senate Indian Affairs Committee in 2000, Louis Roybal, the governor of the Piro/Manso/Tiwa Indian Tribe of the Pueblo of San Juan de Guadalupe (currently seeking recognition through the BAR), made this quite clear. He told the assembly, "Unacknowledged tribal religious leaders were asked to disclose sacred sites, ceremonial practices, and sacred knowledge in order to prove the cultural validity of the people, which goes against every instinct and norm which says this information is not to be shared, filmed, or recorded in any way."[61]

Political scientists Anne McCulloch and David E. Wilkins show how an "ongoing tendency by a number of federal agencies to treat Indian tribes monolithically" is based on an obsolete and fictitious concept of the mythic aboriginal Indian.[62] By socially constructing a mythic Indian and then measuring demands for recognition against it, federal recognition processes seem more often to depend on how many aboriginal traits the petitioning tribe retains in common with the mythic notion of Indian or tribe, than to truly understand the history and reality of the petitioning group.[63] Because they are not constructed as authentic, unrecognized tribes are rendered invisible to the federal gaze. They become, according to Rachael Paschal, "unseeable."[64]

Some critics further argue that the BAR's reluctance to credit oral history and its determination to have a cohesive narrative of tribal life perverts the past of petitioning groups, making the tribe itself unrecognizable to its own members, as well as to others in Indian Country.[65]

The second part of the critique of FAPs as racialist endeavors deals with the BAR's seeming reliance on physiognomy, or phenotype—the visual differences among groups of people often attributed to race—and blood quantum. Indian activists argue that tribal membership decisions like blood quantum and miscegenation rules belong to the tribes themselves. They report worrying that petitioning at the BAR has forced hopeful tribes to adopt restrictive, racist membership criteria that will reproduce the U.S. racial hierarchy in the short run and will ultimately lead the group to extinction.[66]

Many also argue that high rates of intermarriage or out-migration seem to affect a group's chances for recognition in disproportionate ways. The BAR appears to have been inconsistent in determining these matters, and many argue that racism is at the core of this inconsistency. Some tribal leaders told me that "black blood" has been treated as a contaminant of pure "Indian blood," and that "white blood," though problematic for recognition, has been viewed with less suspicion at the BAR. Groups like the Mowa Choctaws (Alabama), Golden Hill Paugussetts (Connecticut), and Ramapough Mountain Indians (New Jersey) complain about the racial attitudes they've encountered at the BAR. All feel that they have been "accused" of having too much black blood; all have been denied acknowledgment by both the BAR and Congress.

Put simply, critics charge that the BAR's requirements replicate white outsiders' views of what constitutes an Indian tribe. In the process of making themselves visible to the federal government, Indians seeking acknowledgment are forced to make most visible those traits that are stereotypically tribal; in the absence of such traditions, they may even need to create and develop them, in order to be seen. In addition, the BAR's requirements replicate white-Western views of democracy.[67] Determinations of what constitutes legitimate forms of democratic governance are predicated upon a separation of church and state, representative (rather than participatory) democracy, and separations of powers and functions of leadership. None of these are necessarily natural to Indian tribal organization, nor do all indigenous people find them particularly desirable.

## COLONIALISM: THE BAR AS A COLONIAL HOLDOVER

Much of the critique of acknowledgment as a racist endeavor dovetails with critiques that take American Indians' neo-coloniality as their starting points. Authors who locate Indians as primarily colonial subjects argue that the idea of tribalism found in acknowledgment processes is part of a larger colonial "discourse of the Indian."[68] They point out that the racial construction of American Indians served the interests of colonial expansion, which fed Indians' marginal class position, and that processes of colonial and imperial normalization and racialization are still occurring within the BAR.

Though he was not speaking of American Indians, Frantz Fanon wrote that part of the colonial project is to pervert the past of the oppressed. Colonialism, he wrote, "is not satisfied merely with holding a people in its grip and emptying the nation's brain of all form and content. By a kind of perverted logic, it turns to the past of the oppressed people and distorts, disfigures, and destroys it."[69] In their evaluation of, and ruling on, acknowledgment petitions, BAR professionals and other "Indian experts" may be seen as reinforcing colonial stereotypes of authentic Indian identity, while perverting, disfiguring, and destroying tribal histories.

A further implication of this theory is that, since the idea of an "Indian Tribe" is in reality a colonial construction, tribal status is unobtainable by any authentic means. Any attempt by an indigenous group to develop visibility to the federal government, even when done for primarily instrumental and material reasons, must, according to these theorists, be a form of false consciousness, a capitulation to a colonial ideal, and a voluntary donning of the oppressor's shackles.[70]

## Colonialism, Sovereignty, and Self-Determination

Until the mid-1970s, U.S. policy toward Indians was not usually termed "colonialism" in the academic literature. This changed when anthropologists and historians, building on scholarship emerging from Latin America and Africa, as well as the literature developing an understanding of "internal colonies" coming out of Ireland, Great Britain, and Scotland, developed a model of the continuing colonial experience in North America. Heavily influenced by dependency theorists, U.S. authors Robert Bee and Donald Gingerich; Patricia Albers and William James; Nancy Lurie; Jack Forbes; and Roxanne Dunbar Ortiz all focused on the economic aspects of continuing colonialism.[71] They highlighted the circular creation and maintenance of impoverished, dependent enclaves (reservations), and they showed how surplus Indian labor was being moved, as a course of government policy, to urban centers.

Ward Churchill further developed an analysis of U.S. colonialism as a genocidal practice, including the cultural extermination of Indians and military occupation of their lands.[72] At the same time, literary and cultural critics in Indian Country turned to theories of the subaltern,[73] which focused less on the materiality of colonialism and more on what one author, Chandra Mohanty, has termed "the relation of structural domination and discursive or political suppression of the heterogeneity of the subject(s) in question."[74]

The political logic of internal colonialism as it pertains to American Indians encompasses the annexation of land, the creation and maintenance of economic dependency, the imposition of foreign laws and cultural norms, and the oppression and assimilation of a large minority population by a dominant aggressor.[75] The situation of neo-, or internal-, colonialism in the United States is characterized in particular by an official denial of its continued existence (sometimes in the form of multiculturalist arguments toward inclusion) and by the extension of the possibility of semiautonomy and semisovereignty in the form of "domestic dependent nation" status for Indian tribes.

Authors in this vein view what some may call "success," as, in fact, capitulations to colonialism. They argue that things like Indian gaming and other forms of economic development are themselves opposed to true indicators of tribal sovereignty. For some traditionalists, "to sacrifice culture knowingly in the effort to attain increased powers of self-government and economic self-sufficiency is unacceptable."[76] Russel Barsh makes the point that, increasingly, tribal governing structures, which include business arms, political arms, and cultural or traditional arms, serve to separate the "tribe" from the "people," and seek external, rather than internal, legitimacy.[77] He notes that many tribal government officials do not seem to put traditional views into practice.

> Indian and non-Indian institutions have converged far more than tribal leaders or scholars want to admit. Reservation econo-mies are centralized, industrialized, and bureaucratic. . . . Gross domestic product has replaced unity, family, integrity, personal dignity, and mutual respect as a standard of good gov-ernment. Tribal officials proudly show visitors their police cars, jails, mines, and factories. . . . They publish financial reports like the business corporations they emulate.[78]

Certainly, my experiences at the Poarch and Mashantucket, and, to a lesser extent, the Mowa Choctaw reservations, reflected the reality, if not the tone, of Barsh's comments. As a visitor, I was proudly shown the hotels, police cars, tribal government buildings, housing projects, and future plans. Though Barsh recognizes the needs of impover-ished groups, he takes a dim view of this aspect of tribal government. He writes, with obvious dismay, "Tribal governments are growing indistinguishable from white governments."[79]

Ward Churchill makes similar criticisms, and spares no words in doing so. He writes:

> At this point, with the codes of colonial domination embraced by many Native people as comprising their own traditions, and articulation of the latter often perceived as a contravention of indigenous sovereignty, the colonized become for all practical intents and purposes self-colonizing. In this most advanced and refined iteration of imperialism, confusion accomplishes much more cheaply, quietly, and efficiently what raw force was once required to achieve.[80]

For these authors, and those who share their views, the heart of the problem is this: tribal governments have adopted a Western, legal view of sovereignty that divorces politics from spirituality in an unnatural dichotomy. This is opposed to a traditional approach, which "does not separate the secular from the religious, the political from the legal," and which "unifies all aspects of life. The spiritual, secular, political and legal are indivisible; symbolized by a sacred circle representing the integration of the land, the people, and all animal and plant life into a whole."[81] In the disjuncture between traditional and modern, between ancient lifeways and assimilation, a measure of sovereignty, they argue, is lost. This transformation of tribal government, then, may be the rather inevitable effect of unchecked colonialism.

Yet it is clear from histories of their resistance and renaissance that Indian tribes have not merely been duped into submission; nor are tribal governments always and only arms of the colonial power. In their legal strategies and campaigns, Indian activists repeatedly point to the disorientation caused by the colonial system around them and the "obvious extent to which the government had complete control of their lives."[82] Penobscot tribal governor James Sappier, telling a reporter about his tribe's political struggles in the 1970s, said that during that time, he constantly reminded himself of a 1755 Massachusetts proclamation that offered twenty-five pounds sterling for each scalp of an Indian child. Indicating that he felt modern government was little different from a 1755 colonial regime, he said ruefully, "You've got to know who you're dealing with." Indians are aware of their history, and they're aware of the potential to subvert the oppression of the past.

Tribal governments and Indian activists have had considerable, though measured, success in their struggle to "be in a position to control one's own economic, social, and political destiny."[83] Charles Wilkinson notes the successful efforts of tribes to maintain a "measured separatism" from U.S. culture;[84] Frank Pommersheim argues that reservations inhabit a "geography of hope."[85]

Current tribal practices of self-government, as Carole Goldberg-Ambrose put it, in 1994, are "an amalgam of traditional identifications and organizations, federal pressures, and Indian improvisation."[86] The variety of forms and expressions of self-government is as wide as the diversity of the tribes. Some of the most widespread practices are those undertaken by tribes to foster economic development, establish tribal governance and social service provisions, access and gain power in dominant society, and revitalize lost or dormant aspects of their indigenous culture. Many argue that success in these realms is a very real manifestation of tribal sovereignty. Certainly, such success is on the agenda for groups currently seeking federal recognition of their tribal status.

## CHAPTER FOUR

# Pioneers in the Process

Between 1978 and 2000, the BAR recognized fifteen tribes, and seven more achieved congressional recognition. These twenty-two tribes represent incredibly different populations. They are quite different from one another in membership, geography, history, and politics; to make generalizations about them, or to generalize from one instance of recognition to another, would be foolhardy.

There are things to be learned, though, from a close study of two cases. In particular, a close study of two pioneers in the process can highlight areas of tension for possible petitioners or groups seeking congressional recognition and can help understanding of regional political and economic pressures at play in tribal recognition. Such a study can also examine national discourses surrounding acknowledgment, particularly those emphasized by the media.

The Poarch Band of Creeks, in Atmore, Alabama, was among the very first to go through the administrative recognition process. As the only federally recognized tribe in the state of Alabama, it holds considerable political power. The Poarch Creek Tribe has also been a trailblazer in developing Indian bingo in the region and has (so far, unsuccessfully) sought casino gaming on trust lands.

The Mashantucket Pequot Tribe, in Ledyard, Connecticut, was recognized by Congress in 1983. Though it was certainly not the first tribe recognized by Congress since the creation of the BAR, the Mashantucket Pequot recognition bill (and subsequent gaming compact) has politicized recognition in a new and profound way. The

Tribe's gaming establishment, Foxwoods, is the largest in the country, and has come to represent Indian gaming in the minds of many people, including those concerned with the ramifications of tribal recognition, both at the BAR and in Congress.

The Poarch Creeks and Mashantucket Pequots, then, are pioneers in several regards. Each has led the way in achieving recognition, in establishing bingo and gaming, and in using newfound political power. Their stories are important for understanding the political aspects of federal recognition, the backlash associated with gaming and acknowledgment, and the strategies used by tribal leaders to counteract attacks on tribal legitimacy and to consolidate tribal power.

## The Poarch Band of Creeks

Members of the modern-day Poarch Band of Creek Indian Tribe are descended from a remnant Creek band whose chiefs and warriors were allotted a square-mile reservation as signatories to the 1815 Treaty of Fort Jackson. Though the treaty also granted the band members the opportunity to avoid Removal, many of them chose not to take their allotments and instead traveled with relatives to Oklahoma. Some of those who stayed had already acculturated and intermarried; they became prominent whites in the county. Others, the poorer and more "Indian looking" Creeks, of the McGhee, Rolin, Adams, and Colbert families, settled on the allotment in Escambia County, in the vicinity of the current Poarch Reservation.[1]

From 1816 to 1924, they lived on this land, which was held in trust but was without entitlement to federal services, such as Bureau of Indian Affairs policing or Indian Health Services facilities and staff. The federal government removed the land from trust status in 1924, but the families retained the right to compensation from timber interests as well as tax exemption on some of the land grants. The church activities of the Holiness, Episcopal, and Free Will Baptists congregations of the early 1900s became the focal point of tribal activism and leadership and continued to be so through the acknowledgment period.

Similar to what later happened in Connecticut, where Pine Tree Legal Service's land claims opened the door for Mashantucket Pequot recognition, legal battles peripheral to Poarch Creek acknowledgment became central to the development of tribal government, and to the Poarch Creeks' eventual push for recognition. In Alabama, desegregation litigation and social movement activity spawned by the early civil rights movement mobilized the Indian community and resulted in the creation of a core of activist families that would later push for acknowledgment.[2]

Throughout the South, segregated education meant that black children were stuck in schools with minimal funding and facilities; many felt stigmatized and degraded by the separation. Indian children were not allowed to attend the resource-rich white schools, but Poarch members refused to send their children to the impoverished black schools. As a compromise, they were allowed to attend an Indian School, run by the county. However, tribal leaders felt that the education there was of poor quality; they continued to mobilize for admittance to the white schools. The BAR's Final Determination for Poarch Creek recognition shows how the community activists sought educational access for their children.

> "One parent organized a boycott of the Indian school and another blocked the passage of the white school bus through the Poarch Community until the driver allowed the Creek children to board. With the support of these parents and other Poarch Creeks, Calvin McGhee initiated a lawsuit against the County Board of Education in 1947.[3]

This lawsuit resulted in the opening of the white high schools to Indian children and led to improvements in the quality of elementary education at the Indian School.

Building on this success, Calvin McGhee established a tribal council in the mid-1950s. He served as its chair and chief until his death in 1970. A charismatic leader, McGhee "curried the favor of state and national politicians, and willingly posed in Plains-style Indian costumes for news photographers."[4] After his death, Calvin McGhee was immediately replaced by Willis Kent McGhee, who was instrumental in forming the Creek Nation East of the Mississippi, Inc. (CNEM), a nonprofit tribal organization chartered in late 1971.

Before it was ultimately recognized as the Poarch Band of Creeks, the CNEM Tribal Council was reorganized twice. The reorganizations and disputes culminated in a split in the larger group (the CNEM) and the formation of the Poarch Band of Creeks Tribal Council. Though the name and governing structures changed often prior to the solidification of the Poarch Band of Creeks, it is clear to anthropologist Tony Paredes that "during the post-Calvin McGhee era, though not always fully cognizant of where they were headed, the Poarch Creeks and their Council moved inexorably toward the establishment of the government that is that present tribal council of the Poarch Band of Creeks."[5]

From the beginning, Poarch leaders were astute actors within pan-Indian politics. Calvin McGhee had always extended his political efforts "far beyond building merely local organizations of Indian descendents for pressing the land claims and other local causes."[6] McGhee attended the 1961 Chicago Conference and was a member of a delegation to the White House in 1962; he was well respected in a wide variety of Indian circles. Willis McGhee's protégé, Eddie Tullis, was groomed to follow in the footsteps of the two men, and Tullis became even more adept at using his political alliances with state officials and pan-Indian organizations to further the Tribe's cause.[7] Tullis was sent as a Poarch emissary to intertribal events and attended the meeting that formed the Coalition of Eastern Native Americans (CENA), in Boston, in 1971. Just prior to assuming the position of Poarch chair, in 1978, Tullis formed important ties with the National Congress of American Indians (NCAI), an organization within which he ultimately held high leadership positions.

Perhaps even more important to his Tribe, Tullis was an active member of Escambia County's Young Republican organization. It was at meetings of that group that he developed a friendship with Alabama's governor, George Wallace.[8] Even before ascending to tribal chairship, Tullis discussed the Poarch Creek recognition claim with Wallace. In 1975, after talking it over with Tullis, Governor Wallace requested that the United States accept eight acres of state land and place it into trust for the Poarch. This land would include the Indian School the Tribe had fought so hard for and would form the base of a new reservation.

The BIA's eastern area director at the time advised the Creeks' lawyer that Wallace's request, and the Creeks' demands for acknowledgment, "could not be considered until the issue of the Secretary's [of Interior] authority to recognize tribes [was] resolved."[9] At the time, acknowledgment was purely ad hoc; no regulations existed to

extend acknowledgment to a tribal group. One tribal leader told me
the following:

> A lot of people don't realize it, but the Bureau had not had
> anybody come forward like Poarch Creek was. And up until
> that time, you know, the Congressmen took real pride in get-
> ting people recognized and all, but there was a lot of opposi-
> tion, and there was growing opposition to Congress doing that.
> Some of the recognitions by Congressional action just did pass,
> and only if they were the right political party and everything.
> So, we fell into that situation where never before had anybody
> come to the Bureau and made the same argument we did.[10]

The bureau was initially unresponsive; accordingly, Poarch leaders
mobilized their pan-Indian ties, as well as their state congressmen
and senators, to lobby the BIA for the creation of acknowledgment
criteria.

The Poarch were at the forefront of the push for such criteria, and
they were adamant that the process be housed within the BIA.[11]
Nevertheless, once the petitioning process was instituted, the Poarch
Creek Tribe was, to its leaders' disappointment, not the first tribe recognized under the new regime. One leader told me the following:

> [BAR staff told us] if you all want to be considered under the
> new process, you all are going to have to file, and meet these
> criteria. As the negotiations went on, we would try to make
> sure that the new procedures said something that we already
> had up there. We knew what we had up there in our petitions
> for them . . . but the procedures were not adopted just like
> that. And that's another thing that you come to realize in this
> area, is that politics is not an exact science. You never know
> what you're going to get. Unless you're there to the last
> minute. So it caused us a delay. We kindly felt that since we'd
> been used as almost a test model, or almost as the prime exam-
> ple of why they should do this, we thought we would be first.
> Now we were not the first tribe. Sometimes I admire some of
> those people [who got recognition prior to Poarch], I think
> they realized a lot sooner than we did that it was going to be

adopted, and they evaluated, and got their petitions in, although some of them had been pending much longer than we had been. But it did work for us, the process did; I like the process as it's in place now.[12]

The Poarch Band of Creeks was the thirteenth petitioner to complete a file at the BAR; its claim was evaluated after nine other decisions had been handed down. It was the sixth tribe to be recognized by the BAR.

A key development within Poarch political history up to this point had been their victory at the Indian Claims Commission (ICC), which provided the Poarch Band of Creeks with a share in a land settlement with the Creek Nation in Oklahoma. Prior to their recognition, the potential for a share in the claims money had been a lure for tribal enrollees. The "Poarch News" column of the *Atmore Advance* issued numerous calls for Indian people in the region to register at the Poarch tribal office. However, the Tribe was not eligible for the money until after recognition, when it accepted the share on behalf of all Alabama and eastern Florida Creek Indians. The Poarch Creeks received 18 percent of a $1,346,000 settlement granted to the Oklahoma Creek Nation by the federal government.

The distribution of the money to the Poarch embittered members of the Creek Nation East of the Mississippi, who were not included in the settlement dispersals because they were not a recognized tribe. Under this pressure, the CNEM again split into two groups, the Creeks East of the Mississippi, headquartered in Florida, and the Principal Creek Indian Nation of Alabama. Both filed their own acknowledgment claims, which were rejected by the BAR in 1981 and 1985, respectively.

Don Sharon, council chair of the Florida Tribe of Eastern Creeks, said at the time, "In a sense the Senate stole the money and distributed it to a certain group of people."[13] He went on to explain that the 1,460 Poarch Creek members represented only a portion of the estimated nine thousand Creek Indians living in the Southeast.

Tullis defended the legislation, but did so in a way that may have angered many even more. He pointed out that a lump sum given to his Tribe would be of more benefit than "$20.00 given to each Indian." He told reporters, "The money will be better spent and have more benefit to the Indian people" if given directly to the Poarch Band of

Creeks.[14] Poarch tribal leaders distributed some of the share on a per capita basis, but used a majority of it, in conjunction with BIA start-up funds, as seed money to begin reservation revitalization.

Throughout the 1980s, Poarch tribal leaders instituted a number of economic development initiatives, including Indian ManPower programs, the construction of a Senior Activities for Independent Living Center ([SAIL], funded in part with a nine-thousand-dollar federal grant), and the construction of new quarters for the tribal council.[15] Poarch women developed sewing and quilting initiatives and produced Native handcrafts for sale. The Poarch lured industry to the area by erecting a speculative building (or "spec." building) and touting the region's eligible and well-trained workforce. Federal recognition gave the Poarch access to economic opportunities that had previously been closed to them. One leader told me that, prior to Poarch recognition,

> about five families controlled Atmore. And, we only had two banks for a long time, but brothers were presidents; each of them was run by brothers. . . . [There was] Swift Lumber Company, which was the biggest employer in the area, and then Vanity Fair came along. And so there's been a very small group of people, excluding the Indians, no Indians involved in it at all. So it's always kind of been a company town. . . . [This] kept a lot of our people from realizing their real potential, too, for years. . . . My people used to depend on migrant farm work or working in the fields, and so it's now where we control the jobs now, and we provide some services that our people did not have access to, and all.[16]

Clearly, the most successful venture has been the Bingo Palace. The drive up to Atmore, Alabama, from the Gulf Coast and Mobile is gorgeous. After the flat, coastal plains of the shore areas, the next forty-five minutes of rolling hills and thick forests offer the opportunity to cross the vast Tensaw, Mobile, and Alabama Rivers on bridges that hang as though they were suspended from the sky. There is not much traffic, and the off-ramp for the Poarch Creek Bingo Hall is never congested, not even on a Friday evening.

The Bingo Palace was initially managed by Native American Bingo Management, Inc., based in Dallas, Texas. The Palace was financed with a $5 million Liberty National Bank loan, also out of Dallas.[17] It is housed in a cement block-and-steel-frame building on an eleven-acre site off of Alabama's Interstate 65, and boasts 27,000 square feet of bingo action that draws patrons from across the region. It opened in 1985 to great fanfare: on opening day, twenty-eight charter buses from more than forty different Southern cities and towns brought approximately fifteen hundred people to Atmore to play bingo for fifty to one hundred dollars a card.[18] One Bingo Palace official offered reporters this early assessment, "It is not unusual to find people from Texas, Tennessee, Ohio, Kentucky, Mississippi, Florida, Louisiana, Georgia, and Alabama on any given weekend," and estimated that the parlor drew seven hundred to eight hundred people on a Saturday night, and five hundred to six hundred on a Sunday.[19]

Unlike most other gaming establishment operators, Poarch leaders decided early on that they would not allow liquor on the premises and that no minors would be permitted, even in the company of their parents. These provisions helped to guarantee the Palace's success among the Deep South's religious bingo patrons. Many of these visitors are repeat players. One New Orleans resident told a reporter, "We usually stay at the Best Western and go to church at St. Roberts for Mass"; she estimated that her group of bingo partners visited the Bingo Palace three or four times a year.[20]

Within only ten months of opening the bingo hall, the Creeks used its profits to purchase the nearby Best Western Hotel and adjacent Good-N-Plenty Restaurant. The Tribe converted the Good-N-Plenty into the "Creek Family Catfish Junction" and announced long-range plans to expand the hotel from sixty-seven to one hundred rooms.[21]

By its second year of operation, the Bingo Palace had generated nearly $800,000 in profits, and the Creeks were investing even more heavily in building tribal infrastructure.[22] Using bingo proceeds and a Housing and Urban Development (HUD)–Indian Community Development Block Grant, the Poarch opened a $1 million tribal complex in 1987, set on four acres of tribal land on Jack Springs Road. Ross Swimmer, then the assistant secretary of Indian Affairs, attended the ribbon cutting, as did several other national and local leaders.[23] The attendance of these leaders is certainly a measure of the clout of the Poarch Band of Creek Indians.

By the time I began my inquiry in Alabama, the Poarch Bingo Palace had been open for twelve years and had been a successful enterprise for the Tribe both financially and politically. The success of casino and bingo enterprises rests largely with the state of the economy in the region—most people do not gamble unless they have extra disposable income associated with a robust economy. As such, the Poarch Creek enterprise has undergone the fluctuations normal for the business. It has also weathered upheavals more significantly caused by the opening of the Mississippi Gulf Coast casinos and the Mississippi Choctaw Casino in nearby Philadelphia, Mississippi (about three hours away).[24]

The Tribe had also been waging a quiet battle with the state to open a Class III (casino style) operation on tribal trust lands in Wetumpka, Alabama (near Montgomery).[25] There are dog tracks in Alabama, which pull in a considerable amount of state tax revenue,[26] but the state has no lottery and does not authorize casino gaming. It is, as one Indian official said to me, "a state that basically just doesn't want gaming,"[27] and the Poarch have been unable to push the envelope against a strong state legal team. Another tribal leader told me that Alabama had "five assistant attorneys general that don't do anything but try to best us on gaming."[28]

Casino gaming aside, bingo alone has made the Tribe relatively wealthy. As a result of their bingo profits and political ties, the Poarch, like a number of newly recognized tribes, have an increased role in state and national politics, local economies, and pan-Indian affairs. The Tribe has been able to use its clout to accomplish a considerable amount. Significantly, leaders were able to get an interstate interchange built near the Reservation in 1992. Prior to its construction, tribal members had been forced to travel sixteen miles to get around and over to Exit 57, but "today it's a little over a mile here, and then head south and north, and wherever, whatever direction you're going in."[29] The Tribe has held a position of power as the only federally recognized Indian tribe on the Alabama Indian Affairs Commission (AIAC) and has used its power to become both a helper and a gatekeeper for other tribes in the state and region seeking federal recognition.


## The Mashantucket Pequots

Former Poarch Creek chair Eddie Tullis has much in common with the former Mashantucket Pequot chair Skip Hayward. Neither has much formal education; neither was raised on the reservation; both returned to Indian land in their young adulthood. Both were plant foremen (Tullis at Monsanto; Hayward at the Electric Boat Company) who returned to the reservation and were instrumental in their tribes' recognition; both brought gaming to their tribes. Both have a gift of gab. Tullis speaks highly of Hayward, and the Foxwoods operation, and hopes to emulate Pequot success with a planned-for casino development near Montgomery, Alabama. Certainly, Tullis is not alone in finding the financial success and political clout of the Mashantucket Pequot Tribe enviable.

In truth, there are few words adequate to describe the magnitude of the Foxwoods Casino, both its physicality and its financial success. Foxwoods is, in both regards, magnificent, dazzling, unparalleled, and unprecedented.[30]

From the vantage point of Connecticut's Route 2, a relatively peaceful winding road north and west of Mystic, the Grand Pequot Tower, the newest of the Foxwoods facilities, raises its emerald tips out of the surrounding lush forest. From five miles away, Foxwoods looks like a small, space-age country surrounded by trees.[31] Its pristine white towers are capped in green, and the circular front drive is tented with green glass trimmed in bronze. At night, the lighting effects make the entire building glow nearly silver. Traffic, especially bus traffic, is heavy once the casino is in view, and increasingly so once you've passed the turnoff to enter the reservation, or to visit the museum or tribal offices. After passing by Two Trees Inn, the smallest hotel within the Foxwoods complex, the entrance to the casino proper appears, as do signs directing drivers to various parking facilities.

Aside from the Two Trees—which promotional brochures tout as "quaint [and] rustic . . . Northeastern hospitality at its finest"—guests of the Mashantucket Pequots have two other Foxwoods lodging options: the Great Cedar Hotel and the Grand Pequot Tower. Great Cedar features 312 guestrooms, an indoor swimming pool, and fine dining. Its décor has a woodsy feel to it—the rooms and lobbies are all decorated in dark purples and greens, accented with a warm shade of cream. The lobby of the hotel is accessed through the lower level of the casino complex and features a stunning sculpture of a kneeling Indian man offering thanksgiving to his Creator above.

The Grand Pequot Tower is a stark contrast to the Great Cedar. Decorated in rich gold and orange tones, the 825 guestrooms and suites suggest more cosmopolitan luxury than woodsy comfort. A giant relief reminiscent of the Pequot tribal seal highlights the lobby and reception area. The floors are marble and covered in thick Oriental tapestries; fresh flowers abound. The penthouses hold a number of villas described by the *Pequot Times* as "sumptuous" and "opulent."[32] The Mashantucket Suite, for instance, is five thousand square feet and is offered as an amenity to "high-end players."[33]

Connecting the two hotels is the Foxwoods Casino. Though a visitor may not need a tour guide to fully appreciate the facility, the maps provided at nearly every possible stopping point are quite useful. Slot machines are ubiquitous: Foxwoods has more than 5,750 of them, ranging in stakes from a quarter to one hundred dollars. There are hundreds of table games as well: keno, baccarat, blackjack, craps, roulette, and pull tabs are the main draws, as is the "Race Book," where off-track pari-mutuel betting takes place. Guests can navigate through the Great Cedar Casino, the Grand Pequot Casino, and Rainmaker Country (which houses the high-stakes bingo parlor and an innovative, smoke-free casino on the mezzanine level) via a number of "Trails"—the Pequot Trail, the Bingo Trail, and the Rainmaker Trail.

These Trails are improbably, and, disconcertingly to those expecting primarily an "Indian" theme, modeled on early-twentieth-century New England villages. The "Theatre District" portion of the Great Cedar Casino typifies the theme: patrons line up at a food court that looks like little clapboard houses with shutters and gaily painted trim. All that's missing from the image is a row of white picket fences, and a couple thousand fewer people.

In the center of it all, in the midst of twenty-four restaurants, cafes, and nightclubs, at the apex of the casino complex—the intersection of Rainmaker Trail and the Bingo Trail—sits Rainmaker Square. A twelve-foot-tall urethane structure, *The Rainmaker,* portrays a male Indian bent down on one knee with a bow pointed skyward, ready to shoot an arrow into the heavens to bring needed precipitation. His knee rests on a rocky platform over a small waterfall; his entire body appears crystalline. The laser show that occurs every twenty minutes changes him from white to peach to shades of blue and reflects the lightning from the thunderstorm his arrow unleashes.

Featured prominently in tribal advertisements for the casino, as well as in journalistic accounts, the Rainmaker statue is given the awesome responsibility of speaking for the Tribe in this place. The recorded voice that accompanies the laser show tells of the Pequots' past and present—a journey from the brink of extinction to the threshold of sovereignty. This story, told in tandem with films in the aptly named "Federal Acknowledgment Theater," in the Mashantucket Pequot Museum and Research Center, provides an account of the Pequots' understanding of their place in history and present-day Indian affairs.

The initial contacts between the Pequots and colonial settlers set the tone for later interactions and led ultimately to the Pequots' non-recognition. In the lower Northeast, contact-era tribal-colony relations were complicated by tensions between the major tribes of the region (Pequot, Mohegan, Narragansett, and Niantic); conflicts between the colonial governments of present-day Connecticut, Rhode Island, and Massachusetts; and conflicts and alliances made between those colonial governments and some of the tribes. Northeastern tribal-federal relationships were unique when compared with relationships in the rest of the country, in that the federal government did not make treaties with the tribes; treaty relationships were established between the tribes and Great Britain, and, in some cases, recognition of tribal existence and authority was recognized by local and town authorities. However, like members of many other northeastern tribes, the Pequots lived "at the will" of the colonies and the states those colonies became.[34]

The Pequots numbered approximately ten thousand members prior to contact, and the Pequot Nation held control of the wampum trade in the region. Its membership was largely wiped out by disease and war—in particular, the Pequot War of 1636 and the Massacre at Mystic on May 26, 1637, which decimated the population.[35] In 1666, the colonial government of Connecticut placed some of the remaining Pequots on a twenty-five-hundred-acre reservation. The colony sold others into slavery in the Bahamas, placed some Pequot prisoners with the Mohegan, Narragansett, and Eastern Niantic Tribes, and relocated others to an "Eastern Reservation"—the Lantern Hill Reservation, which is located about two miles from the Western Mashantucket Pequot Reservation.[36]

In 1761, Connecticut's general assembly reduced the western reservation from 2,500 to 489 acres; immediately following the American Revolution, land sales further diminished the reservation to 184 acres. The reservation land was managed by a system of

Indian overseer—non-Indian individuals appointed by the state; these overseers did not usually act in the best interest of the Tribe, and their actions facilitated the further diminishment of the reservation.[37] The impoverished economy failed to support tribal members. Pequot workers took jobs off the reservation: female tribal members became domestic workers in neighboring cities, and many of the men either farmed or continued the tribal tradition of whaling. Those who stayed struggled "to prevent their tribe's disappearance," earning money with wreath making in the winter and berry picking in the summer months.[38] In the mid-1800s—according to historians,[39] modern-day journalists,[40] colonial records, tribal oral histories,[41] and even Herman Melville[42]—the Pequots were nearly extinct. By the 1970s, only 168 acres and one inhabitant remained of the western reservation.

That one inhabitant was Elizabeth Plouffe George (usually spoken of as Elizabeth George), the matriarch of the modern Mashantucket Pequot tribal nation, and the grandmother of the first tribal chair of the federally recognized Mashantucket Pequot Tribe, Richard "Skip" Hayward. George and her sister lived in a small farmhouse on the reservation for many years, and later, George lived alone in the farmhouse, which lacked running water, electricity, and indoor plumbing.[43] George refused to leave the reservation; she believed that if she did leave, the state would turn it into a recreational area, or that it would serve as a home for relocated paupers from the Eastern Pequot Reservation. She was vocal in her opposition to those possibilities, and has become known in Mashantucket Pequot oral history as "the one who held the land."[44]

After Elizabeth George died, in 1973, her grandson decided to live out her legacy and fulfill a promise he had made to her to return to the reservation.[45] At the time, Skip Hayward was a nuclear pipe fitter with the Electric Boat Company. His mother was Elizabeth George's daughter; his father was a Navy corpsman who "traced his lineage back to the Mayflower."[46] Through George and her sister, Martha Hoxie, Hayward had an extended network of cousins, aunts, and uncles, all with Pequot blood and a claim to the land. He gathered a number of them and laid out his plans to make the reservation viable again. They began by funding a small housing complex and apartment building with HUD grants, and by starting a greenhouse. At this time, members of the Tribe had no idea that federal recognition was a possibility.

However, a revolution in Indian law was under way. Attorneys Tom Tureen and Barry Margolin were pioneering the use of Non-Intercourse Act claims to retrieve Indian lands in the Northeast and force the federal government to acknowledge a relationship with, and responsibility to, the northeastern tribes. As part of a proactive outreach to Indian Country's unrecognized tribes, Tureen sent contacts out to talk with every unrecognized tribe he could locate. He and a Passamaquoddy tribal leader personally contacted Skip Hayward and were impressed by his initiative in drawing his relatives back home. Tureen spoke with Hayward about the possibility of filing a land claims suit and was soon representing the Mashantucket Pequots in court, at the BIA, and before Congress.

In 1976, the Pequots filed a land claim in Connecticut court.[47] They sought not only a return of reservation land and financial recompense but also federal recognition. Though it appeared likely the Tribe would win congressional approval of a negotiated settlement prior to the BAR's review of its petition, after 1978, tribal members worked to prepare documentation for administrative processes. As one tribal member noted later, however, "BIA wasn't trying to make it easy."[48] Indeed, covering all of its bases proved a good idea: the Tribe won unanimous backing from the Connecticut delegation for a bill to settle the land claims and recognize the Pequots.

Senator Lowell Weicker (I-Conn.) and Congressman Sam Gjedenson (D-Conn.) proved key allies in the fight that would follow. The BIA disapproved of congressional recognition for the Pequots, and President Reagan vetoed the first bill, which passed both houses in 1982. Reagan cited an unacceptably low level of state contributions to the settlement and the seeming inability of the Mashantucket Pequots to establish tribal status through the BIA as the leading causes of his veto.[49] But, as one tribal member put it, "We're not a people to give up." With the help of the Native American Rights Fund (NARF) and the Indian Rights Association, the Tribe launched an intensive lobbying and negotiation effort, and a compromise was reached in the Senate Indian Affairs Committee by July 1983. Later that year, President Reagan signed the bill to acknowledge the Mashantucket Pequots and resolve the land claims.[50]

Using a HUD grant to offer free reservation housing to all returning relatives, the newly recognized Mashantucket Pequot Tribal Council, led by Chair Hayward, was able to draw even more members back to

Connecticut. The Pequots tried reservation development through a number of enterprises, including a maple syrup operation, a pizza parlor, a hydroponic greenhouse, and a hog house. Then Skip Hayward befriended Seminole Chief James Billie, and was his guest at the Hollywood Reservation and Bingo Hall.

Contemporary accounts differ as to whether or not Hayward had always planned to open a gaming establishment, though all stress the important role he played in bringing casino gaming to the Mashantucket Pequots. Some argue that the possibility of a casino was always foremost in Skip's mind,[51] others that he had never considered it.[52] The truth is probably somewhere in between; ultimately, once Hayward decided to establish Pequot gaming, whenever it was that he made that decision, there was no stopping him. One tribal member described Hayward's return from a trip to Florida in this way: "He came back with flaming arrows trying to convince us that Bingo was the way to go."[53]

Convincing the Tribe's members, who now numbered more than fifty, was difficult. A majority of them were Jehovah's Witnesses or Baptists with strong moral and religious views against gambling.[54] Many wanted to continue reservation revitalization by other means. Nevertheless, just as he had worked two angles on federal acknowledgment, Hayward secured financing for the eventual bingo establishment, even as he struggled to win the Tribe's approval.[55]

Using a loan from the Arab-American Bank, guaranteed by the Bureau of Indian Affairs, the Pequots opened a high-stakes bingo parlor.[56] They ran that business successfully for a number of years, making solid profits and investing the money wisely. Within a few years they decided to expand. They wanted to bring high-stakes, casino-style gaming to Connecticut and envisioned luring New York patrons away from Atlantic City, while drawing others from Boston and Providence.

Originally, the state of Connecticut opposed the expansion of the Mashantucket Bingo Parlor into high-stakes, Class III gaming. The state, under the leadership of Governor William O'Neill, took the hard-line position that Connecticut's Las Vegas–Night law, which allowed charitable gaming and wagering on jai alai games, did not allow the Tribe to run its own casino. O'Neill's administration refused to negotiate with the Tribe, and, in November 1989, attorneys Tureen and Margolin sued on behalf of the Mashantucket Pequots. Federal

District Court Judge Peter Dorsey found that the presence of the Las Vegas–Night law, combined with the Pequots' federal status, mandated compliance with the recently passed Indian Gaming Regulatory Act (IGRA). Judge Dorsey ordered Connecticut to negotiate with the Pequots. The state appealed and lost in the Second Circuit.[57]

Though the state officially began compact negotiations in the summer of 1990 and even entered into third-party mediation, it maintained an anti-casino position and pursued an appeal of the Second Circuit decision. While waiting to hear if the Supreme Court would grant certiorari, Connecticut refused to accept a federal mediator's plan, even though the mediator essentially chose the regulatory scheme originally proffered by the state. When the Court refused to hear the appeal, new governor Lowell Weicker (a former ally) launched a last-ditch effort to stop the Pequots, pushing a bill to outlaw all charitable gaming in the state by repealing the Las Vegas–Night law.[58]

In response to Weicker's initiative in the legislature, the Pequots and their lawyers initiated a three-week lobbying blitz in Hartford, under the slogan of "No More Broken Treaties."[59] A number of things could have influenced the outcome of their efforts: the lobbying itself; the overwhelming probability, based on precedent established in *California v. Cabazon*,[60] that the Pequots would win any appeal that the Supreme Court might eventually choose to hear; the fact that anti-casino Weicker owned two race horses; the unpopular 6 percent income tax increase the state was considering, even as its citizens faced massive layoffs from the defense industries and computer companies located on the coastline;[61] or, as one observer charged, the recent popularity of the movie *Dances with Wolves* and a romantic desire to "do good" for the Indians.[62] It was probably some combination of these factors that led to the failure of the Las Vegas–Night repeal, by a vote of eighty-four to sixty-two, on May 16, 1990.

This failure forced the governor to negotiate in good faith, and the two parties established a compact to allow Class III gaming on Pequot tribal lands. Using funding in excess of $60 million from Malaysian investors,[63] the Pequots built a world-class gaming facility in rural Ledyard, Connecticut, which opened in February 1992. Their first negotiations with the state had proven fruitless in getting the Pequots their much-desired permission for slot machine operations. However, in early 1993, the two parties negotiated an addition to the gaming compact that included an agreement that, in exchange for permission for, and a monopoly over, slot machine operations, the Pequots would provide the state with $100 million a year in payments in lieu of taxes. This was renegotiated shortly after the Mohegan Tribe was recognized by the BAR, and before the Mohegan Tribe broke ground on its incredibly successful casino. The renegotiation granted both tribes such a monopoly.[64]

By 2000, the facility contained 190,000 square feet of gaming space. It is vast even in comparison with the MGM Grand in Las Vegas, which had previously been the largest casino in the United States, with 175,000 square feet of gaming space. Foxwoods employs more than ten thousand people from the area and enjoys estimated profits in excess of $470 million a year, with revenues from slot machines alone averaging nearly $40 million per month. In addition to the three hotels, Foxwoods houses expansive conference facilities that are used by Indian and non-Indian groups alike. And the profits from Foxwoods have enabled the Pequots to buy land (some of which is held in trust for them by the BIA) in excess of the 250 acres they had been relegated to by Connecticut's colonial governor so long ago. The Pequots guarantee higher education to any tribal member who desires it, provide housing for tribal families, and offer sure employment in a number of tribal enterprises. One account, the story of tribal member Patricia Fletcher, speaks volumes.

> From a life of poverty, she moved into a brick colonial the Tribe had purchased. . . . The Fletchers's 3,500-square foot house had two fireplaces, a sauna, a Jacuzzi in the master suite, two staircases, an upstairs music room, and a wooded yard surrounding a fancy outdoor pool. The Fletchers "purchased" the home from the Tribe for $1,500 down and a nominal monthly "mortgage" payment. Under the agreement with the tribe, Fletcher would be refunded the money she put into the house when she left. She was also informed that she was eligible for free driving lessons and tuition free classes at the local community college. Her son's $2,650 tuition to North Stonington Christian Academy was paid for by the tribe, as were tutors. Medical services were free, as were day-care and health club memberships.[65]

This success is stunning, especially considering that, prior to recognition and gaming, the Mashantucket Pequot Reservation had no running water, and the county did not even provide sewage and waste removal. When Hayward returned to the reservation, everything had to be built from scratch.

## Consequences of Acknowledgment: Gaming and Racial Identity Come into Play

Taking their cue from stories that detail the rags-to-riches rise of the Pequots and their success with Foxwoods, impoverished and unrecognized groups increasingly see acknowledgment as a prerequisite for gaming enterprises as a tribal economic development policy. Their ability to offer gaming is conditioned on two things: their recognition, either through the BAR or Congress, and the Indian Gaming Regulatory Act. The conflation of these two needs—recognition and economic development through gaming—has had an enormous impact on the federal acknowledgment process.

When the tribes that I studied first began petitioning for acknowledgment, high-stakes casino gaming was not an option; it was not even on the horizon. In the United States in 1978, when the BAR was developed, Nevada was the only state that allowed casino gaming, and, though Reno also developed a casino culture, Las Vegas held the corner on the market. Gaming ventures expanded to Atlantic City, New Jersey, in the late 1970s, and those three cities—Reno, Las Vegas, and Atlantic City—were the prime places for casino-style gambling in the United States. The expansion of tribal bingo operations in the 1980s, and the subsequent growth of Class III Indian gaming, has had an unexpected and unheralded effect on tribal acknowledgment:

> In the Northeast and throughout the country, the economic and legal standing of thousands of Native Americans rests largely on their skill and luck in dealing with the often-tangled process of recognition—a backlogged system widely seen as subjective and unfair. Until recently, no one but the tribes, a few members of Congress, and a smattering of specialists paid much attention to all this. Then came gambling.[66]

Now, community groups, anti-gaming organizations, and town council members are keenly aware of acknowledgment cases. Some established tribes closely monitor and guard access to the process, and states' attorneys general bring suits challenging BAR decisions. Where the BAR once engendered controversy among only a select group of scholars, and interest among those seeking recognition, its activities are now dinner-table discussions for average people in affected communities.

## CHAPTER FIVE

# *Perceptions of the Process I*

## Federal Acknowledgment in the Context of Indian Gaming

Since the reconstitution of their governments under the Indian Reorganization Act, tribal leaders have struggled against seemingly insurmountable obstacles to successfully incorporate economic development plans. Some small tribal enterprises—jewelry making, the sale of Native arts and crafts, and tax-free cigarette and gasoline sales—have produced marginal profits, but have not provided enough revenue to fund extensive infrastructure development or to create large-scale educational and employment opportunities.[1] Government programs such as the facilitation of relocation and urbanization, cooperative federal-tribal development efforts, enterprise zones, Indian preferences in agency hiring, and training programs have largely failed to turn the tide of dependency on reservations.[2] Some larger tribally initiated enterprises—ecological and cultural tourist operations, industrial lumber and cement plants, furniture making—are occasionally successful at improving reservation economies; however, such enterprises are dependent on a skilled labor force and a strong resource base. Large-scale reservation industries have also usually relied upon a previously successful enterprise purchased, rather than started, by the tribe. Such successes have not been widespread.

Bingo halls combine the labor and resource needs of the smaller industries with the larger profit margins of the grander development schemes. By opening bingo halls, tribes can provide jobs for less-educated workers. In addition, these jobs do not depend on the development of external resources such as wood or oil. And finally, bingo operations have extremely low overhead. These factors, plus the incredible popularity of bingo among the nation's large retirement-age population, make it an attractive economic development option for many tribes, even those in rather remote locations.

One remote tribe, the Seminoles, began the trend of explosion in gaming when the Tribe opened its first bingo palace, in Florida, in the late 1970s. The Seminole Tribe has a long history of activism and leadership in national and regional Indian politics. It has been a leader in an intertribal coalition of Indian tribes geographically located in the southern and eastern portion of the United States: United South and Eastern Tribes (USET); it is active, as well, in several other intertribal organizations. Rather unsurprisingly, the Seminoles soon became leaders in the gaming industry. Though a majority of the Tribe's members live on the Big Cypress Reservation, deep in the sparsely peopled and inaccessible Everglades, the Tribe also has reservations located in more densely populated areas adjacent to the urban centers of Miami and Fort Lauderdale. Using a $1 million construction loan to build their operation, the Seminoles opened the nation's first Indian-run bingo hall on the Hollywood Reservation, near Miami. Bingo there was wildly successful. The Tribe paid off its construction loan within a six-month period and was soon recording substantial profits. In 1980, the Seminoles opened a second bingo parlor, this one on the Brighton Reservation. The bingo halls reduced Seminole unemployment by 50 percent, and the profits were used to fund a reservation police force, gyms on the Brighton and Big Cypress Reservations, senior citizens' centers, and a cultural heritage project.[3]

The state of Florida allows charitable bingo run by churches and civic organizations; other gambling, however, is illegal. Almost immediately after the Seminole bingo hall opened, Florida challenged its legality. Florida officials cited Public Law 280, a Termination-era law that transferred criminal jurisdiction over Indian land from federal authorities to several states. Florida insisted that PL 280 gave it the power to regulate, and even prohibit, bingo on the reservation. On May 6, 1980, the U.S. District Court for Southern Florida held that Florida's charitable bingo statute was not criminal law, but was instead part of the civil-regulatory code. Therefore, the anti-gaming statute did not apply to Indian land. Even with PL 280 jurisdiction, bingo

could not be prohibited on the reservation if it was allowed anywhere else in the state. Since Florida has no regulatory authority
over noncriminal activity on Indian land, Florida could neither prohibit nor regulate any aspect of tribal bingo games. Almost as
quickly as the state of Florida lost its Fifth Circuit challenge to the
Seminole operation[4] tribes across the nation turned to bingo as a
way of making money.[5]

The next legal challenge to Indian gaming came from the state of
California. Between February and May 1980, the Cabazon and
Morongo Mission Indians passed tribal ordinances authorizing the
bands to operate for-profit bingo halls and card clubs, including
draw poker games. The state of California authorized both forms of
gaming, when run by nonprofit organizations for charitable purposes. But Riverside County, where the tribes were located, explicitly
prohibited card clubs. The Cabazon and Morongo Bands continued
to operate the halls and clubs, despite threats from state and county
officials, until 1983, when sixteen Riverside County sheriff's officers
raided the card clubs, confiscated three thousand dollars and cards,
chips, and financial records, and charged more than thirty people
with violating the county ordinance prohibiting card games.[6]

Riverside County's actions were defended in litigation by the
state of California. Both the district court and the Ninth Circuit
Court of Appeals rejected California's attempts to halt the card
games on PL 280 grounds, but the state continued its legal challenges. The U.S. Supreme Court, in *California v. Cabazon Band of
Mission Indians,* affirmed the lower court decisions.[7] *Cabazon,* published on February 25, 1987—seven years after the Cabazon and
Morongo Bands first passed their pro-bingo tribal ordinances—
affirmed the inherent, sovereign rights of Indian tribes to engage
in their chosen path to economic development, even if that path
was bingo or card gaming.

Before *Cabazon,* members of the U.S. House and Senate had been
concerned enough about Indian gaming to hold hearings on the
topic. However, it was not until the Supreme Court delivered the
*Cabazon* decision that legislators were sufficiently spurred to action
and forced to make law.[8] As Rebecca Tsosie notes, "After *Cabazon* . . .
most states were not content to seek voluntary agreements with
Indian tribes. Instead they lobbied furiously for passage of congressional legislation on Indian gaming."[9]

Part of the congressional delay before that point was due to the diversity of interests involved in the process. Some states welcomed tribal gaming; others did not. State governments argued that they should be able to control gambling in their territory. If the citizens of the state did not want high-stakes gambling, they reasoned, they should not have to have it. Indians saw the issue quite differently. Tribal leaders refused to acknowledge any possibility for state government infringement on tribal sovereignty. They reasoned that the only jurisdiction to apply was federal, and, since Indian gaming was not breaking any federal laws, it should continue unregulated by state government. For its part, the federal government, through its representatives at Interior, sought to mediate between state and Indian demands, while maintaining its historic posture of being "above" gaming concerns.[10] A fourth party, the Atlantic City and Las Vegas casino interests, and dog- and horse-track owners across the country, were already a powerful lobbying voice in the capital; they did not want to see *any* expansion of Indian gaming—but it became clear, as the Indian Gaming Regulatory Act (IGRA) took shape, that they would lose that fight.

Several bills to regulate Indian gaming failed in the 1986–87 sessions. In 1986 a bill calling for a five-year moratorium on tribal casino enterprises passed in the House (HR 1920) but did not reach the Senate floor for a vote. Seven bills were introduced in 1987 alone. A "grand compromise," written by Senator Daniel Inouye (D-Hawaii), was finally voted on and codified in 1988,[11] when President Ronald Reagan signed into law Senate Bill 555, the Indian Gaming Regulatory Act. The IGRA, as it is known, was recommended by the Senate Committee on Indian Affairs and passed unanimously through both houses.

That does not mean, however, that the IGRA was necessarily the ideal solution to an increasingly complex issue. Senator Harry Reid (D-Nev.) said at the time that it was, instead, "the only bill that could pass." One writer, quoting Reid, notes that the IGRA was "the ultimate compromise that pleased no one."[12]

## The Indian Gaming Regulatory Act, 1988

Though it did not completely please anyone, and certainly did not do anything to allay the fears of Las Vegas and Atlantic City casino

owners and others with gaming interests, the compromise did manage to offer something to three of the interested parties. It kept
intact the federal government's hands-off approach to gambling, by
enabling tribal-state compacts to govern the regulation of tribal
gaming enterprises. It also pleased federal officials, because this
form of economic development generated revenues more rapidly
than others, and could be expected to quickly reduce some tribes'
dependence upon federally funded development programs.

The IGRA's compact negotiation provisions allow states, for the
first time, the power to regulate an Indian enterprise. The IGRA also
offers state officials the power to disallow Indian gaming by refusing
to legalize any gaming within their territory. The IGRA also offers
political cover; by requiring governors to negotiate in good faith
with any federally recognized tribe that desires to operate gaming
facilities on tribal lands, the compacts provision of the IGRA also
shields state governments from potential negative voter reaction and
citizens' anti-casino outrage—governors can tell their citizens that
federal law mandates the state to allow casinos.

As it already had casino-style gaming and a large Native population,
Nevada was the first to voluntarily enter a tribal-state gaming compact,
and in 1988 the Fort Mojave Indian Tribe opened a small casino near
the town of Laughlin, on the Arizona-California-Nevada border.[13]
Some states with legalized charitable gaming took a much different
route; they considered repealing those statutes in order to avoid
Indian gaming altogether. Connecticut unsuccessfully flirted with that
approach, but to date, no state has been successful in repealing pro-
gaming statutes.

Those states, such as Nevada, that already had legal gambling had
immediate access to a new piece of the economic pie. Although
Indian casino profits are not subject to taxation, wages paid to non-
Indian employees are subject to state and federal income tax with-
holding. More important, through the compact process, states can
negotiate for substantial portions of gaming revenue in the form of
payments in lieu of taxes. In addition, tribally funded regional infrastructure improvements that extend beyond reservation and casino
boundaries decrease burdens on the state and provide the general
citizenry with needed development, jobs, and services.

The third set of actors interested in resolving the state-Indian
conflict over gaming, the various Indian tribes, was disappointed

with what it saw as state infringement on its sovereignty through the IGRA's stress on tribal-state compacts. Tribal leaders argued that they should only negotiate with federal officials, because, under the Constitution, states have no jurisdiction to negotiate treaties or agreements with tribes. They maintain that the IGRA itself infringes on tribal sovereignty by offering state governments an unprecedented level of control over, and access into, tribal governance and lands.[14] Roland Harris, chief of the Mohegan Tribe (Connecticut), told Congress in 1997, "From the tribal perspective, IGRA was a substantial compromise, a setback to efforts to maintain tribal government control over tribal territory."[15] Tsosie agrees: "Despite the popular sentiment that the IGRA conferred a gaming 'right' on Indian tribes, it is important to note that the IGRA is not the source of the tribes' right to engage in gaming; rather, the statute places limitations on those sovereign rights. The IGRA thus exemplifies the use of federal power to constrain tribal sovereignty."[16]

However, tribes also realized that they had won big in this compromise—they gained the right to operate gaming in states that allowed lotteries, charitable bingos, and other forms of games of chance. The IGRA states it clearly at 25 USC., sec. 2701.

> Indian tribes have the exclusive right to regulate gaming activity on Indian lands if the gaming activity is not specifically prohibited by Federal law and is conducted within a state which does not, as a matter of criminal law or public policy, prohibit such gaming activity.

The IGRA's regulatory structure recognizes three levels of jurisdiction over Indian gaming, congruous with the three interested parties: federal, state, and tribal governments. The 1988 legislation established the National Indian Gaming Commission (NIGC) to provide oversight at the federal level. Its three members originally met to issue formal rules and regulations, define the classes of gaming subject to the commission's oversight, and establish federal guidelines for Indian gaming operations. The NIGC continues to meet quarterly to investigate violations of its guidelines and to impose civil fines.

The chair of the NIGC is a presidential appointee who serves a three-year term. He or she has the statutory power to temporarily suspend business at casino operations suspected of violating NIGC guidelines. The secretary of the interior appoints the other two members of the commission; one of them serves a three-year term, the other serves for one year only. Two of the members of the commission may be from the same party, two must be Indian, and none can have ties to any gaming facility.

The IGRA further defines three classes of gaming. Class I is subject solely to tribal regulations and encompasses all traditional tribal games and social games for prizes of nominal value. Class II is considered to be low-stakes wagering at slots (a nickel is the maximum bet per pull) or table games (five-dollar maximum bets). It also consists of bingo, lotto, punch cards, and manual card games legal anywhere in the state—basically it encompasses all those games not played against the house. Class III gaming consists of all other gaming, including pari-mutuel betting, such as wagering on horse racing, jai alai, or dog tracks, as well as Off-Track Betting (OTB) on these races and games; and casino-style gambling, including table games played against the house and higher-stakes slot machines.

The IGRA also mandates how Indian gaming money can be spent. It provides that substantial percentages of tribal gaming revenues must be spent on tribal governance, economic development, and tribal welfare initiatives. Additionally, tribes can use their gaming money to make donations to charitable organizations and to help fund the operations of local (non-Indian) government agencies. As part of fulfilling their responsibilities to economic development and tribal welfare, tribes can opt to give per capita payments to tribal members; they must first provide a detailed plan of proposed payments and infrastructure expenditures to the NIGC.

Only Class III gaming requires the negotiation of a tribal-state compact; the IGRA mandates the "good faith" negotiation of such a compact. However, in 1996, the Supreme Court severely curtailed the power of the IGRA's compact provision. Subsections 2710(d)(7)(B)(i) of the IGRA enabled tribes to sue a state in federal court if the state refused to negotiate in good faith. In *Seminole Tribe of Florida v. Florida et al.,* a five-to-four majority of the Court held that the 11th Amendment prohibited Congress from waiving states' immunity from suit.[17] Chief Justice Rehnquist's opinion struck that portion of the IGRA as unconstitutional. In the wake of the decision, states that refuse to negotiate for a Class III compact are immune from legal challenge of their refusal, and the Court declined to clarify how disputes over gaming should be resolved by states and the tribes. Significantly, with the decision in *Seminole Tribe*, all Indian tribes lost an important enforcement mechanism for the IGRA, and an important measure of sovereignty in the ability to bring suits for compliance.

During such negotiations, the state regulatory structure is worked out according to the needs and desires of the parties. The final compacts vary widely from state to state, and even within states, as different tribes enter the negotiations. The outcomes of such negotiations may include allocations of regulatory authority between the tribe and state, a division of labor in criminal justice cooperation (including payments from the tribe to the state to cover enforcement costs), agreements for tribal payments in lieu of taxes, remedies for breach of compact, and standards for the gaming operation. In some cases, a state grants tribal monopolies on certain kinds of gaming (such as slot machines) in order to ensure that non-Indian gaming will not come to the state; this allows greater state control over gambling within its boundaries, and insures profits for the tribes. For all of these differences, though, one thing is similar in every state: during negotiations, the agreement of all parties on all aspects of the compacts is key to policymaking. Tribal-state gaming compacts are always the result of concerted effort and compromise between the parties.

In their 1995 study of tribal-state compacts, authors Stephen Cornell, Joseph Kalt, Matthew Krepps, and Jonathan Taylor provide detailed information on five tribal regulatory structures that they deem representative of the vast array of gaming regimes. They examined the gaming operations and state compact agreements of the Ho-Chunk Nation (Wisconsin), the Mohegan Tribe (Connecticut), the Oneida Tribe (Wisconsin), the Sault Ste. Marie Chippewa Tribe (Michigan), and the Standing Rock Sioux Tribe (North and South Dakota). Their investigations show that tribal regulatory structures routinely employ regular economic audits, gaming room and clientele monitoring, and employee background checks. Additional regulatory controls include licensing schemes, compliance monitoring, and third-party oversight of selected management functions.[18] Gaming tribes often have a business arm nominally separate from the tribal council and a gaming regulatory body separate from both. Cornell and the other authors report that the Mohegan Tribe, for example, established two tribal gaming regulatory bodies, known as the Mohegan Tribal Gaming Authority and the Mohegan Tribal Gaming Commission. According to Mohegan tribal chairman Roland Harris, these entities "ensure the integrity of the Tribe's gaming enterprise through vigilant oversight and enforcement of tribal law and control of all gaming-related development, construction, management and operations."[19]

In addition to the IGRA's mandated structure, tribes have formed powerful regional and national alliances of gaming organizations. In particular, the New Mexico Indian Gaming Association (NMIGA) is successful in backing political candidates and lobbying for important legislation.[20] The Minnesota Indian Gaming Association (MIGA), which represents ten of Minnesota's eleven gaming tribes, collects and analyzes socioeconomic data related to gaming in the state; and in Wisconsin, the tribes joined to form the Wisconsin Indian Gaming Intelligence Association (WIGIA), which shares information and resources in the monitoring and apprehension of criminal activities regarding Wisconsin gaming.[21]

The IGRA's three-pronged regulatory structure has, then, informally expanded to include an effective regulatory network of inter-tribal and regional institutions. It has also expanded to include the National Indian Gaming Association (NIGA). Tribal leaders formed the NIGA as a counterpoint to the federally appointed NIGC; the NIGA board of directors and operating officers are nominated and voted on by the gaming tribes themselves. The association serves as an effective information clearinghouse and lobbying effort headquartered in Washington, D.C. The NIGA initiated and coordinated the development of a set of Minimum Internal Control Standards (MICS), which standardized tribal regulatory regimes across the nation. In addition, the NIGA worked in cooperation with the National Tribal Gaming Commissioners and Regulators to formulate a set of "best practices" for tribal enterprises.

## The Magnitude of Indian Gaming since the IGRA

Literally thousands of newspaper articles have been written on the topic of Indian gaming,[22] and billions of dollars have been made;[23] there are more than 360 Indian tribes offering some sort of gaming, and twenty-four states now have casino-style operations run by tribes.[24]

Some enterprises have been amazingly successful. Though Florida has refused to negotiate with the Seminoles about Class III gaming, the Seminoles' five small casinos—offering penny-ante poker, bingo, and low-stakes electronic slots—make nearly $80 million a year.[25] The Mohegan and Mashantucket Pequot Tribal Nations of Connecticut, who do have Class III gaming, gross nearly half a billion dollars each, every year, on slot machines alone.[26]

Some see in tribal gaming an ironic (and welcome) reprisal of the trickster role. As the *60 Minutes* report on Mashantucket Pequot success put it, "It's a story rich in irony; rich because it involves lots of money, irony because it's about Native Americans finally turning the tables on the white man—the craps tables, the blackjack tables and the roulette tables, to be precise."[27]

Others reject the irony argument with vehemence. Robert Porter (Seneca) argues that casino operations and other entrepreneurial ventures are depressing signs of true assimilation, and constitute an infringement on tribal sovereignty. He writes, "Entrepreneurs [have] built gas stations and smoke shops and sold gasoline and cigarettes to non-Indians eager to drive to the reservation and exploit the absence of state taxes. Gaming . . . became the next developing industry, attracting even more non-Indians and their money. No nation has been immune from these new developments."[28]

Clearly, Indian gambling facilities are a financial boon to some tribes, a break-even scheme for others. Casinos may be seen as an ironic twist on white exploitation, or as a cultural bane and blight on indigenous values. They are controversial in almost all regards. Most accounts acknowledge that gaming has both benefits and costs. Says one (non-Indian) analyst, "Gaming represents operating in 'white' society, which carries potential threats to tribal sovereignty and cultural traditions in exchange for control over revenue."[29]

Certainly, gaming success has resulted in a threat to tribal acknowledgment claims. Across the nation, gaming has provided resources and power for some recently recognized tribes, while casting shadows on the legitimacy of other petitioning groups and contributing to factionalism across the board. Gaming has also engendered an incredible backlash against Indians in general, which can be seen in the public outcry over new acknowledgment attempts.

## The Effects of Gaming on Acknowledgment Law

Gaming is a constitutive element of the debates surrounding unrecognized Indian groups. It is constitutive in three primary ways. First, the resources generated by the gaming tribes can be effectively used to help or hinder the efforts of unrecognized groups in the region. Second, it has become possible for unrecognized tribes to finance work on acknowledgment petitions or lobbying efforts by cooperating with gaming backers. Finally, and most significantly for tribes seeking federal acknowledgment, gaming has created a backlash against high profile, recently recognized tribes that extends to backlash against hopeful groups.

### RESOURCES OF GAMING INTERESTS AND GAMING TRIBES: HELPING AND HINDERING RECOGNITION EFFORTS

As detailed in chapter 3, petitioning the BAR and lobbying Congress for acknowledgment are expensive propositions. Traditionally, hopeful groups have sought funding from the federal government and some humanitarian organizations. The Administration for Native Americans (ANA) of the Department of Health and Human Services provides grants to groups petitioning the BAR. The ANA has provided grants to most hopeful tribes, including some who have been unable to achieve recognition (such as the Mashpee Wampanoag), and some whose petitions at the BAR have been successful (such as the Eastern Pequots of Connecticut, to whom the ANA gave numerous grants in the early 1990s). ANA grants can be used to document the petition, preserve vital tribal records, or fund other necessities of tribal governance and cultural survival. Humanitarian and religious groups, such as Lutheran Brotherhood, the Baptist Council, and the Quaker Friends Committee, have also provided funding to petitioning tribes.

Although these sources of funding have proven invaluable to most of the tribes seeking acknowledgment, they are often inadequate to pay for the research demands of the BAR, the lobbying and research demands of Congress, or the legal demands of the court system. The gaming industry, seeing a need in the community and a payoff in the form of potentially lucrative tribal casino contracts, has rushed to fill in the gaps left by other sources of funding.

At times, Connecticut seems awash in casino cash; it appears that enormous sums of money are going to aid and hinder tribes seeking recognition. The press reports that Donald Trump's Hotels and Casinos Division financed the petition of Connecticut's Paucatuck Eastern Pequots, which received recognition from the BAR in spring 2002. In addition, leaders of one faction of the Golden Hill Paugussett Tribe, in Connecticut, acknowledge that they have received in excess of $4 million from a New York State real estate developer, and that they have plans to join with him in a casino enterprise, if they receive recognition.[30]

Just as the Poarch Band of Creeks has aided several tribes in its region in seeking recognition, the Mashantucket Pequots have used their money and experience to the benefit of hopeful groups. The Mashantucket Pequot Tribe recently donated substantial financial resources to the Eastern Pequots' recognition efforts. In 1996 and again in 1998, the tribal leadership of the Mashantucket Pequot Nation wrote to Interior on behalf of the Eastern Pequots' petition.[31] Mashantucket tribal chair Kenny Reels attended the BIA's formal Technical Assistance Meetings on the Eastern and Paucatuck Eastern Pequots' acknowledgment decisions as a supporter of the Eastern Tribe, and *The Pequot Times* regularly includes stories and information about the Eastern Pequot Tribe and tribal members.

In addition, the excellent resources on Connecticut Indian history and governmental affairs in the Mashantucket Pequot Museum and Research Center (MPMRC), made possible by gaming wealth, are available to any regional tribe desiring to use them in documenting their petition, and the Pequots go to great length to advertise this availability. Aside from the MPMRC and *Schemitzun* (the Pequots' annual Feast of Green Corn and Dance), the Mashantucket Pequots host numerous regional and national intertribal events and symposia.

As a result, then, of investments made by casino developers and gaming tribes, some hopeful groups are able to finance massive work on their petitions, or hire lobbyists in aid of legislative recognition. This certainly helps to ensure that some deserving tribes will not be denied recognition simply because they could not afford to hire the research work necessary for their petition. It may also, however, create or exacerbate tribal splits over the idea of gaming, which could lead to economic and power disparities within the petitioning groups.

It is, in part, the availability of gaming financing and the publicly aired factionalization of some petitioning groups that have led to gross oversimplifications about acknowledgment, such as the Connecticut television station that reported the following when the Golden Hill Paugussetts were denied by the BAR: "Golden Hill Paugussett Tribe denied a gambling permit by the Federal Bureau of Indian Affairs."[32] A year later, when the BAR's decision was reaffirmed at the IBIA, reporters at WVIT-TV stated, "It means they can't build a casino."[33] And even when BAR officials talk about the recognition prospects of the Golden Hill, they cannot resist using gambling metaphors. In response to Chief Quiet Hawk's 1994 prediction that the tribe would win recognition in several months, an anonymous BIA official "familiar with the tribe's application" said "the odds of that are a million to one."[34]

## BACKLASH: THE CONFLATION OF GAMING WITH ACKNOWLEDGMENT LEADS TO A QUESTION OF MOTIVES

The conflation of gaming with acknowledgment by the media and BAR staff alike is unfair for those groups who sought recognition long before the passage of the IGRA, and are merely taking advantage of new laws to achieve economic self-sufficiency. A full 117 letters of intent to petition were filed prior to the IGRA's passage in 1988, and nearly 130 were filed before the opening of the first Indian casino in 1990. Certainly, there was a marked increase in the arrival of letters to petition following on the heels of the success of recently recognized groups in establishing gaming facilities in the early 1990s, and it makes sense that more unrecognized groups would seek acknowledgment in order to take advantage of opening economic opportunities. However likely it is that gaming is part of the motivation for groups seeking recognition, especially those who have filed since 1990, it is unclear if that spike in letters can be attributed *solely* to gaming options. Though more than half (55 percent) of the tribes recognized or restored by Congress have signed gaming compacts, only 33 percent of tribes recognized by the BAR have signed such agreements (admittedly, quite a few of the remaining 77 percent operate bingo parlors).[35]

Resentment against Indian tribes as they pursue land claims or economic development is nothing new. As early as the mid-1830s, attorneys for the Cherokee Nation reported that their efforts on the tribes' behalf had caused them grave personal danger and economic harm.[36] In the late 1960s, lawyer Tom Tureen reported receiving threatening anonymous phone calls and hostile public commentary as a result of his work on the Maine Land Claims Settlement Act.[37] And, at least since the Golden Hill Paugussetts' armed standoff with the state of Connecticut over cigarette taxes, tensions between that state and its Indian leaders have often run high.

However, at least one political scientist has noted a dramatic escalation of tensions between the towns, the tribes, and unrecognized groups in Connecticut since the advent of casino gaming. Robert Bee, speaking before a small crowd at the MPMRC, argued that this backlash is changing state-Indian policies in Connecticut, and that it has ramifications for federal acknowledgment.[38] In the most pressing instances, Connecticut legislators have called for the dissolution of state recognition for the Golden Hill Paugussetts, and for a federal investigation into the acknowledgment of the Mashantucket Pequots.

The tensions have also risen to a national level, with a number of anti-gaming bills being introduced since the IGRA. A plethora of bills has been introduced to limit the power tribes have in controlling their finances and policing their lands. Bills in 1999 and 2000 proposed to relieve tribes of their sovereign immunity from suit;[39] debate in committee focused on the Mashantucket Pequots' unwillingness to pay some personal injury damages or be sued for intellectual property violations.[40] Attorney James Ferdon stated the following in testimony before Congress:

> The doctrine of sovereignty immunity is antiquated. When Congress first established the doctrine, over one hundred and fifty years ago, Indian tribes were not gloriously successful entrepreneurs. It was not foreseeable then by Congress that Indian tribes today would be operating major casinos where thousands and thousands of people come to play and work each day. The law must change with the times. In this day and age, when Indian tribes are reaping the rewards of their commercial success, they must also fulfill their responsibilities as

property owners. All property owners in this country, except Indian tribes, are subject to tort law.[41]

A second type of proposed legislation seeks to tax Indian casino profits. The House Ways and Means Committee in 1997 came very close (in a 22–16 vote) to recommending that an additional 35 percent tax be assessed on Indian tribes' commercial ventures. Bill Archer of Texas, chair of the committee, offered the proposal, but it was replaced with J. D. Hayworth's (R-Ariz.) proposal for a $15.50 arrivals and departure tax on international airline passengers. In addition, other initiatives have been made to reduce funding to the BIA and tribal programs. These initiatives are based, in large part, on the misperception that all tribes have "made it big" in gaming.[42]

Nationally and regionally, those who resent Indian casino success have voiced three primary concerns. These concerns focus on the supposed immorality and criminality of gaming, the perception that local towns and cities are not benefiting economically from Indian gaming, and the perception that the tribes are using their increasing political power to steamroll citizens concerned about uncontrolled development of tribal lands.

## Gaming, Crime, and (Im)Morality

Though the American public has generally become more tolerant of gambling, while becoming less tolerant of other "vice" activities, such as smoking, drinking, and drug use, local lawmakers continue to characterize Indian gaming as an illicit activity.[43] In 1992, then-governor of Connecticut Lowell Weicker made a statement that epitomizes this characterization; he asked a crowd of supporters, "Is this a gambling state? Or is it a family state?"[44] Backlash around Indian casinos often focuses on the possibility of increased rates of organized crime, neighborhood and property crime, and family crime, as well as the economic hardship that gambling often places on the poor.[45]

Although it is clear that residents of the new casino counties have well-founded concerns about some crime and quality-of-life issues, a number of recent investigations of Indian gaming agree with Dennis Nelson's 1996 finding that "there is little statistical or anecdotal basis to support a claim that Indian casinos are either a magnet for, or

direct contributor to, the crime rates in any jurisdiction. . . . The crime
rates in these jurisdictions are (with very few, but explainable exceptions) *below* the crime rates for counties of similar size."[46] Although
there are prominent voices on both sides of the debate, most analysts
will agree that an important deterrent to casino-related criminal
activity is the extra surveillance and high-quality policing provided by
tribal police and casino task forces. Nelson writes, "By federal law,
state compact, and tribal ordinances, casinos are among the most vigorously regulated of any businesses. . . . Primary responsibility for
assuring this high degree of regulation is on the tribes themselves,
where effective self-regulation is a matter of pride."[47]

Gaming revenues have allowed some tribes to establish or improve
their own fully certified police departments; many of them are able
to offer specialties such as bomb- and drug-sniffing dogs and extra
personnel, who are often lent to non-Indian police forces in the
region. Many Indian casino areas, especially those in rural regions,
have higher ratios of law enforcement to civilians than other parts of
the state.[48]

Many tribal members have little use for statistics or studies on
either side of the issue. One told me that, while she acknowledges
the social ills of gaming, and respects the religious views of those
who oppose it, gaming is a matter of tribal sovereignty, first and foremost. She told me, "It's not the state's responsibility, nor does the
state have the right, to tell a sovereign nation what it can or cannot
do. It is our decision to make; right or wrong, it's our decision." She
continued thus:

> And I know that gambling has social ills and all that. . . . Every
> economic development industry has social ills, it has problems,
> it creates some. But people also don't look at the other side of
> it, too. Lack of something creates social ills. You talk about
> Indian tribes, with the drinking and the alcohol, the drug
> abuse. Can you imagine the hopelessness of no job, no job
> future, and no hope? Think about the social ills that causes:
> domestic violence, suicide, robberies. . . . So you have to look
> at [gambling] and see, yeah it causes social ills, but so does the
> other side of the scale, it causes social ills, too. . . . We all put
> some sugar in our tea and in our coffee. And we don't ever
> think about all the social ills and problems that sugar caused.

with the sugar cane and the cotton. Growing all this cotton. We put on our cotton shirts and we don't say, "Well I can't put on this cotton because look at all the people that died because of this cotton." You know, "Don't go to the casino, that's dirty money. That's sin money." Well, cotton and sugar cane we fought a civil war over the social ills of all of that stuff. People don't think about things like that.[49]

### "Gaming Is a Cannibalization of the Local Economy."

Indian gaming facilities, like other gambling establishments, "reap tremendous profits from their various operations, at the cost of their patrons."[50] Because of the contribution casinos make to the local tax base, citizens often tolerate them as an entertainment venue where people spend their luxury dollars. However, because Indian gaming facilities are not subject to federal and state income taxes, sales taxes, or municipal real estate taxes, many people think they operate completely free of taxes, and are just parasites of the local economy.

In fact, tribal recipients of per capita distributions do pay taxes on that money, and non-Indian employees of tribal enterprises have federal and state payroll tax deducted from their pay warrants. In addition, construction and tourism booms in the region caused by casino development generate additional taxable dollars. Finally, as large employers in their regions, Indian casinos pump substantial amounts of extra consumer dollars into their local economies, and reduce expenditures on programs like welfare, food stamps, and unemployment insurance.[51]

James Klas and Matthew Robinson's discussion of Indian gaming in Minnesota shows that employment in gaming counties has increased at a rate 67 percent faster than in non-gaming counties in that state; "If Indian gaming were a single entity, the combined employment would rank ninth among Minnesota employers," above industries like Wal-Mart, Fingerhut, and Honeywell.[52] Minnesota's Aid to Families with Dependent Children (AFDC) roles decreased by 15.1 percent in counties with Indian gaming; Indian recipients of federal aid decreased by 58.1 percent statewide from 1990 to 1995; the Twin Cities region experienced an 11.4 percent increase in federal aid during this time, and aid rates decreased only by 5.6 percent in rural, non-gaming counties in the state.[53] The Evans Group's econometric analysis shows how gaming (Indian and non-Indian) adds $5.9 billion to federal taxes and $2 billion to state and local tax rates nationwide. This study shows that, nationwide, gaming directly employs 337,000 people, and indirectly employs another 328,000.[54]

Even with the positive impact of these successes, the common perception that gaming is a "cash cow" providing incredible wealth to all tribes is patently false. In fact, most Indian gaming falls far short of the grand scale of the Connecticut casinos; it is even rare to have an Indian bingo parlor fare as well as the Poarch Creek establishment. As the National Indian Gaming Association puts it, gaming is not a "white buffalo" for every tribe.[55] According to the NIGA, "only a small portion of the tribal gaming operations [nationwide] raise enough to generate income."[56] In fact, a mere 8 of the 198 existing tribal casinos represent a full 40 percent of all tribal gaming profits.[57] Most gaming tribes appear successful at raising their people above oppressive poverty; they elevate tribal existence to one above subsistence, but not one of dazzling wealth. Gaming often has the effect of bringing tribal members into the lower middle-class, not of making them the economic elites of their region.

After payouts like wages and other operating expenses, only about 4 percent of gross wagers at the casinos typically go the tribes as profits. Additionally, as discussed in the overview of the IGRA, the statute places strict rules on how that average 4 percent is distributed. Tribal gaming revenues may be spent only for tribal government operations, to promote the general welfare of the tribe and its members, to promote tribal economic development, to make charitable donations, or to fund the operations of local government agencies. Cornell, Kalt, Krepps, and Taylor report that between 40 and 50 percent of tribal casinos' profits is spent on tribal government, and that an additional 25 to 35 percent goes to tribal welfare expenditures. If per capita payments are chosen, they are specifically apportioned to tribal members based on net income of the casino and the IGRA requirements. Typically, an additional 10 to 20 percent of profits goes to further economic development; between 5 and 15 percent of profits are spent as charitable contributions or payments in lieu of taxes.

*Gaming Backlash Leads to Recognition Backlash*

Though most of its premises are unfounded, the backlash against casino operations is quickly spilling over into a backlash against recognizing new tribes. And, while BAR staff maintains that its processes are above such backlash, congressional processes certainly are not. Grassroots anti-recognition and anti-gaming organizations form interesting partnerships of seemingly odd bedfellows. Liberals and environmentalists opposed to expansionism and development are joined by fundamentalist Christians opposed to gaming of any sort; together they are vocal and visible at Senate hearings on recognition, and are frequent visitors to congressional offices.

It is hard to judge whether the BAR's outcomes and processes are affected by the casino issue; none of the tribes that have been recognized since 1978 were post-1988 petitioners. In other words, none of the fifteen newly recognized tribes are likely to have been motivated solely by high-stakes casino gaming when they filed their first correspondence with the BAR. Only one of the fifteen groups denied by the BAR was a post-1988 petitioner;[58] this leaves no argument that the BAR staff's decisions against tribes came about due to concerns regarding the petitioners' gaming motivations.

One significant aspect of BAR processes and decisions, however, has been affected by casino gaming. The accelerating rate of litigation of BAR decisions, as states side with their non-Indian residents in suits fighting tribal acknowledgment, subjects the BAR to increasing scrutiny, costly research and litigation, and a sense of being embattled on all fronts. BAR proceedings are subject to backlash, like it or not. Certainly, the same is true for groups hoping to achieve acknowledgment. As chapters 7 and 8 show, mitigating this backlash is key to legitimating tribal recognition and, also, to ensuring economic survival and political power.

## CHAPTER SIX

# Perceptions of the Process II

Indian Racial Identity and
Federal Acknowledgment

The prevalence and importance of public and official perceptions of Indian racial identity in contestations over federal acknowledgment have already been touched on. Chapter 3 discussed racial stereotypes of Indians and how some authors believe that these stereotypes affect some groups' chances for achieving recognition. Using those critiques as a basis of analysis, this chapter looks briefly at the racialized language inherent in acknowledgment struggles, and examines how the tenor of that language is affected when money and land are perceived to be at stake. As Gail Sheffield notes in her examination of the Indian Arts and Crafts Act, "The confusion of the political with the cultural (or ethnic) and both with the racial seems to be endemic in all Indian matters in this country."[1] Certainly, race has long been a concern of those interested in federal acknowledgment processes (FAPs); by undertaking an analysis of the racialization of Indian identity, as well as an analysis of the changes in such racialization in recent years, it is possible to gain a broader understanding of contemporary racial considerations and their implications in acknowledgment.

## Public and Official Perceptions of
## Race and Acknowledgment Law

Most of the current public discourse on acknowledgment tends to confuse the role of acknowledgment in recognizing tribal existence with the idea of *authenticating Indianness.* Most public attacks are not attacks on the *tribal* nature of the recently acknowledged tribe or hopeful group, but rather on the perceived *racial identities* of the membership. In other words, not many will charge that a group is not a tribe; the typical person hostile to a tribe's acknowledgment is more likely to argue that the group's members are not real Indians. Those hostile to acknowledgment continually racialize Indian identity.

Though BAR processes do not certify Indian identity, as such, but rather establish the maintenance of tribal political authority, it is clear that conferral of tribal status does have the effect of legitimating some Indians' racial identities while possibly delegitimating others'. One former Alabama State Indian official, and a member of an unrecognized group, put it this way: "I've also met people in federal tribes that were less blood quantum than I am. So those people are [considered] Indian because they're federally recognized, and I'm not because I'm not federally recognized? I mean, that's all a big joke to me."[2]

I have observed three types of statements about Indians that racialize Indian identity; they can be summed up in the phrases: *Indians are red; Indians are primitive;* and *Indians are poor.* Anthropologist Katherine Spilde calls the confluence of these types of erroneous statements "Rich Indian Racism." Claims that "Indians are rich" can and have been used to deny treaty rights and trust status to tribal governments on the basis that "[those] Indians don't need them anymore."[3] Although I focus on the tribes I have spent the most time studying, including the incredibly wealthy Mashantucket Pequots, it is important to note, as Spilde does, that other tribes have fallen victim to similar mischaracterizations of their ethnicity and tribal government needs based on wrongheaded economic and cultural criteria.

INDIANS ARE RED

Dominant U.S. society has a very fixed idea of what an Indian looks like. That fixed idea has been reproduced photographically and cinematographically since the turn of the twentieth century. The male Indian is red skinned, with high cheekbones and an aquiline nose; he has long, braided black hair and an erect posture. His skin is craggy, his eyes are wizened, and he often has with him the accoutrements of indigeneity: horses, blankets, feathers, and tomahawks. He is silent, illiterate, and ancient—whether he is depicted as a noble warrior on the plains or a bum on a street corner in Denver.

There is, as well, a plethora of images of American Indian females. Artists portray Indian women as either hypersexualized, or as "maidens," in poses of submission and subservience. Again, long braids, feathers, and horses are in abundance, as are improbably diaphanous leather and skin garments.

Sometimes, members of recently recognized tribes meet these imagined expectations—with a quick glance, an average person would probably characterize them as Indian. For instance, one well-meaning observer mentioned to me that members of the unrecognized Mowa Choctaws, when you meet them, "make a strong case *just on visual,* [emphasis mine] and on personal meeting, that absolutely they're Indians."[4]

This is not always the case though. The membership of these tribes is often quite racially diverse, which is to be expected given their patterns of intermarriage and measured assimilation. They have not lived on isolated and self-contained reservations, but have rather farmed and worked next to other people in their region. The scholarship of Jack Forbes makes clear that African Americans and Indians have been interacting for at least five hundred years, in a variety of settings, and for a variety of purposes. As a result of such interaction, membership in many tribes often includes black Indians, as well as those who have intermarried with whites.[5]

Intermarriage and a lack of Indian phenotype, or appearance, confuse the public, and tend to throw motives for self-identifying as Indian into question. A 1960s newspaper account of a Poarch Band of Creeks tribal meeting provides a typical comment.

> The Eastern Creek Indian Nation has refused to bury the hatchet in its fight with the Great White Fathers in Washington. . . . [Chief Calvin] McGhee and his top adviser, C. Lenoir Thompson, a lawyer, addressed the 200 braves, squaws and papooses who gathered for the powwow. *Many of those attending showed few signs of Indian heritage but all claimed Creek blood and a share in the wampum.* [emphasis mine][6]

Lebaran Byrd, a Mowa Choctaw Indian and former principal at Reed's Chapel school, was reported in a local paper to have said that tribal members "resented being saddled with preconceived ideas about how an Indian should dress or act." The reporter noted that "stock images of how an Indian should look have occasionally caused the Mowa community to question its own identity." Byrd told him that "[tribal members] were seeing things on TV [and saying] 'No I don't look like that. No, I'm not an Indian.'"[7]

The prevalence of language concerned with looking, or, rather, not looking, Indian has not waned with the times. Nor is it relegated to the unique racial politics of the Deep South. In fact, such language has been mobilized in recent days to negatively highlight the diverse physical appearances of the Mashantucket Pequots in Connecticut. Before 1999, when African Indian Kenneth Reels took over as chair of the Tribe, the Pequots were very visibly represented by Skip Hayward, who was identified (and at times self-identified) as white on important documents such as marriage certificates and school enrollment, until he returned to the reservation in the 1970s.[8] At 1992 Senate hearings on proposed changes to the IGRA, after acknowledging that his remarks might not be "politically correct," casino mogul Donald Trump told the senators, "When you go up to Connecticut and look—now [the Pequots] don't look like real Indians to me, and they don't look like real Indians to other Indians."[9]

INDIANS ARE PRIMITIVE

A trend in television comedy of late has been to set skits in Indian casinos, or make jokes about Indian gaming, with the goal of showing how un-Indian the proprietors of these establishments are. Jay Leno joked on the *Tonight Show* that the Pequots were a "group of Italians running around in the woods, running a big casino."[10] On a 2002 episode of ABC's *My Wife and Kids,* Damon Wayans helps his daughter and her friends learn about indigenous cultures during a sleepover, during which they sleep in the backyard in homemade teepees. When one of the little girls asks Wayans's character why he has built an extra teepee, he responds, "That's the casino!"[11]

But Leno and Wayans's quips are lightweight confections when compared to the raunchy ten-minute opening skit of *Saturday Night Live*'s "25th Anniversary Special," which featured Bill Murray playing a role that could only be a parody of Skip Hayward.[12] Murray posed in a number of comedy sketches set in an Indian casino in which he characterized the tribal leader as lacking Indian-style social graces and exhibiting overwhelming tendencies toward gambling, womanizing, and, of course, drinking.

Even television animators have found ways to capitalize on questions of authenticity raised by some critics of Indian gaming and acknowledgment. On one episode of the Fox network's now-defunct *The Family Guy,* the cartoon characters are driving through the northeastern woods when they stop at an Indian casino ("Geronimo's Palace") and wager enough to lose their car.[13] When the father of the family demands to see the tribal elders in an attempt to regain possession of the automobile, which he alleges they have swindled him out of, he is ushered into a corporate-looking office and met by a racially diverse group of men in business suits, whose only indigenous accoutrements are bolo ties and the ubiquitous feathers. They command him to go on an American Indian vision quest in order to get his car back, but they are unable to offer him any guidance, since, they shrug, they've never done one. The "Family Guy" successfully completes the vision quest and retrieves his family car, and, in the course of doing so, proves that even he is more indigenous than the so-called Indians running the casino.

These jokes unwittingly mirror a frustration about acknowledgment processes that some unrecognized groups are quick to express. One member of the Mowa Choctaw Tribe has argued that any petitioner capable of getting through the federal process unscathed *cannot* be a real Indian tribe. While serving as the Mowas' legal counsel, he told the *New York Times* that his people were "too Indian" to be recognized through the process. He drew an unflattering comparison with the recently recognized Poarch Creeks.

> If you could meet the criteria set up by the BIA then you probably weren't Indian, because that means you've stayed in one spot, could read and write, kept a journal of everything you've done for the past few hundred years, and were economically stable. If we had all that, [we would not be Indian] we would be middle-class white people.[14]

Other tribal leaders are quick to compare the high expectations of the BAR criteria with the low expectations the general public has for Indian tribes. Pequot chair Skip Hayward notes the following:

> Maybe if we were still getting water from an open well and going outside to two-hole outhouses and using human manure

to fertilize our gardens, nobody would be paying any attention to us. Now, we are coming back to be leaders again. Now, there seems to be a problem.[15]

Another Mashantucket Pequot council member told a reporter that people just did not realize tribes could be modern *and* traditional: "Most folks in the general public, without having any malevolence toward Indian people, would be comforted if they came here and found my people in wigwams and long-houses and buckskin dress."[16] And Chief Taylor of the Mowa Choctaws in Alabama, while serving as the state Indian commissioner for Alabama, was compelled to explain to the local press that "rather than using bows and arrows and war paint, we now use computer chips and attaché cases."[17]

## INDIANS ARE POOR

Much of the primitivism attributed to Indians assumes their poverty. After all, rich people do not have to sell baskets or firewood to afford subsistence housing. Pequot tribal member Joey Carter ties the anti-Foxwoods racial backlash to both money and power: "We're not supposed to have enterprises like Foxwoods. Indians are supposed to be poor people, they're supposed to live on a reservation, grow their corn, pick their berries, and be exploited. That's what [the Pequots' critics are] scared of. They realize money is power—that's what it's all about."[18]

In some regards, Carter is right. Even popular culture accounts that are sympathetic to the Mashantucket Pequots' enterprise fall into the trap of equating indigeneity with primitivism and poverty. One journalist writes that

Indians are still in these [Connecticut] woods, but most of those who live on the Mashantucket Pequot reservation are hardly recognizable as such. None is native to the reservation, and what they trade is mostly illusory. . . . There is no basket weaving, no pottery or firewood for sale here. . . . In place of pickup trucks and subsistence housing, Jaguars and boats dot the front lawns of split- level homes.[19]

Yet it is undeniable that some gaming tribes perpetuate stereotypes about Indianness that many critics fault the BAR criteria with embodying. Several aspects of the Pequots' operation open it to criticisms of primitivizing, racializing, and gendering tribal relationships in an unacceptable way. A National Public Radio report noted that "cocktail waitresses at Foxwoods wear short—extremely short Indian print shifts slit above the thigh—[it is] sort of an adults-only Pocahontas costume." The reporter, Scott Simon, is obviously embarrassed. He tells a tribal member the following:

> I—I guess the part I noticed more [than the skimpiness], believe it or nor, was—was less the—the, kind of what some people would call immodest nature of it than the way it did seem to be some kind of a—I mean, for example, if somebody opened a restaurant off the reservation a few miles from here and they had waitresses dressed in those kind of style costumes with, you know, with—with feathers in their hair, it seems to me there might be some Native Americans who would protest that and say "You're—you're mocking us."[20]

This phenomenon is not limited to the Mashantucket Pequots, and it surprises few engaging in tourism scholarship, who have found that the tourist industry often perpetuates ethnic stereotypes, which are promoted as indicators of authenticity. Stuart Kirsch writes, "Foxwoods casino in Ledyard, Connecticut, is the economic wellspring and ideological vehicle of the recently reconstituted Mashantucket Pequot Tribe. Both the status of the Pequots as 'real Indians' and their entitlement to their gaming enterprise are vigorously contested within and beyond the native American community. The Pequots supply counter-authorization of identity by constructing and deploying several discourses of authenticity within the casino."[21]

Gaming analysts in particular argue that legitimacy and political acceptance are essential for a casino's success.[22] Indian casinos have a double burden for legitimacy: in order to be politically palatable, their business practices and entertainment must be perceived as legitimate; at the same time, the identity of the entrepreneurs must be perceived as legitimate. In non-Indian cultural tourism there is usually no license for cultural and heritage resources, and no ownership of such resources can be claimed;[23] through federal acknowledgment law, such "licenses" for cultural representation through tourist enterprises such as gaming are granted and used to re-create the political identities of the tribe. This necessitates the visible markers of Indianness that dominant society has come to expect, and which are part of the conflict over the racialization of Indian identity at federal acknowledgment venues.

Not all claims to authenticity will bow to Western stereotypes, however. Gaming profits facilitate the translation of Indian culture into educational tourist sites, many of which are outstanding examples of display of tradition, history, and culture. Those who have studied the tourist industry closely argue that "the conservation of cultural resources and the process of transformation into tourism products can be a real incentive to the process of reviving cultural identity."[24] Through this cultural revitalization, formerly marginal groups commemorate their history with tourism. This has long been true of Indian tourist sites. One author points to Indian experiences of retranslation and revitalization in examples like the Wounded Knee Memorial on the Pine Ridge Reservation, the Trail of Tears corridors in the southern United States, and the Mashantucket Pequot Museum and Research Center.[25] Such reappropriation of historical and cultural material complicates and contradicts the view of Indians as primitive, and is possible only through the accumulation of wealth.

## Only "Real" Indians

The previous chapter made it clear that the IGRA has forever changed the acknowledgment process. Gaming monies are a source of potential funding for petitioning groups to use to engage in greater depth of research, resulting in a potentially more- professional product to present in the petitioning process. Gaming monies are also sources of potential funding for established tribes that wish to aid, or work against, petitioning groups. In any case, gaming has drawn a shadow across many acknowledgment claims, and has made public relations difficult for petitioning tribes, even for those not seeking casinos. This backlash has, at the same time, made Indian racial identity an ever-touchier subject in popular culture, regional associations, and BAR deliberations.

The mayor of Hartford, Connecticut, recently said this about Indian casinos: "Folks are really mad because the *Indians* are making all the money down there." Those same "folks" increasingly want to use acknowledgment to see to it that only *legitimate Indians* can make "all that money." While this concern—that only *real* Indian tribes get recognition and gaming—is certainly justifiable, how the recognition claims of Indians are legitimated, and reported upon, by the media is complicated by perceptions of race and racial identity at play in different regions in the United States. Something as seemingly clear as "Indian identity" is actually *much* more complex than most would grant. The next two chapters, which examine intersections of cash, color, and colonialism in Alabama and Connecticut, make this abundantly clear.

## CHAPTER SEVEN

# Cash, Color, and Colonialism in Alabama

William W. Quinn, a historian of federal acknowledgment processes, wrote in 1990 of his belief that a "Southeast Syndrome" would soon sweep the nation.[1] He predicted that hundreds of "Wannabe Indians" and "Phantom Tribes" would somehow manage to get recognition from the federal government.[2] He further predicted that most of these "Indian Recruitment Organizations" (IROs) would originate in the confusion that typifies tribal-state affairs in the Deep South.

I agree with those who call Quinn's message alarmist.[3] Given the slow pace of federal acknowledgment proceedings, the care the BAR staff takes with the petitions, and the number of groups who have been denied administrative acknowledgment, the scenario Quinn predicts is highly unlikely.

However, it is evident that IROs do operate across the nation, and that they are particularly prevalent in the South. And, because southern state officials have had fewer interactions with their Native populations than officials in states with more established tribes and American Indian programs, there is a reasonable fear that they are less able to distinguish between real and hobby tribes, and are at risk of extending state recognition to illegitimate tribal entities seeking primarily financial advantages. As such, the fear that hobby groups, even though they obviously do not meet the federal criteria for tribal status, will seek, and be awarded, that status, and use it for financial gain, is hard to shake.

Indeed, prior to the codification of rules for state recognition of Indian tribes and Indian organizations, the proliferation of Indian chiefs in Alabama could have been confusing for citizens and officials alike. In the community of Coffeeville, near the Mowa Choctaw settlement, J. C. Roberts, "Chief River Rat," was appointed Clarke County's Choctaw Indian chief in 1982. The local paper reported that he became "the first Clarke County Indian Chief to be appointed since the time of William Weatherford, who was also known as Red Eagle." Roberts wore a "traditional turkey feather costume" and explained that his "Indian name" was River Rat because he operated a fishing camp on the Tombigbee River.[4]

That same year, the paper published a number of editorials and letters to the editor denouncing the recognition hopes of one Alabama tribe, the Echota Cherokees. These communications called the tribe a "hobby group," and urged others not to support their claims.[5] The archived files of the Alabama Indian Affairs Commission (AIAC) contain a number of letters from that period asking for AIAC advice on which IROs were legitimate. One, written in shaky, perhaps elderly, script, tells the author's family history (a grandmother who was an enrolled, full-blood Creek) and adds, "I have not affiliated myself with a tribe in Alabama because I am reluctant due to possible money schemes. I would like to, if you can advise me. I did join one in Geneva Florida and never received a thing. They accepted my check."[6]

Certainly, there are unscrupulous people in the world, even those who would falsify tribal enrollments and heritage. Just as certainly, there are economic and social advantages to be gained for individuals by claiming their true Indian identity, in having tribal membership, and in legitimating tribal status. Anthropologists Anthony Paredes and Sandra Joos note that, in Alabama, Poarch Creek tribal members' status as Indian has continued to be to their economic advantage.

> Compared to local Black people the Creeks of recent years appear to have become more socially accepted by Whites, and to have been preferred by employers required by governmental policies to improve minority-hiring practices. Thus, in certain respects, Indians recently have achieved a social position more clearly superior to that of Blacks.[7]

Many in Alabama would agree that it is better socially to be identified as Indian rather than as black. Discussing racism in the state,
one Native American woman acknowledged that

> it's more anti-black. . . . We're less than one percent of the popu-
> lation; blacks are almost 25 percent of the population. Wherever
> you have a high number of minorities in the state, those are
> the ones that are resented. . . . And, see, down here—because
> for so many years people have readily accepted that all the
> Indians were removed to Indian Territory—it never occurred
> to them that there were so many Indians. So we're kind of a
> novelty. . . . And, it's to the point where, because they get tired
> of the issues that they deal with, with blacks, whether they're
> right or wrong is not even an issue. . . . I've had people say to
> me, "I hope you people get this and this and this because I'm
> tired of the blacks getting all this."[8]

These distinctions between black, white, and Indian seem overwhelmingly important in Alabama. Indeed, nearly everyone I met
there, when this project came up in casual conversation, confided
that they "had Indian blood in them." Even the chief of staff to Representative Sonny Callahan (R-Ala.) used the congressman's part-
Cherokee heritage to vouch for his interest in and concern for the
Mowa recognition claim. Callahan is not an enrolled member of any
Cherokee Tribe, but his aide told me, "Sonny's got some Indian
blood in him. So he certainly understands the importance of this."
The Mowa Choctaws, as an unrecognized group in Alabama, also
understand the importance of "Indian blood" and "black blood,"
and their role in federal acknowledgment.

### Race in the South: The Mowa Choctaws, "A People Whom Time Forgot"

Some early work by anthropologists and historians that focused on
the Deep South erroneously reinforced the common assumption
that the Indian population indigenous to the region had been made
extinct by the late 1800s. The incidence of prolonged Indian-white
conflict was lower in the Southeast than in the Northeast, in California,

or on the plains.[9] Yet the Native population was still decimated by
wars and diseases, which were exacerbated through contact with
French, Spanish, and British colonists. Early antimiscegenation laws
governed the sexual and familial contact of the different races, forbidding free whites from marrying or having sexual relations with
Indians, blacks, or mulattoes. To do so was to forfeit their own, and
their children's, racial privileges. A Virginia Act of 1705, for example,
defined a mulatto as "the child of an Indian, and the child, grandchild, or great grandchild of a Negro" so that " all half-Indian children
were legally mulattoes."[10]

Tribal numbers were further devastated by federal Removal-era
policies directed explicitly at the tribes of the Deep South. Beginning in 1832, members of what were known as the Five Civilized
Tribes were led on forced marches from their homeland to Indian
territory in present-day Oklahoma. The Creeks signed the first Removal
treaty on March 24, 1832; the Seminoles were removed beginning in
May of that year. The Treaty of Dancing Rabbit Creek, governing
Choctaw Removal from Mississippi, Louisiana, and Alabama, was signed
in October 1830, just a few weeks after the Chickasaws had begun
their long trek north and west. The official Cherokee government
held out the longest, but finally, in 1835, a number of dissident chiefs
signed the Treaty of New Echota, and began the formal process of
exile of the Cherokee Nation from North Carolina and Georgia.

Those few Indians who remained faced a further threat to their
identity and survival: their extinction through reclassification.[11]
Though slavery and its eventual demise necessitated a complex system
of classification throughout the entire nation—the coding of people
of color as "free" or "slave"—such classification became obsessive in
the South. In the racial paranoia of the time, "it was no longer toler-
able to be considered merely a free person of color. One had to be
able to prove what kind of non-white [sic] one was."[12] Aside from
white, Indian, or slave, people of color in the South had seemingly
endless classificatory possibilities forced upon them—"Free Person
of Color," "Free Black," "Mixed Blood," "Mulatto," or "Creole."[13] It is
clear that "Mulatto" was used for Indians, even those with no African
ancestry; and, in Alabama, since the mid-1800s, "Colored" had been
used for similar persons.[14] Each category carried with it its own
perks and perils.[15]

More often than not, people flowed between the categories, switching official identities depending upon context. Yet one pernicious rule nearly always applied, the "One-Drop Rule," whereby any person with any amount of "Negroid blood" could be considered black for purposes of law. Ward Churchill notes that "any racial admixture at all, especially with Blacks, was often deemed sufficient to warrant individuals, and sometimes entire groups, to be legally classified as non-Indians, regardless of their actual standing in indigenous society. On this basis, most noticeably in the South but elsewhere as well, whole Native peoples were declared extinct via the expedient of simply classifying them as mulattos or coloreds."[16]

As a result of the loss of their Indian identity due to classificatory structures, and the decimation of their tribal structures due to Removal, the remnant groups found it difficult to control their own governance, and faced losing the ability to maintain their public ethnic boundaries.[17] Detribalized, these "mixed-bloods" either assimilated so much as to appear culturally indistinct from poor whites and blacks in the region,[18] or went so deep into isolation that they were easily ignored by federal and state officials.[19] For these Indians, it may have seemed easiest *not* to challenge the dominant community's perception of them. If they did not get married in an official ceremony, break the law, or buy and sell property, most members of these groups would not even be listed in county records. These Indians might have felt that the more invisible they became, the safer they remained.[20]

Few groups know the isolation and racial tension that Indians in the Deep South experienced as well as the Mowa Choctaw Tribe of Alabama, who call themselves "A People Whom Time Forgot."[21] Located on the border of Washington and Mobile Counties, they live at the center of Alabama's history.[22] Washington County was the first county government established in what Congress named Alabama Territory, on March 3, 1817. At the time, Washington County held the territorial capital, St. Stephens, and encompassed twenty-five thousand square miles. Twenty-six counties in Alabama and Mississippi now occupy what used to be Choctaw stomping grounds. The Tombigbee River flows through the county, meeting the Alabama and Coosa as they flow into the Gulf of Mexico—the Tombigbee Valley was home to the Creeks and Choctaws, and St. Stephens had a Choctaw Trading House, where a number of Indians served as translators, and

facilitated commerce and governance. Commercial hunting replaced
the Choctaws' subsistence agriculture as the Indians entered the
colonial cash economy.

The Choctaw Nation extinguished its claims on lands east of the
Mississippi by becoming signatories to the Treaty of Dancing Rabbit
Creek, in 1830. The federal government was to sell the land and use
the money to remove the Indians to Oklahoma. The majority of
Choctaws were removed, but a large number remained, both
because the government's Removal efforts in the region were not
complete and because Indians took evasive action: they hid in the
salt flats and pine groves of their "Old Stomping Grounds" and in
the structures of the Choctaw hunting camps.[23] Fearful of mob violence against them, the remaining Choctaws retreated; according to
one account, they went so deep into the forests that white men had
never been there. The result was to make the remaining Choctaws
"literally refugees in their own country . . . with a strong feeling of
alienation from the White man."[24] When Alabama voted to secede
from the Union at the start of the Civil War, some Choctaws hid in
bails of cotton, as well as in the swamp, to avoid conscription; others
joined local militia units, including the Chunchula Guards, which
were organized by Captain Benjamin Toomer and were composed
of "primarily established Indian families," many of whom were later
listed as "Free Persons of Color" in the Mobile and Washington
County censuses.[25]

As the Civil War segued into Reconstruction, there was considerable violence by groups of white militias remaining loyal to the southern ideal perpetrated against other whites, as well as Indians and
blacks, in Mobile and Washington Counties. As a result, one account
notes that "Choctaws living near the Escataupa River retreated deeper
into unoccupied public or railroad land."[26] Farmers and timber interests eventually encroached upon this land, and the Indians endeavored
to establish a patron-client relationship with individual landowners in
the area. As one historian for the Mowa Choctaws writes, the price of
Indian cooperation was to "clear cut the forests that had been their
home and deliver the profits to others."[27] During Reconstruction,
some Choctaws were able to apply for and receive homesteads on
the land that they held and lived on through the close of one century
and into the middle of another. Further difficulties would come as a
result of Allotment-era policies.

It has long been U.S. policy to quantify Indians and take note of their movements. However consistent this policy of enumeration has been, the United States has sent mixed messages about mixed-blood. When the goal of government policy was to reduce Indian land and facilitate assimilation, mixed-blood was desirable because government officials felt mixed-blood Indians would be more amenable to change. In addition, in the Dawes era, mixed-blood leaders were courted, since they were much more likely to speak English and to have had some Western education. Already more assimilated, these Indians appeared more likely to support Allotment policies.

At the same time, however, racial intermixture served to dispossess a large number of potential allottees. Local Dawes commissions were empowered by the Burke Act to set blood-quantum standards for individuals seeking allotments.[28] In addition, local Dawes commissioners in several parts of the country (but especially in the South) used their power to disqualify African Indians by defining their ethnicity as Indians "by marriage" or "by freedom," rather than "by blood."[29] Jacqueline Matte, a historian who prepared the Mowa Choctaw acknowledgment petition, notes the consistent inability of the Mowas' ancestors to get listed on the Dawes rolls. She writes that they did the roll applications "incorrectly."[30] The Mowas' incorrect entries onto Dawes rolls may reflect their inability to translate the conflicting messages of the General Allotment Act and its practice, as well as their inability to translate their own mixed-blood heritage into an Indian identity visible to Dawes commissioners. Members of the Mowa Choctaw Tribe argue that Dawes-era practices effectively kept mixed-heritage Indians like them from appearing on government (and, thus, official) versions of tribal membership lists.

As Jim Crow extended its reach throughout the Deep South, the Mowas, who had intermarried with blacks and had no tribal status, felt increasingly alienated and threatened. The "contamination of Indian blood by Black blood" was soon experienced as an incredible social and cultural liability to the assimilated and previously ignored populations. Such "contamination" was, in the age and place of lynching, a physical liability as well. Uneducated as a result of segregation policies, and consequently unable to find work in local manufacturing plants, the remaining Choctaws slipped deeper into poverty, and much of their land was lost to timber companies and paper mills.

Education became a flash point for tribal activism; "disputes over school attendance resulted in the development of official 'Black lists' designed to aid school personnel in identifying Indian children who might be able to pass" and receive a white child's education.[31] As with other racially marginalized groups in the United States, the Mowas turned to church activities to maintain their kin ties and community structures. Reed's Chapel was especially important in this regard. The Southern Baptist Mission Board had been the most prominent religious and educational influence on the Mowas, and they continued a tradition of religious education and practice in the Southern Baptist faith.[32] School- and church-related activities and activism helped to forge a bond among the core group of families—the Weavers, Rivers, Taylors, and Reeds—just as such activism was doing across the river and twenty-five miles east, on Poarch Creek land.

The civil rights movement occurring around the Tribe also informed Mowa tribal activism. Gallisnead Weaver, who was a central player in the fight for recognition, told one newspaper writer, "What we are really trying to do is develop pride among our young people. Jesse Jackson tells Blacks, 'I am somebody,' we say we are MOWA Choctaw and proud."[33] Weaver wrote a number of treatises on the topic of his Mowa identity that highlight the complex racial composition of the Tribe. These papers include "Minority among Minorities" and "I Led Three Lives Because of Jim Crow." He stated in 1981 that he had begun, at age seventeen, to research his heritage and educate himself about the Choctaw lineage.

> I wanted to interact with other Indians. We had a white stereotype of what [we] felt were Indians in this area. Indians were denied jobs and economic opportunities. Soon we began denying our own heritage so that we could get those jobs, so that we could be like Whites. But, as time went by, people began to realize their own rich heritage and take pride in it.[34]

Political and social activism was complemented by governmental development, and, in 1979, the Mowas created a tribal council, with the expressed goal of formalizing the "long-standing system of informal leadership that has characterized the native populations of the Southeast since the majority of the Indian population was Removed."[35] The council's governing structure recognized the dispersed population's differing needs, and accounted for them by electing delegates to the council in proportionate numbers from each county. The tribal offices, however, were to be located in Washington County— three miles from Highway 43, on Red Fox Road. This caused a continued split in the Tribe between members residing in Mobile County and those in Washington County. Though the drive between Mowa settlements in the counties is fifty miles at most, the population was so impoverished, and Alabama's roadways so poorly maintained, that the trip to tribal offices for cultural meetings, business planning, or government-sponsored food distribution was exceedingly difficult. The isolation was so complete that, in 1978, an outbreak of hepatitis caused great concern because parents could not drive the twenty miles from Citronelle (in northern Mobile County) to the city of Mobile in order to get their children vaccinated, even after Citronelle's homecoming queen died of the disease.[36]

In 1981, the Mobile County School Board attempted to close Reed's Chapel, the Indian School at Calcedever, as part of its continuing commitment to desegregation. Just as George Wallace had intervened on behalf of the Poarch Creeks in their fight to improve, and later, keep, their Indian School, so too did Virginia (Jennie) Dees, a Poarch Creek tribal member then serving as the executive director of the Alabama Indian Affairs Commission, intercede on behalf of the Mowas to keep their school open. At the same time, the AIAC provided technical assistance to the Mowas for the Tribe's petition to the BAR.[37]

The Mowas were recognized by the state of Alabama through acts of Congress numbers 79-228 and 79-343, on December 10, 1981. State officials accepted Mowa tribal traditions and oral history, and decided that the Mowa Choctaws were indeed Indian by heritage. They decided this even though ancestors of tribal members were often listed (even when given the opportunity to self-identify) as black on official records, and the group was widely known as Cajun and Creole. Alabama's attorney general specifically noted an 1890 Alabama State Supreme Court case, *Linton v. State*,[38] in which the court held that Alabama's census and county records had so confused racial identification that blacks, Indians, and mulattoes were legally indistinguishable.

In the 1980s, the Mowas began in earnest to develop their reservation, which consisted of a cluster of tarpaper shacks, many without indoor plumbing. A grant from HUD, received shortly after their state recognition, helped the Mowas erect brick houses with modern conveniences, pave the driveways in the small housing development (the road off the highway to the reservation remains a narrow, red dirt lane), and build a tribal office complex.

Though they have not reached the level of political influence exerted by the Poarch tribal leaders, there is some evidence that the Mowas have gained political clout in the region. As a result of the Mims Act of 1982, which wrested control of the Indian Affairs Committee from the sole power of the Poarch, the Mowas and several other federally unrecognized tribes took a place on the Alabama Indian Affairs Commission. And a tribal member, Darla Graves, served for a number of years as the executive director of the AIAC before stepping down in 2000. In addition, the Mowas constitute a large and disciplined Democratic voting block in a primarily Republican state, and some politicians did court their favor.[39]

There has been, however, a racialized backlash against even the slight progress made by the Tribe. A 1986 political cartoon published in the county paper indicates local non-Indian discomfort with tribal leaders who were exerting their influence as *Indians*. The cartoon features a crowd at a political rally, and one member of the panel is in a headdress; an aside shows an aid telling the candidate, "Sir, I think in your speech you should mention that you're a *native* of the area."[40] More than ten years later, Alabama statehouse members engaged in an embarrassing show of ignorance during discussion of a bill to allow the Mowas to police their own reservation. One legislator asked the sponsor of the bill, "How will they patrol? On horseback? With tomahawks and bows and arrows?" Members of the statehouse then engaged in a round of "war whooping" and stomping.

In response, the Mowas have begun the important work of reconstructing their history, using their voices, their powwows, and their handicrafts to show their continuous habitation of the land. The Mowas used HUD funds to move and restore a small clapboard house that now sits behind their powwow grounds and highlights the history of the Tribe and the land. The Tribe was able to secure a HUD grant to develop its library and museum. The museum displays maps of proposed projects: if it achieves recognition, the Tribe hopes to build a "pioneer" theme park with an RV campground and a well-stocked fishing pond; it also hopes to revitalize its tradition of agriculture and hunting. In the meantime, the Mowas provide Choctaw language classes for tribal members, hold an annual powwow, and meet for a festival at Reed's Chapel, combining the annual tribal membership meeting with church-related homecoming activities.

One Mowa leader made it clear to me in conversation that he considered it a tragedy that so little was known of his Tribe by the outside world. He explained that since the group had been largely illiterate, they were never able to read the stories written about them. When they became educated, and could read those stories, they found inaccuracies that were ridiculous: one account described them as dangerous cannibal savages. According to this person, local merchants throughout the 1920s and 1930s told visitors, "You better not go out there [to the Mowa Reservation], them people will kill you." Now, he points out, his Tribe welcomes scholars and journalists, even friendly curiosity seekers.

> We can sit down and talk and have a conversation with you in your language. Before, we didn't know what people were talking about. . . . People come here and find that we're real decent people . . . now, we have educated people, educated leaders now, there's no threat to your life anymore [laughter].[41]

The Mowas prepared their petition for acknowledgment with the help of local historian Jacqueline Matte and legal anthropologist Susan Greenbaum. They have been supported financially by the Native American Rights Fund, and at times by the Mississippi Choctaw Nation. They have never denied their mixed racial heritage; one leader told me, "We're poly-racial. . . . We are a mixture of Spanish, French, Creole, Cajun, white, black, red."[42] But the Mowas' first letter of obvious deficiency (OD letter) from the BAR, which they received in February 1990, detailed a lack of evidence that they had maintained a distinct tribal community to present times.43 Since then, the BAR has found an even bigger problem with the group's claim to Indian identity.

In their original petition, the Mowas claimed ancestry from Cherokee, Apache, Chickasaw, Choctaw, Creek, and Houma individuals. In their response to the 1990 OD letter, the Mowas' amended petition claimed only Choctaw, Cherokee, and Creek ancestry, and reduced the core ancestors they claimed from thirty to five. However, BAR staff was able to verify the Indian ancestry of only one core ancestor, Alexander Brashears. The BAR further estimated that only about 1 percent of the four thousand–person tribe (or forty people) could prove their Indian heritage through ancestor Brashears.

Though the Mowa petition's narrative proved connections between current Mowa members and the other four core ancestors, BAR staff was unable to verify that these ancestors—Ka-li-o-ka, Nancy Fisher, Lemuel Byrd, and David Weaver—were Choctaw Indians, or, indeed, that they were Indian at all. The technical report reads as follows:

> The BIA also searched the extensive records concerning the historical tribes from which the petitioner claimed descent and did not find any of the MOWA core ancestors connected with any of these historical tribes. The MOWA core ancestors do not descend from the signers and beneficiaries of 1830 Treaty of Dancing Rabbit Creek nor from persons listed on the Identification Rolls of the Dawes Rolls. Nor were the core ancestors identified as an Indian entity on the 1910 U.S. Census.[44]

The BAR determined that since it was clear the other four listed core ancestors could not be proved to be Indian, the Mowas failed essential criteria 83.7(3), and should be slated for expedited review. The expedited Final Determination denied the Mowas' recognition.[45]

Even with this failure to prove ancestry, the Mowas were able to garner senatorial and congressional support for a number of federal recognition bills. They were able to do so, in part, by deploying the grounds on which they had been granted Alabama State recognition. Alabama law had clearly denied Indian people their identities, by labeling them both racially and ethnically with contradictory and ambiguous terms such as "black," "Cajun," "Caucasian," "Creole," "French," "mulatto," "Spanish," or "white."[46] Though the BAR staff took these records to reinforce its contention that "none of the primary records revealed their documented known ancestors are Native American or Indian," sympathetic Alabamans believed they understood such classification as a way of denying Indian identity in a time when antimiscegenation laws in the state applied only to blacks and mulattoes (not Indians), and mulatto status was extended to even fourth-generation descendants of one black ancestor, regardless of other parentage.[47]

Richard Shelby, a prominent Republican senator from Alabama, has sponsored and fought for the bills to recognize the Mowa Choctaws as an Indian tribe. In 1991, one such bill made it out of the Senate Select Committee on Indian Affairs with two votes against it, but it did not reach the floor for a vote.[48] In 1992, the full Senate passed a bill for Mowa recognition, but President Bush opposed the bill on advice of the BIA, and it never reached debate in the House. In 1995, a Senate vote again approved a Mowa recognition bill; it died on the House floor, without debate.

In 1998, I attended the Mowa Choctaw summer powwow near Mt. Vernon, Alabama. It was just after the Mowa acknowledgment petition had been placed on active consideration at the BAR, and their chances for both administrative and legislative recognition were occasionally brought up during the course of the annual celebration. The powwow's head caller (master of ceremonies) identified himself as a Poarch Creek tribal member, and his opening remarks revealed his own and his Tribe's hopes for Mowa recognition, to a warm reception from the crowd. At the time, the Mowas were optimistic about their chances.

When I spoke to Poarch leaders a year later, and after the Mowas' appeal at the BAR had been denied and they were again seeking legislative recognition, many expressed their hopes that the Mowas would be recognized; however, they stressed that Poarch officials favored Mowa recognition only if the group went through the BAR, and not Congress. Many Poarch Creeks feel that BAR processes offer safeguards necessary to ensure tribal legitimacy, and that these safeguards are not present in congressional recognition. I do not doubt that the Poarch would support Mowa recognition through the BAR. However, the Alabama State Archives contain a well-documented study commissioned by the Poarch meant to discredit Mowa claims in Congress; it could certainly be mobilized against them at the BAR.[49]

Poarch tribal leaders insist that their opposition to Mowa Choctaw recognition is based on the Mowas' inability to prove to the BAR their descent from a historic tribe. Although a good reason for opposing a petition, key political leaders in the state point to a different motive—they argue that leaders of the Poarch Creek Band of Indians oppose Mowa Choctaw recognition as a way to keep a monopoly on their bingo operations.

In Alabama, the Poarch alone have federal recognition. There are six additional state-recognized tribes, and only three of them have actively pursued federal recognition: the MaChis Lower Creek Tribe, the Principal Creek Indian Nation, and the Mowa Choctaws. The Principal Creek Indian Nation was denied by the BAR in 1985, as were the MaChis in 1988, and neither Tribe has maintained contact with the BIA since that time. The Mowas are alone in their continued pursuit of recognition, and are the sole viable competitor for Poarch gaming profits. A larger, more-disciplined voting block, the Mowas constitute somewhat of a political, if not financial, threat to Poarch power in Alabama.[50] However, the Poarch have had great success at the federal level, and have close friends in positions of power within the state; it appears to some that this power extends to activities against Mowa recognition bills and their petition.[51]

A former member of the AIAC, and a state representative of the Poarch Creek congressional district, told me that a "good friend of Eddie Tullis," namely, U.S. Representative Sonny Callahan, "double-crossed" the Mowas. According to the representative, though Callahan told the Mowas that he supported their bid for federal recognition, he did not push for it once it passed the Senate, and later "made up an excuse" to make sure it died in the House in 1995.[52] Callahan's office has offered a different explanation for his inaction—that suspicions about Mowa gaming had put a damper on his enthusiasm.

Even though the Mowa Choctaws' Southern Baptist tribal council has a constitutional amendment forbidding gaming, state-elected officials do not believe their resolve for a minute. One told me, "I know what it takes to change a charter. One quick vote."[53] In addition, the chief of staff for one U.S. representative reported that the reason his boss did not follow up on the Mowas' recognition bill was that

> quite frankly, . . . there was a distraction. There were numerous reports that the sole motivation for recognition was not for a new school, or for a new library, or for a health-care facility, but because at that particular time there was a real push for casino gambling in Alabama. There was no referendum; there was never a political mechanism to actually have the casinos. But Donald Trump had an office in Mobile; the mayor of Mobile, Mike Dow, was pushing casinos strongly. So there were some who believed that, well, if we can't get them through a vote of the people, because the South, as you may know, is very conservative . . . then we will insure that we are able to put casinos on

the Indian tribes [sic]. And [the representative] was just, quite frankly, concerned that the emphasis was shifting.[54]

It seems that most decision makers in Alabama believe that the Mowas would quickly change their charter, begin bingo operations, and attempt to set up Class III gaming. This is the case even though tribal elders have voiced strong opinions against gaming. The local paper made this clear in 1992, after a bill to recognize the Mowas had passed the Senate, stating that the Tribe wanted recognition in order to access "programs designed for Indian reservations." It went on to state that "light manufacturing and small business enterprises are anticipated, but gambling has been all but outlawed [emphasis mine] by the tribal leaders."[55] Another article in the same edition of the paper quoted a tribal leader saying, "We'd rather starve than have gambling," and explaining that "gambling takes advantage of the poorest in society."

However, a headline appeared in the local *Call-News Dispatch* just eight months later ringing out, "Choctaw Indians Plan to Build a Gambling Casino!" This type of confusion makes it politically difficult for the Mowas to continue to receive any political or financial support for bills of acknowledgment or recognition through the BAR. They have not been able to mitigate the backlash associated with gaming, racial identity, and recognition; instead, they have fallen victim to it.

Yet another explanation for the death of the Mowas' 1995 recognition bill seems plausible, and it is one that takes into account the important context of continuing black-white racial tensions in Alabama. In his conversation with me, one congressman's chief of staff said, "I believe it was 1995 after Congress had changed hands and the new majority took control, Congressman Hilliard from Birmingham introduced legislation [for Mowa recognition] in the House." When I noted that Birmingham seemed an odd place from which to launch Mowa recognition efforts, as it is a good four hours north and east of the southern tip of Washington County, the chief of staff agreed. He said that

it did not make sense to us. [Hilliard] did not inform the congressman of this. And suffice it to say that [the congressman] was not pleased. We have a small delegation in Alabama, one

that works well regardless of party labels. . . . When it comes to
an issue of importance in Alabama, we try to work in lockstep.
[He] was none too pleased to have a colleague coming in and
introducing legislation on behalf of his constituents.[56]

Hilliard was a first-year congressman, but the chief of staff did not
think that the faux pas had been a simple "freshman mistake." He
concluded our conversation by reiterating that Hilliard's support for
the Mowas made no sense, and that it had been in large part responsible for the congressman's lack of interest in supporting the Mowas.
   What this individual, who was very forthcoming in most other
regards, failed to mention was that Hilliard, an African American
who had been elected as a result of massive redistricting in the state,
intended to increase the proportion of African Americans representing Alabama in the capital. Hilliard was elected from a newly
created district, the seventh, which had been gerrymandered to be
68 percent black. It had previously been only 33 percent African
American, and 3 percent of the increased black population had
been drawn from the congressman's First District. Throughout the
process, redistricting was incredibly controversial—critics called it
secretive, time consuming, unfair, and wrongheaded. To have an
African American freshman congressman from a newly drawn legislative district centered in Birmingham, Alabama, propose Mowa
Choctaw recognition over the head of the senior representative
from the coastal plains, could, I imagine, be just as harmful to the
Mowas' cause as gambling rumors.
   And, although Poarch opposition to Mowa recognition could be
harmful, it is just as clear that such opposition is not an aberration
in acknowledgment politics. There are numerous examples of federally recognized tribes opposing the recognition of other groups. The
tensions are often regional, and in some instances, legendary. In the
Pacific Northwest, for example, the Tulalip Tribe has opposed the
recognition of the Snoqualmie, Samish, Steilacoom, and Duwamish
Tribes.[57] In the Southeast, the Eastern Cherokee Tribe of North Carolina has long opposed full recognition for the Lumbee Nation.
None of this opposition started as a result of gaming wealth, and
such opposition was in place long before the IGRA came on the
scene; in fact, most of this opposition lacks any apparent financial
motive. It is undeniable, however, that gaming profits do allow a

tribe that is already opposed to a group's recognition to spend more money fighting it. It is also undeniable that gaming profits do sometimes provide motivation for a tribe to act against the recognition of a contender in the region.

On the other hand, appearances in the Mowa case to the contrary, Poarch Creek leaders are adamant that they are willing to help other groups achieve recognition through the BAR and in Congress. One tribal official told me the following:

> That's one of the things that I've always argued, is that it wouldn't bother me at all [for other groups to be recognized]. It's kind of one of those things that I know how hard it was for us. And I've spent a lot of time with the other groups, I know a number of people I went and spoke to. My whole wish is to make sure that this is what you want to do . . . so I advise groups to, look, be sure you know what you're talking about, be sure that you've got a good firm foundation, be sure that you've got someone committed to following this thing through. If somebody goes through the process, I guarantee you that they can depend on Poarch Creek. Of course, the Catawbas went through legislatively, but we had people here, the Catawbas, asking, before the legislation even went through. They sent delegations here; we sent people out there. . . . We feel that that's an obligation we have here. So we stand ready to help any tribe.[58]

Another Poarch tribal member reiterated this position, and stressed that there was an informal mechanism by which information was shared between recently recognized tribes and unrecognized groups in the region.

> It's just like how we're talking now. They'll say, "We're running into a problem here, and we got back our letter of deficiency" . . . and they'll say, "We need some more information on this, what did ya'll use? Where did you find it?" . . . Now like with us, I'll say, "Well, we used so-and-so" and I'll ask them, like, "Well, have you looked in your military records? Have you checked the census records? Did you check the old community newspaper records? You know, you might could find some articles that will help you." So it's not anything that's real, real technical. It's

just sharing, "Well, we did this and we didn't have any luck with that." . . . So, I'd never [say no] if I knew the answer. Now, if I don't know, I don't know; I don't know everything![59]

This informal sharing is actually much more formal than it appears, and more important in recognition claims than many might initially believe. In fact, intertribal ties may prove to be of singular importance in determining which tribes gain acknowledgement. Particularly, tribes that were members of the Coalition of Eastern Native Americans (CENA) or of the United South and Eastern Tribes (USET) have been overwhelmingly successful in achieving recognition. Only three of the fourteen CENA members who petitioned for acknowledgement have been denied.[60] The Catawba Tribe, which was helped by the Poarch Creek, had overlapping membership in the CENA and the USET, as did the Mashantucket Pequot, the Narragansett, and the Mohegan Tribes. I asked a Poarch leader about the role of the CENA and the USET in sharing information about acknowledgment and he answered, "That was the whole purpose [of the organizations]. We were able to get some Department of Labor Grants. . . . We relied on one another to help. That's the kind of support we gave each other."[61] And, though the Poarch Creeks' role as a gatekeeper has engendered some perplexed hostility within the state Indian population, it has seemed to increase their stature in pan-Indian affairs, as well as magnified their perceived legitimacy as Alabama's "only Indian tribe" for local non-Indians.[62]

## THE POARCH EXERCISE SELF-DETERMINATION AND SOVEREIGNTY

In distinction to the Mowa Choctaws, who have been unable to gain recognition in any fashion, the Poarch Band of Creeks has not only achieved administrative acknowledgment, but has also amassed political clout and local goodwill. Tribal members have been exemplary in mitigating backlash attendant recognition and gaming, and in avoiding racialized attacks on their Indian identity.

This is perhaps the case in part because Poarch leaders quickly learned the truth of an old sports adage: the best defense is good offense. They have always moved rapidly and effectively to dispel any rumors that would threaten their legitimacy. They have done so by creating a clear tribal structure and persona, constantly educating and reeducating the local community on Poarch history and future plans, and making judicious use of the press to stop rumors before they catch hold. An example of this type of clarity is an article placed in the *Atmore Advance* explaining the new Poarch police force. The article reads, in part, "The idea of the Poarch Band of Creek Indians having their own tribal police has some people in the Atmore area wondering what's going on. It's something new here, but in other places it's old hat. The right to have a tribal police force and an inferior court system to handle minor criminal and civil complaints was just one of several privileges that came with federal recognition of the Poarch Band of Creeks as a distinct people. In fact, it entails far more responsibility, says tribal chairman Eddie Tullis." The article goes on to quote Tullis at length.

> Says the chairman, "Some people incorrectly assume that it means there is refuge on the reservation, but there's not. . . . If you come on this reservation there is just as much law enforcement as anywhere else, maybe more." Two police officers [have been hired] for 230 acres [which] means the reservation . . . has more law enforcement per capita than any place in Escambia County right now [*sic*]. . . . Tullis said he expects to see a tribal police department with a chief of police and three tribal officers in place and providing full-time coverage.

The article then concludes, "Officers now attached to the Sheriff's department are being paid out of tribal funds, so their training will not be at county expense. . . . 'We are in effect in the process of setting up a new government and it is an exciting but very challenging time to us,' Tullis said. 'Above all, we want to do it right. We want to fulfill our responsibility to our own people while becoming an asset to the rest of Escambia County, as well.' "[63]

Poarch leaders explain the development of the police force as simply one part of the Poarch tribal government's increased responsibility to its people, and to the surrounding area. This increased responsibility was a frequent topic in my interviews with Poarch leaders. They pointed out that the Tribe operated like a county government, providing assistance for those in need of welfare programs, Head

Start and daycare for their children, and senior citizen assisted living and community centers. The Tribe also has a fire department, which provides protection even outside of the reservation community, a health clinic, and a community recreation facility that is open to the general public.

At other times, Tullis spoke to the press directly about the various rumors surrounding Poarch activity, and met them head-on with the tribal version of the facts. Prior to announcing the purchase of the local Best Western hotel, press reports quoted Tullis as admonishing the public, "Unexpected pitfalls can and do occur before transactions are closed. At the proper time, and that's several weeks away, announcements will be made, but it's probably now the right time for comments in general about what we intend to do, *instead of leaving things to the rumor mill*" [emphasis mine]. When the Poarch Creeks bought the Best Western hotel and adjacent restaurant, the *Advance* reported, "Wishing to dispel rumors that the Poarch Creek Band of Indians was getting heaps of federal money with which to buy land and property, [Tullis] emphasized that the motel complex was being purchased with a twenty-year loan from First National Bank of Alabama." And, when rumors began to fly that the Poarch had only wanted recognition for economic reasons, Tullis and the tribal council acknowledged the kernel of truth in the gossip, while using the opportunity to lay to rest even more rumors about the Tribe's plans. Tullis told the paper, "Talking turkey, economic development for the Poarch Band of Creeks *was* a primary motive for seeking federal recognition as an Indian tribe." The article's author then states that the Poarch "wish to dispel some rumors" about the Tribe's plans.

> Firstly, the Poarch Band of Creeks are not buying land with which to go into the Country Club business, secondly they will not be getting federal grants with which to finance their business ventures. "We intend to borrow money from a local bank, so nobody is giving us the money" [Tullis] emphasized.[64]

By addressing questions of motivation directly, Poarch leadership acknowledged what locals feared: Indian tribes sought recognition for monetary gain. In the same breath, however, Tullis conveyed his strong belief that Poarch recognition would benefit everyone in the county; later Poarch programs sought to make good on that prediction.

Even when not addressing rumors, the Poarch were exemplary in using the press to reassert their legitimacy as a tribe. They often took out full-page adds to explain their business ventures, their powwows, and their tribal history, reminding the communities of their continuous presence in the Atmore area and the contributions the Tribe makes to Escambia County. Finally, they often invited government officials and national Indian luminaries to the reservation. These events got good press coverage, and guests of the Poarch were often quoted in ways that reinforced the image Poarch had built for itself.[65]

In addition to their political and economic successes, the Poarch have been unique in avoiding prolonged periods of racialized attacks on their identity.[66] Though some members have a mixed heritage, combining Indian, white, and black descendants, the only negative comment I heard about the Poarch, unrelated to tribal plans for a casino in Wetumpka—which generated hostility nearly everywhere—came from a librarian at the state archives who told me, "Calvin McGhee couldn't wait to prove he was Cherokee, 'til he found out it was easier to prove he was Creek."

Otherwise, the Poarch Band of Creek Indians' use of the media and public relations strategies has helped them avoid racial backlash. Their intertribal ties and obvious acceptance by national pan-Indian organizations have been enormously important as well. Former Poarch chiefs Tullis and McGhee were actively involved in many intertribal organizations, and held leadership positions in the NCAI, the CENA, and the USET. Membership and leadership have helped the Poarch maintain local, regional, and national legitimacy as a Tribe.

The Poarch had hoped that their small cultural center would serve a similar purpose of ingratiating the Tribe in the non-Indian community while teaching that community the history and culture of the Poarch. One tribal member said in 1990, "I believe this [cultural center] will do something about changing people's perceptions of Native Americans. It will demonstrate that Native Americans wear hats and suits like everyone else. They don't just wear loin cloths and dance around."[67] Although it is successful, the cultural center is also quite modest. It is housed in an old gymnasium (formerly the tribal community center). On its walls hang quilts made by tribal members, and stationery cases hold a small number of artifacts that the Poarch have managed to excavate or have returned. The front desk of the museum doubles as a candy counter; people drive from quite a distance for Poarch Creek pralines, fudge, and taffy.

By far, the Thanksgiving powwow is *the* main event in the cultural representation of the life of the Tribe. It is an event that draws not only tens of thousands of non-Indian visitors, but also a large number of Indian Country luminaries like Ron Andrade (in 1981, when he was executive director of the NCAI), Choctaw chief Calvin Isaacs (in 1978), Chief Rueben Snake of the Winnebago (in 1986), Billy Mills (Sioux Indian and Olympic gold medalist), and Seminole chief James Billie (a rock star and alligator wrestler, as well as an astute businessman and tribal leader).[68] BAR investigators found that the Poarch powwow tradition played a very important role in "enhancing local non-Indian support of the group *as Indian,* [emphasis mine]"[69] and remains a very important "barometer of tribal life."[70]

Prior to recognition, the Poarch Tribe was successful in receiving Indian Education grants and Comprehensive Employment Training Act (CETA) monies. After recognition, in a time of federal cutbacks and an extremely depressed Alabama economy,[71] the grants became even more important to the tribe (and the surrounding non-Indian community), and the Poarch used them to build an independent, viable economy. In 1985, Alabama State senator Jeremiah Denton and U.S. congressman Sonny Callahan released a joint statement congratulating the Creeks on a $350,000 Federal Economic Development Administration Grant for Community-Building;[72] shortly afterward, the Poarch announced their plans to take over the local restaurant and Best Western hotel, buying the complex with a local loan backed by grant money.[73] Soon, the Poarch Tribe was being used as a role model for local non-Indian development.

At times, Tullis has been none too subtle in offering advice, and in suggesting that the local non-Indian community model itself on Poarch success. In 1987, the Poarch bought an empty industrial building on Highway 21 and marketed it to regional businesses as a "speculative building" (or "spec." building). This was a new approach to inviting industry into the area. At a press meeting to discuss the spec. building, Tullis advised town leaders that "the first thing any industry asks anymore is whether you have a building. We felt such a building was important. It is something any community, and I think especially Atmore, needs to do. Atmore has a beautiful industrial park and a speculative building would increase the chances of landing an industry. I say that because I believe anything that helps any part of this area helps us all."[74]

The building soon attracted an aluminum smelting plant, employing between ten and fifteen people. Shortly afterward, the editor of the local newspaper named the Poarch Creeks' economic and cultural successes as the number-two story of the year, behind only the failure of the local savings and loan and attendant lawsuits. Poarch was the top success story of the county.[75] And, sure enough, in February 1988, the editorial section of the *Atmore Advance* proclaimed, "Construction of Speculative Building Is a Move Forward for Town of Atmore"—the town had taken the Tribe's business advice.[76] More important, the Poarch Tribe proved successful in showing that Indians can be modern, as well as traditional, and do not need to wear poverty as a badge of authenticity.

Of course, none of this is without some amount of controversy. There has been resentment over Poarch leaders' attempts to monopolize power in the Alabama Indian Affairs Commission, which at one time was called the Alabama Creek Indian Affairs Commission. Records from the AIAC show that when the Poarch Tribe's recommendation that only *federally* recognized Alabama tribes should have power on the committee failed, its involvement in the AIAC dropped off. Whereas the Poarch had once been the main grant writers behind projects like the Southeastern Indian ManPower Development Project, Native American Media and TV Workshops, and Indian Education Grants, after recognition, the Poarch Creeks' local and state Indian educational activities seem to have dropped off. In addition, Poarch leaders' outspoken desire for gaming has brought some backlash to the Tribe.

For instance, though I saw absolutely no proof of the accusation, several non-Indians in Alabama told me that illegal Class III gaming, in the form of off-track pari-mutuel wagering, was occurring at the Poarch Creek Bingo Palace. This rumor contributed to fervent ill feeling against the Poarch Creeks' proposed casino in Wetumpka, by intimating that they were already grossly overstepping legal limits on their bingo operations.

Religious leaders have also reacted strongly to Poarch Creek attempts to locate a casino on land in Wetumpka, Alabama. The casino, funded by Harrah's, Inc., would be located at Hickory Grounds, which some call sacred Creek land, and which the Department of the Interior put into trust for the Poarch in 1984. Wetumpka lawmakers say they have a "moral and legal responsibility" to block any form of gaming in Wetumpka, which is "a small town . . . a very religious community."[77]

In essence, unlike the resentment engendered by Pequot financial success in the Northeast, the Poarch have found themselves the unlikely recipient of white praise and imitation. And, unlike the Mowa Choctaws, who have not been able to prove Indian ancestry to satisfy the BAR, the Poarch have achieved recognition and legitimacy as a tribe; they have used that recognition, and their economic success, as a platform from which to increase the reach of self-government and practices of sovereignty. In fact, with the exception of controversies over their planned casino operation in Wetumpka, the Poarch have achieved outward manifestations of local non-Indian respect and support at a level unprecedented for Indian tribes in rural and poor regions.

## CHAPTER EIGHT

# Cash, Color, and Colonialism in Connecticut

Unlike the relative calm attendant Poarch Creek recognition, the recognition of the Mashantucket Pequot Tribe, in Connecticut, has been subject to intense scrutiny and controversy. Not only has the Pequots' casino been a political hot potato, but their identity as Indian has been impugned by several sources. Connecticut is now home to two grassroots organizations dedicated to limiting casino growth in the state, and has been the site of intensive litigation meant to stop the federal acknowledgment of two recently recognized tribes, the Eastern Pequots and the Schaghticokes. (The Schaghticokes' proposed finding, delivered in 2004, has not been finalized.) There has even been debate in the U.S. Senate over bills to rescind Mashantucket Pequot recognition. In Connecticut, gaming and acknowledgement are incredibly intertwined, as are public perceptions of Indian racial identity.

## Grassroots Opposition to Casino Expansion

Many area home- and landowners are deeply concerned about the expansionist tendencies of the Pequots, and about the land claims being brought by several unrecognized groups in Connecticut. Once a land-claims suit is filed, homeowners find their titles to the property clouded, which makes it impossible to sell, refinance, or insure their property. One man, trying to buy a home in the region, told a reporter, "I really wanted to live on this piece of property. I mean, this was my retirement. I—we had big dreams for this place, and now all of a sudden, it's—it's got to go on hold."[1]

This puts the traditionally more politically liberal Connecticut landowners in the uncomfortable position of fighting against an old political cause célèbre—the Indians. Although many in Connecticut express sympathy for the land claims and a desire to see the Indians come out ahead, they also argue that they and their children cannot be held accountable for wrongs more than three hundred years old. Many of them also report feeling that the casino tribes are pushing the envelope; rather than just moderate development on reservation lands, these longtime Connecticut residents see huge-scale building, massive parking lots, and towering structures. Railing against increased noise, air, and light pollution, these residents see their struggle as one to preserve Connecticut's rural image and small-town heritage. Increasingly, they see their struggle as one against the recognition of any new tribes.

Opponents of the Mashantucket Pequots' expansionist tendencies have organized to form CasiNO! and members of that organization travel to neighboring states, spreading the news about what they say have been the horrible side effects of casino gaming on their communities. At a town meeting, they told residents of West Warwick, Rhode Island, about "roads thickly littered with coin slot cups and miniature liquor bottles, mushrooming traffic, a rise in the number of special education students, the climbing crime rate, and other strains on town services."[2] Against claims that Foxwoods has brought new businesses to the region, CasiNO! members argue that the only economic development has been "two doughnut shops and a pawn shop," and that the Tribe "has bought up so much undeveloped land, other private development has been stymied."[3] A further upshot of this is that residents' property is now devalued, making the Tribe the only likely buyer should the residents decide to move. CasiNO! members tell others that having a tribe recognized in their backyard has been a nightmare.

One recent account of the Pequots' success reads as follows:

> Suddenly, in what had once been one of the quietest patches of America, crimes were being committed that had been unheard of in the past. In their frenzied rush to the slot machines and

blackjack tables, parents left their children and dogs locked in their cars, sometimes for hours. One New York City man left his five year-old girl and a nine year-old boy in his car for over two hours, with the motor running. A twenty-eight year-old Massachusetts woman left four children ranging in age from two to seventeen alone for seventeen hours while she lost the family grocery and rent money while pulling slot handles. . . . The towns' jails filled on account of drug and cocaine possession arrests. . . . In a three-month period in 1998, Connecticut State Police counted three hundred and forty crimes in tiny Ledyard, most of them drug or disorderly conduct crimes.[4]

Francisco Borges, the Connecticut State treasurer, and frequent advocate of Connecticut's poor, urban population, testified in the state legislature that the idea of Indian casino gaming in Connecticut was "sickening and unspeakable," and predicted that gambling would, like illicit drugs, rip apart families that are already exploited and suffering. Responding to charges that Connecticut's economy would receive a boost from casino-style gaming, run perhaps by the Golden Hill Paugussett Tribe (which does not have federal recognition), Borges told the legislature, "The only shot in the arm a gambling casino would give us is like the ones that the heroin addicts on Hartford's streets depend on for their cheap, quick, dirty, easy, and ultimately death-inducing fix."[5]

A large part of the resentment against the Mashantucket Pequots and other tribes in the state is perhaps due to the growing perception on the part of many non-Indians that "secret deals are being brokered"[6] in "closed door meetings" and "casino summits."[7] And in fact, the Pequots, Mohegans, and the state of Connecticut do routinely engage in closed-door, secretive meetings, sometimes emerging with agreements that leave even the state legislature in shock.[8] The secrecy adds to the illusion of tribes' increasing political power, and to the growing powerlessness of the townspeople—average citizens are "held hostage" by the expansion of the Indian casinos.[9]

Of course, not all townspeople feel antagonism toward the tribes that needs mitigating by charitable donations and cooperative actions. Certainly, visitors to the Mashantucket Pequot Museum and Research Center and gamblers at Foxwoods do not, in general, feel threatened by, or angry with, the Pequots. Some patrons even see a certain kind of justice in the arrangement. One senior citizen gambling at Foxwoods told a national news crew, "More power to them."[10] And Hartford mayor Carrie Sacon Perry put it this way on National Public Radio: "Let them make the money, that's a little payback for all of the trials and tribulations they've had as the original Americans."[11]

However, it is undeniable that the Mashantucket Pequots and their casino typify for many Americans the excesses and problems with federal recognition. They are subject to backlash over the casino and stereotyping of their tribal and Indian identities.

## The Fears behind Indian Stereotypes

Journalistic accounts of the Mashantucket Pequots' success almost compulsively cite growing membership numbers and lessening blood quantum requirements. One reporter quotes Larry Geene, a self-described "real American" from Connecticut (in the accompanying photo he appears to be white), as saying that the Pequots are not "real Indians," and contending that they have simply assumed an Indian identity.[12] Another report quotes former senator Robert Torricelli (D-N.J.), a political ally of Donald Trump, saying, "Under the federal criteria to establish an Indian tribe, the [Mashantucket Pequot] tribe could never be recognized. . . . This was an enormously clever scheme—a clever scheme that has more than aptly paid dividends for those who conceived of it."[13]

Torricelli may not be completely off base; it is unlikely that the BAR would have recommended a positive determination for the Mashantucket Pequots. But it is my impression—based on the BAR's positive findings on the Eastern Pequot and Paucatuck Eastern Pequot petitions—that the Mashantucket Pequot Tribe would not have failed to prove descendance (or to prove their Indianness), but rather, would have had difficulty proving maintenance of a tribal community. Yet journalistic accounts continue to be obsessed with Indianness, and often note that tribal membership has "soared" and "exploded" from 20 people in 1983 to more than 550 in 2000.[14]

Reporters repeatedly question tribal officials about how "easy" it is to achieve membership. 60 Minutes reported, "If you can prove that one of your great-great-grandparents was listed in the tribal census of 1910, you're entitled to membership in what has become Connecticut's royal family—entitled to comfortable housing, free college tuition, a tribal job that starts at $60,000, plus bonuses."[15] That statement was made as flippantly as if the proof were as simple as showing that your grandmother was a woman. The reporter then reassured hopeful tribal members that "for the culturally deprived, the Pequots offer classes in Native American history," before closing on an even more-ominous note for Connecticut landowners: "The casino has brought a lot more than prosperity to the Pequot Reservation; it's brought Pequots to the Pequot Reservation. . . . There's no shortage of aspiring Indians from London to Louisiana, eager to sign up and share the wealth." The specter of "aspiring Indians" has had Connecticut residents in an uproar for the past ten years. Several groups seek recognition, and the state attorney general, Richard Blumenthal, has vowed to fight all of them. In this environment, the Eastern Pequot and Golden Hill Paugussett Tribes have had difficulty rising above the confluence of racial hysteria and gaming growth.[16]

## The Many Branches of the Contemporary Pequot Family Tree

The story of the struggle for recognition undertaken by two groups of Eastern Pequot Indians usefully illustrates the racial tensions in claiming Indian identity in Connecticut. In this discussion of these two acknowledgment claims, I refer to three distinct bodies of Pequots aside from the Mashantucket Pequots. I use Eastern Pequot to mean the group that recently petitioned the BAR for recognition as the Eastern Pequot Tribe (EP). I use Paucatuck Eastern Pequot (PEP) to identify the group that recently petitioned the BAR as the Paucatuck Eastern Pequot Tribe, excluding EP members. By the designation Eastern Paucatuck Pequot (EPP) I mean the unified Tribe during the 1950s, 1960s, and 1970s. It was during those decades that some of the EPP tribal leadership attempted to disqualify members of what is now the Eastern Pequot Tribe. However, in 2002, the BAR published a Final Determination to recognize both groups, on the condition that the PEP merge with the EP and form a unified Eastern Pequot Tribe (EPT).

All of these designations can get confusing! The confusion is exacerbated not only by the tribal splits, but also by the different ways of referring to the historic tribe used by the state of Connecticut. It is further compounded by different spellings for many of the proper names of individual descendants of the groups, as well as overlapping membership, interlocking kinship relations, and a number of individuals with the same name. I have tried to simplify the issues as much as possible without being inaccurate.

EP membership is made up of a number of descendants of Tamar Sebastian (née Brushell), a woman of mixed black and Indian ancestry who married a Mr. Sebastian, a man of Portuguese and perhaps Bahamian descent. Sebastian lived off the reservation, in her husband's household, from 1848 to 1889, but later returned to the Lantern Hill Reservation and was listed on the Indian overseer's rolls from 1889 until her death in 1891.[17]

The Bureau of Indian Affairs held open hearings during the comment period following the preliminary recommendations to acknowledge both groups, in 2000. During that comment period, questions abounded regarding the extent of Sebastian's Indian heritage: the state of Connecticut unsuccessfully attempted to establish that her father, Moses Brushell, was a free black who resided in Waterford, Connecticut;[18] the PEP petition had tried to establish that Brushell and her children were black paupers who were merely occasional (and unwelcome) squatters on Lantern Hill land.[19]

Yet these racialized allegations are not new, and are not merely a result of seeking tribal recognition. Questions about Sebastian's heritage came up far prior to any attempts to receive federal acknowledgment. In 1937, Gilbert Raymond, an overseer to the reservation, made the following observations about the Sebastian clan:

> In 1849, an African Islander, dark complexioned, was married to an Indian maiden named Tamer Brussels. The result of this marriage has been more than one hundred and fifty descendants of different shades of color from blackest black to what appears to be pure white, most of them living in southeastern Connecticut and southwestern Rhode Island. They are very prolific, many of them having ten children or more. . . . This islander . . . was a dark, squatty man, thickset, who always wore a large broad brimmed hat, and with rings in his ears. Some of his children are still alive and one of them is a very estimable woman, Mrs. Calvin C. Williams. . . . Her husband, many years

deceased, was a Negro preacher. The right of this strain to the tribal privileges is denied by Chief Silver Star [an EPP leader] who claims that the Indian girl, Tamer Brussels was not a Pequot Indian.[20]

These older allegations were first revitalized in the 1970s, in the context of the formation of the Connecticut Indian Affairs Council (CIAC). Governor Ella Grasso formed the CIAC in 1973 and charged its eight members with recognizing and protecting the rights and privileges of Indians in the state, determining and enforcing treaty rights of those tribes, surveying the reservations to establish land value and boundaries, attending to the health, safety, and well-being of "Indians residing on tribal lands," and promoting awareness and understanding of Connecticut's Indian population within the state.[21]

Connecticut recognized five tribes at that time, and each state-recognized tribe was eventually invited to send a representative to the CIAC (the governor then appointed three at-large members to serve as well).[22] Helen LeGault, a grandchild of EPP members Eunice Wheeler and Marlboro Gardner, through their twelfth child, Emma, assumed responsibility for CIAC duties on behalf of the EPP, but did so without the consent of the Sebastians.[23] She proceeded to use the CIAC as a platform from which to have the Sebastians removed from the tribal rolls, and on several occasions she used polarizing language to discredit their lineage. In 1961, testifying before the state of Connecticut's general assembly, she stated thus:

> You know very well that those Sebastians are not Indians. If I've got to bring up the name, I will. It's Sebastian. Is that an Indian name, an American name? It's a Portuguese name. I even know where the first Sebastian came from, and how he came to this country, and what [sic] he married, and who he married, and who she was; and you can't claim what kind of Indian she was, because you don't know and no one else knows.[24]

LeGault began, simultaneously, to organize an "authentic" Eastern Pequot Tribe, which, by the 1970s, held the ear of the state.

The Sebastians mobilized against these upsetting developments, and routinely wrote to both the BIA and to the CIAC, demanding both LeGault's removal from the CIAC and an inquiry into the membership practices of the EPP Tribe. They also cast doubt upon Marlboro Gardner's heritage, as part of an attempt to discredit LeGault's Indianness and her authority to speak for the Tribe.[25] In August 1976, the CIAC held its first meeting on EPP membership eligibility. It issued a decision in November that certified that Marlboro Gardner and Tamar Sebastian had both been full-blood Eastern Pequots and declared that members of both families were eligible to vote in EPP tribal elections and certify EPP representation on the CIAC.

This was not the end of the controversy, however. Inexplicably, in 1977, the CIAC issued a second decision. This one confirmed the finding that Marlboro Gardner was full-blood Eastern Pequot, but amended its finding on Tamar—she was found to be only "one half Eastern Pequot blood." This meant, according to the EPP chair Raymond Greer, that only three Sebastian family members would be eligible to vote in tribal elections. Immediately following the CIAC's decision, Roy Sebastian and other family members sued in Connecticut State court, asking the state to investigate CIAC practices, and step in to determine tribal membership. The appeals on this case, as well as separate filings on the issue, eventually took ten years to resolve; the courts ultimately found that the state of Connecticut had no authority to disrupt tribal sovereignty by stepping into tribal membership matters, and therefore could not investigate CIAC or EPP enrollment practices. The state court indicated that federal court would be a more appropriate forum for resolution of tribal membership issues. However, as neither tribe was federally recognized, this option was foreclosed to them.

Raymond Greer had long argued that the issue was a federal one, and that it was more respectful of tribal sovereignty to ask for federal, rather than state, clarification.[26] Greer was dismayed, however, by his Tribe's unwillingness to accept the Sebastian family, and eventually retired from his leadership over the issue. Agnes Cunha then came to power within the tribe, changed the group's name to the Paucatuck Eastern Pequot Tribe, and pursued federal recognition. As tribal chair, she remained firm in her opposition to including Eastern Pequots on the PEP rolls.

In the meantime, the CIAC issued a third finding, which declared that it would determine all membership disputes, citing CIAC administrative regulations that would allow it to do so. By this time, both groups had petitions before the BAR, and their factionalism was becoming problematic to recognition. CIAC leaders urged the two groups to merge in order to present a unified front to federal bureaucrats, but this proved impossible. The BAR staff found that the Paucatuck Eastern Pequot leadership had "scuttled the [CIAC's] proposal."[27]

Part of the "scuttling" of the proposals for unity that the BAR staff appears dismayed by includes rumor mongering similar to what occurs around already-recognized and gaming tribes in Alabama and Connecticut. For instance, BAR records contain a number of letters from Agnes Cunha to the BAR staff, Connecticut politicians, and Interior Department officials. These letters allege that the Eastern Pequots have "forged" and "falsified" vital records. She writes, "The group known as Sebastian has been turning in falsified documents for years, and got [sic] away with it."[28]

Continuing racial assaults on the Sebastian Pequots also seemed destined to scuttle calls for unity. For instance, across the nation, at a powwow in Portland, an "associate" of Helen LeGault spoke publicly about the Sebastian family, saying, "Those people are blacks. The Paucatuck Pequots belong to the red race, not the black race."[29]

BAR officials were clearly uncomfortable with the racialized language used by other Eastern Pequot tribal members to discredit the Sebastians' claims; the technical reports issued by the BAR are repeatedly apologetic about the reproduction of racializing and racist language. The BAR also proved uncomfortable with the language used by Cunha to describe Tamar (Brushell) Sebastian; Cunha told a newspaper reporter, "Brashel [sic] was a prostitute placed on the reservation by a state-appointed white overseer." In the *Eastern Pequot Indians of Connecticut Proposed Finding: Summary Chart*, the BAR staff notes that this allegation was most certainly false. "On the contrary, there is an extensive concatention of evidence which indicates that Tamer (Brushel) Sebastian was, throughout her lifetime, a respectable Baptist woman."

Helen LeGault died in 1990, and in 1991 Agnes Cunha went on the record for the first time acknowledging the African American ancestry of some members of her tribe. She told a *New York Times* reporter, "The problem isn't the Sebastians' black ancestry. The problem is that they are not Indian."[30] Later, in 1996, James Cunha, the treasurer of the PEP tribal council, wrote to Bruce Babbitt, then secretary of the interior under President Clinton, saying that allegations of racism were repugnant to the Tribe, since they *shared* a black ancestry. He restated Agnes Cunha's point, that the black skin of the Eastern Pequot petitioners was not the problem; rather, the EP had simply not proven that they were Indian.[31]

The BAR issued proposed findings in 2000 that showed that the membership of both groups had descended from the historic Pequot Tribe and that as the Eastern (Paucatuck) Pequot Tribe, they had maintained political community and had been recognized as a tribe by various entities, including the state of Connecticut, up until 1960. The BAR staff found that there was not sufficient evidence, however, that this political community had continued after 1960; factionalism was a large, but not singular, reason for this determination. Since the petitioners failed to meet all seven acknowledgment criteria, the BAR staff recommended a finding against acknowledgment.[32] It's important to note that this proposed finding against acknowledgment was based on a lack of political and community cohesion, not on the BAR's acceptance of racialized claims against the Indian identity of particular groups and group members. In fact, the BAR flatly rejected those claims, and found that Indian heritage had been proven by both petitioners.

On the heels of the proposed negative finding prepared by the BAR staff, however, and citing repressive governance by the colony and state of Connecticut as a mitigating factor, Assistant Secretary of Indian Affairs (AS-IA) Kevin Gover took what appeared to be the unprecedented step of ignoring the BAR's finding. AS-IA Gover accepted the BAR's analysis, but not the outcome; instead, he approved a positive proposed finding, which entered a comment period in summer 2000, and was affirmed by the BAR in a 2002 Final Determination for recognition of the two tribes.[33]

At the formal technical assistance meetings, in June 2000, regarding the PEP and EP petitions, it became clear that the state of Connecticut planned legal action if a positive determination was finalized. Connecticut attorney general Richard Blumenthal exasperated BAR staff member Virginia DeMarce with his repeated attempts to deny that Connecticut had ever willingly recognized the tribal existence of the Eastern (Paucatuck) Pequot.[34] That, the impact that the February 2000 Directive had on BAR processes, and Gover's refusal to recuse himself from these decisions though he had served as an acknowledgement attorney for another Connecticut tribe (the Golden Hill Paugussetts), appeared to be the crux of Connecticut's then-anticipated legal action. Gover's actions have become the basis for a lawsuit filed by the state of Connecticut and the towns of Ledyard and North Stonington, alleging that the BIA did not follow its own procedures in making a proposed finding for EP and PEP recognition. The two tribal groups have been named codefendants. Significantly, the controversy over EP recognition has moved from being a controversy over the perceived race of tribal members to being a controversy over the possibility of gaming expansion in the state.

In the meantime, those individuals of the Sebastian clan who were eligible to do so have become members of the Mashantucket Pequot Tribal Nation.[35] These newest members of the Mashantucket Tribe are the great-grandchildren of Annie Sebastian, a sister-in-law of Mashantucket matriarch Elizabeth George, and descendant of Tamar (Brushell) Sebastian. The Sebastians are African Indians with claims to both Narragansett and Mashantucket tribal membership; many of them grew up in poverty in South Kingston, Rhode Island. This second group of "returning" Mashantucket Pequots changed the racial composition of the Tribe, and contributed to what some call the Tribe's recent "growing pains." One reporter notes that the early returnees, "who tended to be White," have expressed resentment over the newcomers' "sense of entitlement."[36] Tensions grew as African Indian Pequots complained that "high-paying, skilled jobs [went] to outsiders, while descendents of the original Pequots [were] relegated to janitorial or gardening positions,"[37] and that they "were being treated as second-class Pequots, receiving less than their fair share of the benefits . . . having to wait for jobs, houses, and educational programs."[38] This resentment also grew from the knowledge that Skip Hayward's grandmother had often expressed contempt for the Sebastians, Gardners, and Wheelers on the Eastern Pequot Reservation, stating that they were "of Negro blood, and squatters." Elizabeth George often wrote to the overseers in colorful language demanding the "niggers [sic] at Lantern Hill" be "run out."[39] Evidently, the racialization of the family feud in the Pequot clan has had a long incubation period.

One of the Sebastian family returnees to the Mashantucket Pequot Tribe is Kenneth Reels, who gained the position of chair of the Mashantucket Pequot Tribe in the late 1990s. Reels moved to the reservation in 1987, with employment as a supply buyer for the bingo operation. He also ran the Tribe's gravel and sand pits. Adamantly against the privilege he perceived the (white) Hayward side of the tribe to be receiving, he ran for, and was elected to, the tribal council. He used his prominence on the council to encourage other Sebastians to join the Tribe, and soon the balance of power shifted. There was a sort of civil rights movement on the reservation, with black tribal members demanding equal opportunity in running the Tribe's businesses, and staging protests such as sit-ins in the casino if they were asked to wait while patrons gambled or ate.

With Hayward often away on business, Reels stepped into a greater position of power in the Tribe. Though he was popular with tribal members, he sometimes alienated the Tribe's most adamant and powerful supporters, such as Senator Inouye, by intimating that the members of his family were impatient with waiting for further progress. Tribal strife turned into intrigue regarding Hayward's handpicked Foxwoods management team. On at least one occasion, the offices of Mickey Brown, the casino's overseer, were broken into by tribal security, with Reels's knowledge. Reels seemed to blunder again, when, in 1998, shortly after being elected tribal chair, he showed open hostility to the area's townspeople, the Connecticut congressional delegation, and the Bureau of Indian Affairs. Skip Hayward had crafted these precarious relationships with care; now they seemed in jeopardy.

Reels's use of a more-radical and political rhetoric may have inflamed local whites, but may also have served a purpose in uniting his Tribe behind his leadership, and aligning the struggles of the Mashantucket Pequots with national struggles for black civil rights and tribal rights of self-determination. In his early months as chair, Reels was successful in reversing what many had seen as an accommodationist stance taken by Hayward's administration.

Since then, Reels and his staff have made a commitment to educating the Tribe, other Indians, and the surrounding communities about the diversity within Indian Country. His cousin, Wayne Reels, who was serving as the director of culture and resources, told a group gathered in 1998 at the Mashantucket Pequot Museum and Research Center (MPMRC) for a workshop on "black Indians," that he found recent white attacks on Pequot identity as ludicrous as they were racist. "It didn't take money for us to be who we were. Poverty only strengthened our identity." He also argued that the internal divisions over skin color engulfing the Pequot Tribe must be understood as the adoption of "outside" society's ways of thinking, and he called for tribal members to resist such "internal colonization."[40]

Members of Connecticut's Golden Hill Paugussett Tribe have watched the Eastern Pequot recognition case, and struggles over Mashantucket Pequot leadership, with interest. A former leader of the Golden Hills, Moonface Bear (also known as Kenneth Piper; now deceased), was an ally of the Eastern Pequots; he used his seat on the CIAC to push for the Sebastian family's inclusion on tribal rolls.[41] Moonface Bear spoke frequently about the racial attitudes he, an African Indian, had encountered, and led those who agreed with him to fight racial oppression.

## Contemporary Perceptions of Race in the Northeast: The Golden Hill Paugussett Tribe of Connecticut

In 1999, after trying unsuccessfully to reach Golden Hill Paugussett leadership through the contact number provided by the BIA, I simply located their two reservations on a map and drove to the one nearest the Mashantucket Pequot Reservation, where I was also conducting research.[42] The small reservation is located in a rural residential area, on a winding paved road about three miles south of Colchester, Connecticut. On both sides of the reservation, as well as across the street, stately middle-class acreages stand surrounded by abundant fruit trees and well-tended lawns. The reservation is on the convex edge of a slight curve, set back from the road and closed off from it by a large metal gate. An American Indian Movement (AIM) flag flies at one side of the gate, a watchtower, or outpost, stands at the other. On my first visit, a large dog strolled the perimeter, but otherwise, no one responded to my presence. There were no cars or trucks in the driveway, and the mobile home appeared empty—on this chilly October day, no smoke came from the smokestack. Heeding the No Trespassing signs on the gate, I left a note with my phone number stuck near the mailbox and drove home.

Within days, two members of the tribal council called to set up a meeting. Shortly after that I met them on the Golden Hills' Colchester Reservation. I had read the press reports, and the BAR findings. I had seen the racist cartoons in the *Hartford Courant* depicting the Golden Hills as a Tribe of six African American opportunists with

names like "Chief So Sioux Me" and "Nike Hide Tanner." So I was prepared to meet two African Indians. I was not prepared, however, to
meet such young leaders. Both were in their early twenties; when I
met them, the oldest was in the midst of his first year in college. They
are responsible for the life of the Tribe on the only inhabited Golden
Hill–held land.[43]

I learned during that first meeting that these two members of the
tribal council represent one part of the Golden Hills, the part of the
Tribe that lives on the Colchester Reservation, deals with the state
government, and tries to keep tribal kin ties and cultural traditions
alive. The other group, headed by Chief Quiet Hawk, Aurelius Piper
(a father to one of the tribal council members, and uncle to
another), is the person spearheading the federal recognition effort,
the one that has access to BIA files and correspondences, and the
one with casino money backing its claims. The extent of the groups'
disagreement was such that I never met Chief Quiet Hawk. The
chasm between the two groups has been so deep that, when I met
them, those living on the Colchester Reservation had not even seen
(let alone approved) the petition under consideration at the BAR.[44]

This all goes back to a fight between brothers Aurelius and Kenneth Piper. Aurelius and Kenneth, two of six children born to Chief
Big Eagle, shared leadership of the Golden Hill Tribe after Big Eagle
left public life and returned to his homestead in Maine. Big Eagle
appointed Aurelius Piper, Chief Quiet Hawk, as the spokesman of the
Tribe; he proclaimed Kenneth Piper, Moonface Bear, to be the war
chief. In his capacity as war chief, Moonface Bear developed both a
militant rhetoric and ties to radical Indian movements such as AIM.
It was, in part, this militancy and the strength of his beliefs that created a deep split between the brothers.

Moonface Bear held a seat on the CIAC, and often acted as an
antagonist, demanding that the tribes and the state "sue the federal
government to force the United States Bureau of Indian Affairs to
take responsibility for maintaining state reservations."[45] He was
twenty-eight, and spoke with an arrogance and hostility that neither
time, nor conversion to Christianity, in 1985, would temper. In one
meeting, he demanded that CIAC members "gird up our loins and
go forward with a sure purpose and commitment to heal old wounds
and make a stand toward prosperity."[46] He and the other tribes' leaders
had complaints against the state for continuing to mismanage tribal

funds and lands, which contributed to the poverty of the residents on the state reservations. In addition, Moonface was able to convince prominent Jewish and African American organizations of the need for solidarity in the struggle, and these groups petitioned for federal reservation status for Golden Hill lands in Colchester.

Quiet Hawk had different plans. He tried to temper his brother's rhetoric, but was just as impatient to reclaim Golden Hill land and move toward prosperity. In 1993 he initiated litigation on behalf of the Tribe, attempting to claim land in the towns of Bridgeport, Trumbull, and Orange.[47] Kenneth and Aurelius quarreled over where the homeland of the Golden Hill should be located—near Bridgeport, or three hours to the east, in Colchester.

They also argued over the lawsuit, which had frightened, angered, and alienated homeowners across the region. Before they are able to mortgage, sell, or refinance a home, Connecticut residents must verify that their property is not subject to any one of the numerous ongoing land disputes between Connecticut and its several state-recognized or federally recognized tribes. Any potential legal activity by these groups is a threat to title stability and potential profit, as well as a hindrance on development or home improvements.

Without federal recognition, the Tribe did not have standing to sue for land, and the state courts lacked subject matter jurisdiction. Through each level of appeals, the judicial message to the Golden Hills was uniform: your claim cannot proceed until you are federally recognized; exhaust your administrative options through the BIA first. However, the Second Circuit Court acknowledged the slow nature of BAR processes, and ordered that if the Paugussett Tribe had not received a proposed finding within eighteen months, it could return to the trial court for a ruling on the merits in the land claims case. Therefore, though nonjusticiable, the suit continued to cloud land title for thousands of property owners in the three towns. The Second Circuit decision also gave Chief Quiet Hawk hope for a favorable resolution, hope that faded as his brother became engaged in an armed struggle with Connecticut state troopers on the Colchester Reservation.

In fall 1993, Connecticut police seized a shipment of cigarettes en route to the Golden Hill smoke shop, where Moonface Bear was using the reservation status of the land to sell the tobacco without imposing taxes. Connecticut charged Moonface Bear with tax evasion, and a warrant was drafted for his arrest. Rather than face the charges, he remained under self-imposed house arrest, and refused to leave the reservation as long as state troopers maintained vigil outside the gates.[48] Members of AIM joined Moonface Bear and a thirteen-week standoff ensued. The war chief's statements at the time did little to ingratiate neighbors to his cause. Fox evening news ran a clip of him speaking from within his gated compound.

> I'm down to go to war. I mean, come on. You don't think I could hurt you, where you think you cannot be hurt? I'm down to burn up the entire world if I don't get no freedom. I'm down to see you, your mother, your father, your sister, and your little baby suffer. Just like mine.[49]

Radical defense attorney William Kunstler eventually negotiated a surrender and Moonface Bear laid down his arms with no bloodshed. He was convicted and jailed, and the rift between him and Chief Quiet Hawk was not repaired before his death, on May 24, 1996, of complications from Lyme disease.[50]

Moonface Bear's death left a void in leadership on the Colchester Reservation that its inhabitants have tried to fill. One spoke to me of the thirteen-week standoff as a crystallizing point in his Indian identity—he, like Moonface Bear, is "down with the struggle" for self-determination and sovereignty. He told me that members of the Tribe have tried to live in a manner that emulates a combination of traditional indigenous and radical movement politics. They have built sweat lodges on the land, developed the pond and hunting grounds, tended Moonface Bear's grave, and established one trailer as an artistic center, where they produce woodcarvings and traditional art.[51] They also plan a cultural center, and progress toward that goal was occurring on my last visit to the reservation in winter 2000—the floor had been laid. The tribal council from the Colchester Reservation also participates actively in Connecticut intertribal activities.

However, the Golden Hill Paugussett Tribe's progress toward self-representation and recognition by others has been made at great emotional cost. In addition to estrangement from Chief Quiet Hawk, this branch of the Golden Hill Paugussetts has confronted racial tensions and stereotypes at every turn, not only from the state of Connecticut, but also in unlikely places.

One story in particular makes it clear how difficult their way of life will be for them to maintain without federal acknowledgment. On a trip to the BIA to read the files on their petition, Golden Hill members were invited by a receptionist at the BIA to attend a large intertribal dance that night. But, once at the door, their attendance was questioned by an Indian man who "carded" them, and said not only had he not ever heard of the Golden Hill Tribe, but also that the two did not look like any tribal people he'd ever run across.[52] Fortunately, a number of Mashantucket Pequot youth were in the line behind them, and "vouched" for their indigenous identity—after all, one young Pequot woman (an African Indian herself) told the doorman, they were just as Indian as she was. Without federal recognition, these types of incidents are likely to become common. Without federal recognition, the future of the Colchester Reservation is in jeopardy.

However, the BAR staff has grave doubts about the Golden Hill petitioners' Indian ancestry, and has found that the group is unable to prove that its common ancestor, William Sherman, descended from the historic seventeenth-century Golden Hill Tribe. The BAR says the group has not proven and, in fact, that it cannot prove, that it is of Indian ancestry, let alone that it is descended from a historic tribe.

When he was an attorney working on behalf of the Golden Hills, former AS-IA Gover asked the BIA to disregard this lack of proof, labeling it a byproduct of the racialized and repressive control exercised over African Indians in the Northeast and elsewhere. Gover and his legal staff pointed out that William Sherman had been identified in the 1860 census as "Black," in 1870 as "Mulatto," and that his designation in the 1880 census was obscured by an ink stain, but *may* have read "I" or "Ind" for Indian.[53] Census takers labeled his children with all three ethnic identifications. Golden Hill petitioners explain these confused racial designations by referring to the historical context: Connecticut's early census policies were similar to those in southern states; enumerators usually classified Indians as either black or white, or listed them as mixed -bloods and mulattoes, rather than give them a tribal affiliation. In the EP summary finding for recognition of that tribe, BAR staff members note that, in Connecticut, there has been "no consistency in ethnic identifications throughout the entire period for which such official records have been maintained."[54]

BAR staff members agree that governmental inconsistencies have caused racial confusion and misidentification. But, relying on tax records and overseer accounts, the BAR determined that William Sherman's actions and relationships were not characteristic of Indians in Connecticut at that time. The decision not to recognize the Golden Hill Paugussetts has been affirmed in two reviews at the IBIA, but was back under consideration again at the BAR in 2002 as a result of a procedural finding for the Golden Hills in Interior's most-recent appeals process.[55]

Struggles for Eastern Pequot and Golden Hill Paugussett recognition have played out in a particular racial context, with a history of state denial of Indian identity. They have also played out in a very large shadow, a shadow cast by the enormous success of, and controversy over, Indian gaming in the state. Connecticut groups seeking recognition may not all be seeking gaming, but few would deny that they aspire to at least some of the practices of self-determination and sovereignty exercised by the recently recognized tribes within the state. It is precisely these exercises of sovereignty that most concern local non-Indian residents of the state.

## Mashantucket Pequot Sovereignty

There are two federally recognized tribes in Connecticut—the Mohegans and the Mashantucket Pequots. Both have successful gaming operations, and both have used their successes to increase the reach of self-government and sovereignty.[56] The Mashantucket Pequots, in particular, have developed practices of self-government in the realms of tribal governance and social service provision, access of power in dominant society, and revitalization of lost or dormant aspects of their indigenous culture.

### ESTABLISHING MECHANISMS FOR TRIBAL GOVERNANCE AND PROVISION OF SOCIAL SERVICES

Tribes nationwide are exercising their rights to self-government through the establishment of tribal court systems, tribal councils, councils of elders, business arms, police forces, fire departments, health care units, and education systems. Through the Tribal Self-

Governance Project of 1988, Congress allows tribal governments more flexibility in administration, and shifts decision making and priority setting from the BIA to tribal governments. As a result of enterprise zone development, self-governance projects, and economic revitalization, "tribes across the country perform virtually all the functions typically exercised by local, municipal, and county governments, many functions exercised by the states, and a few functions unique to Indian situations."[57]

The Mashantucket Pequots have used their rights to self-governance achieved with recognition, combined with their newfound wealth, to establish a unique system of administration. The Pequot Tribe has an extensive tribal court system; a health care center; education vouchers; reservation infrastructure such as roads, sewage, and water systems; and housing developments.

Like the Poarch Creeks, the Mashantucket Pequot Tribe also has a business arm separate from the tribal council; this dual and overlapping structure is meant to insulate tribal leaders from business concerns, and business leaders from traditional concerns.[58] The Mashantucket Pequots tried to further distinguish the economic and cultural aspects of tribal leadership by creating, in 1997, a Council of Elders, which functions as a conscience for the council and business branches. Tribal leaders also say that they have built their court system with "a focus on the coming seven generations."[59] With this phrase, the Pequot Tribal Council attempts to wed two distinct strains of tribal governance: here, a pragmatic, policy-focused approach meets an indigenous conception of "peoplehood," one that transcends contemporary organizations and speaks to the needs of several generations of Indian people—the past, present, and future generations for whose welfare tribal governance is responsible.

## ACCESSING POWER IN DOMINANT SOCIETY

There has been little written concerning the power of American Indian voters, primarily because they have tended to lack electoral power in most jurisdictions.[60] In recent years, however, tribal leaders have encouraged their people to vote as a block, and have engaged in successful "get out the vote" campaigns.

Such strategies are complicated by the complex political needs of tribal government. Like many racial minorities, tribal members have traditionally voted Democratic; tribal governments, however, often benefit from a mix of conservative and liberal ideologies and economic plans. Tribal leaders tend to favor deregulation (a politically conservative position), while they also seek to develop centralized economies with equality of distribution and environmental sensitivity (traditionally more liberal positions). Senator John McCain, a Republican from Arizona, has long been a champion of tribal sovereignty, whereas a fellow Republican from Washington, Slade Gorton, has been tribal sovereignty's worst congressional enemy.[61] Conversely, while Democratic programs tend to benefit tribes financially, they do not always further the goal of self-determination by allowing tribes to administer their own funds and programs. Finally, liberals in the United States have traditionally favored classificatory schemes as the only way to right racial wrongs.[62] For instance, by classifying students as "black," then counting the number of "black students," schools may become eligible for government aid, as they are serving an underserved population. Liberals have favored, then, race consciousness; however, it is clear than an overly racialized view of Indians might in fact be detrimental to tribalism.

Because it is difficult to know which national candidate will most benefit tribal sovereignty, voter registration campaigns and issue drives in Indian Country have tended to focus on local and state races and issues. Recent studies, however, indicate an increasing nationalization of Indian electoral activity, attendant the increase in gaming. Jeff Corntassel and Richard Witmer showed that, when tribal governments did support candidates, the important issues they identified were gaming, sovereignty, self-determination, and treaty-rights enforcement.[63] As I showed in discussion of the Mowa Choctaw case, block voting of this kind can earn the tribe the ear of local politicians.

President Bill Clinton's second-term election certainly benefited from an Indian block vote. Prior to his appointment to assistant secretary of Indian Affairs, Kevin Gover was credited for Bill Clinton's victory in Montana, which traditionally swings Republican. Gover helped the president capture the ten thousand Indian votes that put him over the top in the state. In response, Clinton appointed Gover to head the BIA, and the Democratic National Committee helped to organize the first-ever American Indian Caucus of the Democratic Party, held at the party's 2000 convention in Los Angeles.

Another way that Indians are attempting to have a hand in their own governance and influence politics in the United States is with the rapid growth of tribally funded political contributions and the formation of tribal Political Action Committees (PACs).[64] Although other tribes are also large donors to political causes, the Mashantucket Pequot Nation undoubtedly enjoyed the most clout in the capital during the Clinton administration. The Pequots donated $465,000 to the Democratic National Committee and $100,000 to the Republican National Committee from 1991 to the close of 1993.[65] Then, one report noted, in 1994 alone,

> the tribal council gave the DNC $500,000. When the GOP grumbled, the Pequots gave them $50,000. . . . The Pequots are the first Native American people with enough cash to match the political contributions of big business.[66]

In 1996, the Mashantucket Pequots bought nearly $24,000 worth of tickets to President Clinton's inauguration, and eight tribal representatives were invited to White House fund-raising coffees that year.[67] After being Connecticut's largest soft-money contributor in the 1997–98 election cycle (reversing their trends in giving by donating $260,000 to GOP candidates and $50,000 to Democrats), and the fifth largest contributor nationwide to the Democratic National Committee, the Pequots were again invited, with several other tribes, to meet privately with President Clinton. The Mashantucket Pequots then formed a PAC, arguing that such an organization would allow them to better target their contributions. They left no doubt that they would use their money to target and shoot down proposed congressional restrictions on tribal gaming, tribal sovereign immunity, and tribal jurisdiction.[68]

Not all of the Mashantucket Pequots' politically savvy contributions have been to politicians. They have made well-publicized charitable donations within Connecticut, funding everything from an alcohol-free graduation bash for Ledyard teens to nearby New London's Fourth of July fireworks extravaganza, and a $1 million grant to help launch a tourism board for the Mystic area. The Pequots have made generous contributions to national Indian causes such as the American Indian College Fund, and, in 1997, the Tribe returned nearly

$600,000 to HUD officials, saying that the money should "be sent to poorer tribes."[69] They have been the largest single donor to both the Native American Rights Fund and the National Indian Gaming Association, and the Mashantucket Pequots gave $10 million to the Smithsonian Institution for the building of the new Museum of the Native American on the Capitol Mall.[70]

A final front on the political wars is the stepped-up lobbying efforts of tribes. The Muskogee Nation had a permanent lobby in Washington, D.C., by 1890,[71] and the Navajo Nation became, in 1982, the first tribe since the turn of the twentieth century to open a lobbying office in the capital. It was the dominance of casino money, however, that allowed the next three tribes (Mille Lacs Band of Ojibwa [Minnesota], Wisconsin Oneida, and Mashantucket Pequots [Connecticut]) to open offices in the 1990s, and to use their considerable wealth to buy a large measure of access to government.[72] As Dolores Brosnan notes in her study of tribal gaming, "Gaming tribes have developed expertise and some power for operating in mainstream society. They continue to assert their rights and oppose threats to their sovereignty through negotiations, lawsuits, and lobbying efforts in Congress and with the administration."[73] One reporter estimated that there had been a five-fold increase in the number of Indian-employed lobbyists in the first ten years following the Indian Gaming Regulatory Act's passage. He quoted Senator Nighthorse Campbell (R-Colo.) as saying that there was no question that "the tribes that have casinos and are making a good bit of money now are much more active, and they are hiring much more high-profile Washington-based firms."[74]

Indeed, the Pequots have "the best lobbyists money can buy,"[75] and count former president Clinton and several members of the legislature as their political allies and friends.[76] Certainly they have been the flashiest brokers of influence seen in Washington in recent days. Joey Carter, the tribe's assistant director of public relations told one reporter, "I think I like the idea of Skip being able to charter a Lear jet, fly down, and represent us as a people."[77]

CULTURAL REVITALIZATION

Tribes exercise their sovereignty, as well, in the preservation and revitalization of the cultural life of their people. The MPMRC, with its enormous exhibits of prehistoric and modern-era tribal life, stunning films, and astounding library collections, is a large-scale example of what tribes nationwide are establishing.[78] Skip Hayward's "pride and joy,"[79] the MPMRC brings to life the history and culture of the Tribe, and is known as a center of American Indian research.[80]

The museum's exhibits begin in a large and windowed "Gathering Space"; all five wings of the museum lead back to this central location. The "Pequot Nation" wing is devoted to explaining the contemporary Tribe's industries and governing structures. "Life in a Cold Climate" is a glacier-filled room with life-size statues of aboriginal hunters and prehistoric animals. The centerpiece of the museum, the "Pequot Village," is a true-to-life re-creation of a contact-era Pequot settlement. It features a realistic coastal and woodland environment where visitors can witness "the activities of Pequot daily life [as it was lived in the mid-sixteenth century], hear the sounds of the village and surrounding environment, and even smell the aromas of cooking fires and the forest."[81] The remaining wings are "Pequot War," which chronicles the 1637 Massacre at Mystic Fort, and "Life on the Reservation," which is devoted to the modern-day Mashantucket Reservation and tribal members, and includes a "Federal Acknowledgment Theater" and a replica of the mobile home Skip Hayward inhabited when he returned to the reservation.

The final exhibit in the "Life on the Reservation" wing is a gallery of enlarged photos of tribal members. Some have red hair and blue eyes, others have dark skin and Afros, and still others wear long braids and have high cheekbones. Voiceovers ring out, attesting to what it means to be Pequot, what it means to be Indian. Skip Hayward hopes that, through the MPMRC, people will not only hear this modern, diverse voice, but will also "let that ancient voice speak out. Let that ancient voice have a say."[82]

## Limits on Sovereignty

As noted in previous chapters, some of the Pequots' new access to politicians has engendered a considerable backlash among Connecticut's citizens, who have stereotyped views of Indians as poor, and who feel powerless compared with the wealthy tribal nation. When asked by the *60 Minutes* news crew, "Do they [the Pequots] have a lot of political power?" a woman in Ledyard answered, "Immense." Another added, "Money talks. Money is power. Money is power." As New Jersey representative Robert Torricelli told the reporter, "The Mashantucket Pequots are gaining so much political muscle they're going to be very difficult to control in a few years."[83]

It is true that Connecticut citizens do not get far with their complaints about the Mashantucket Pequots. A tribal supporter in the House of Representatives, Sam Gjedenson (D-Conn.), even called a group of visiting Connecticut homeowners "settlers" when they visited his office to complain about Pequot tendencies.[84] Members of the Tribe may consider the backlash a cost of doing business in D.C., and may perhaps be grateful for the fact that their money can get their feet in the doors of offices formerly closed to them.

Pequot tribal member and casino official Bruce Kirchner notes the ironic turnaround in fortunes his Tribe has encountered. "It used to be we'd have to practically camp out on some government official's doorstep to get anyone to notice us. Now we're the ones who get bombarded with requests."[85] Or, as Kevin Gover put it prior to his appointment to the BIA, "I don't believe in the theory of buying politicians, but I do believe in buying access, and that's what the Mashantuckets have done."[86]

Although tribal members and others in Indian Country see irony, they also see danger ahead. Local resentment has spilled over into an aggressive litigation and legislative campaign undertaken by the state of Connecticut to halt acknowledgment and to stop the expansion of gaming, not only in the state, but nationwide.

Connecticut's state attorney general, Richard Blumenthal, has been a leader in anti-recognition and anti-gaming litigation. Though most of his efforts have been to stop the recognition of tribes within the state, Blumenthal has filed amicus curiae ("friends of the court") briefs on behalf of other states' litigation in Indian matters, and has opposed the recognition of tribal groups beyond Connecticut's borders. He filed one such brief in support of the proposed finding to deny recognition to the Nipmuc Nation of Massachusetts, and another against the Miami Nation's requests for land-into-trust status in Illinois.[87] Speaking to Illinois leaders, and using the Golden Hill Paugussett Tribe of Connecticut (GHP) as an example, Blumenthal said, "They [GHP] held hostage thousands of innocent property owners in the misguided belief that property owners would besiege elected officials to surrender and give the Indians what they wanted."[88]

Blumenthal's office uses his press releases to educate the public as to the "dysfunctional" federal recognition system.[89] He derides the process as "too vulnerable to the influences of money and politics,"[90] and suggests an independent commission be appointed to decide acknowledgment claims, as such a commission would be "insulated from the corrosive influences of money and politics that now pervasively infect recognition decisions."[91]

Other Connecticut town leaders and attorneys mimic the statements made by the attorney general's office. First Selectman Nicholas Mullane told reporters that the public needed to "see for themselves the problems and deficiencies with this decision and the recognition process itself." In the same press release, Ledyard mayor Wesley Johnson noted that "the coalition between our towns and the Attorney General has worked well to give a much-needed voice for community and state interests to the BIA process. I hope that more towns will see the far-reaching ramifications of federal recognition and join with us in our efforts." Even more to the point was Preston's first selectman Robert Congdon, who managed to hit every theme provided by the attorney general's office. He states that the BIA's decision to recognize the Eastern Pequot Tribe is "flawed" and "if allowed to stand, will further weaken an already dysfunctional recognition process. I hope that both Native Americans and non-Native Americans alike will support our appeal and efforts to create a process that is objective and not influenced by money and politics."[92]

Blumenthal's call for a moratorium on federal acknowledgment and the creation of an independent agency to settle acknowledgment claims was also echoed by Connecticut senators Chris Dodd and Joseph Lieberman. Connecticut legislators have also called for the dissolution of state recognition for the Golden Hill Paugussetts, and for a federal investigation into the congressional acknowledgment of the Mashantucket Pequots.

Clearly, though the politicians are from Connecticut, the repercussions are nationwide. Several states' attorneys general offices have begun lobbying in support of two senate bills: S 1392 and S 1393. Bill S 1392 would enforce a moratorium on recognition decisions; bill S 1393 would move the working of the recognition process to an independent regulatory commission.[93] In addition, twenty state attorneys general (including Blumenthal) signed a letter to then-assistant secretary of Indian Affairs Neal McCaleb expressing their serious concerns about what they called arbitrary and illegal changes to the tribal recognition process made by the prior AS-IA Gover's administration. Thirteen states had joined Connecticut in a previous letter asking McCaleb to withdraw the "Gover Rule," or "Directive," mandated by the previous administration to streamline the acknowledgment process by limiting the amount of research the government's professional acknowledgment staff would undertake, and limiting the amount of third party (state and town) research that would be read and analyzed.

This kind of political pressure and threat of litigation from the states only increases the politicization of federal acknowledgment processes nationwide. It is just one more thing with which unrecognized groups must contend.

# Conclusion

The individual states of Alabama and Connecticut, and even the larger regions they represent, may seem very isolated from the rest of national Indian politics and policies. In Alabama, and elsewhere in the Deep South, racism has made it difficult to prove Indian heritage. In this region, white racism against people of color, in particular African Americans, and marriages between African Americans and American Indians, have combined to call into question claims of Indian identity. The Deep South's incredible poverty and its reputation as the nation's Bible Belt lend a regional tenor to anti-gaming voices heard nationwide. In Alabama, Southern Baptists and others oppose the type of gaming expansion seen in nearby Mississippi, and stand ready to rally against Poarch Creek plans to build a casino near the state capital. The unique racial, religious, and political climate in that state makes claims to Indian identity and tribal sovereignty made by the Mowa Choctaws both difficult to substantiate, and increasingly controversial.

Connecticut, and the northeastern seaboard in general, are unique for seemingly opposite reasons. This densely populated, racially integrated, and relatively wealthy region is home to the two most-successful Indian casinos in the United States, the Mohegan Sun and Foxwoods. Residents of Connecticut, traditionally more liberal allies of American Indian causes, have been mobilized for nearly two decades now against the development and expansion of tribal casinos, and against the perceived threat of several more casinos being built in an

extremely small state. Residents of Connecticut also contend with
the growing fiscal and political clout of the recently recognized
Mohegan and Mashantucket Pequot Tribes, and have fought particularly bitterly to rein in the Mashantucket Pequots' sphere of influence in state, regional, and national politics. The initial mobilization
against casino expansionism and Indian political activism has brought
to light latent and, to some, surprising, racial tensions. Connecticut
Indians and members of groups seeking recognition are accused,
variously, of being "too white" or "too black" to be real Indians. In
Connecticut, especially, we can see the mobilization of "Rich Indian
Racism." Connecticut Indian tribes whose members lack traditional
signifiers of Indianness—poverty, primitivism, and phenotype—are
alleged to be inauthentic inventions of greedy people seeking casino
wealth.

Clearly, the recognition struggles of the Mowa Choctaw, Golden
Hill Paugussett, and Eastern Pequot Tribes are particularly informed
by the varying racial and economic politics of the Deep South and
the Northeast, and by the unique responses each group has made, at
different times, to colonizing attempts. Though California tribes are
expanding their casino wealth, the immense gaming success of the
Mashantucket Pequots has not been replicated in the West; nor has
the Deep South's aversion to gaming been as strong or as prevalent
in other regions. In all of these regards, the stories related in this
book are unique.

Yet the particular geographic contexts isolated by this research help
illuminate the intersections of gaming and race—of cash and color—
in public perceptions of acknowledgment practices. These intersections occur elsewhere, and certainly have repercussions nationwide.
This is particularly true, and increasingly so, given the growing power
of recently recognized tribes (and the understandable desire of
unrecognized groups to emulate their success), and given the exercises of sovereignty made available by federal acknowledgment
coupled with the possibilities presented by the Indian Gaming Regulatory Act. It simply is not surprising that federal acknowledgment
has become increasingly politicized and controversial; nor is it surprising that such politicization has been expressed around racial
and economic issues.

Acknowledgement processes, like all other aspects of U.S. law, are
affected by, caught up in, and constitutive of social discourses, his-

tory, and politics. The very need for a process to recognize Indian tribes' relationship with the U.S. government reinforces the proper perception that tribes are, indeed, different from ethnic groups in the United States, and are on a par with other governments. The need for such a regime also, however, reinforces the perception that there is something *essential* about tribal government and tribal peoples, something identifiable, outside of the mainstream, and inherent in Indianness. In other aspects of U.S. law and society, particular views of Indianness have been mobilized to discredit claims to Native identity; this is no different in recognition processes.

The BAR and congressional recognition are both affected by contemporary culture; they are subject to public perceptions of racial identity and resource inequalities. They are subject to public discussions of Indianness, perceptions of racial identity, and historical and contemporary racism that can cloud a tribal member's heritage and identity. These legal processes are touched, as well, by changes in tribal economies and public sentiment brought about by gaming, and by public opinion about controversial development plans.

The racialized language and obsession over resources surrounding acknowledgment claims will not astonish those scholars who recognize the law's embeddedness in society, and the extent to which legal, racial, and class discourses are enmeshed in the United States. But because law presents itself in American life as neutral and objective, and because Americans perceive "politics" as a subjective field of deal making, it is not surprising that BAR staff members, as well as those seeking decisions at the BAR, have the desire to view the proceedings as more legal (thus objective and neutral) than political (tinged with racial bias, perhaps or subject to pressure from towns and localities that dread more casino growth). The acceptance of this "ideology of legalism"—the view of law as neutral and objective[1]—allows participants, observers, and reformers alike to believe that any perceived or real instances of racialized or resource inequality in BAR decisions are natural and inevitable, rather than the effects of history, politics, and power.

With close examination and interpretation of particular cases, however, it is obvious that, as locations of power that deal intimately with the construction of Indian identity, federal acknowledgment processes cannot be value-free, neutral, and objective endeavors. When the ideology of legalism is not accepted, it becomes clear that the realm of acknowledgment law is one of interpretation, where national, public discourses on topics like race and gaming are always in play. To view acknowledgment law without the ideological patina of legalism, then, is to discover that injustices and inequalities in BAR processes are neither natural nor inevitable; rather, they result from existing racial injustices and inequalities in the larger society. Injustices and inequalities in federal acknowledgment are mirroring injustices and inequalities visited upon Indian tribes and people in this country.

Just as acknowledgment law cannot be studied outside of present American legal and social contexts, neither can it be practiced in this way. Recent and ongoing hearings before the Senate Committee on Indian Affairs have stressed the desire to further shield the acknowledgment process from politics. Some argue that an independent commission would be better adept at navigating the politics of the process; others recommend leaving the process at the BIA, but adding additional safeguards such as clearer burdens of proof and expanded rights of review. A recent senate bill would establish an Independent Advisory and Review Board to provide independent peer review of acknowledgment decisions to the assistant secretary of Indian Affairs.[2]

Recommendations to shorten the process, standardize burdens of proof, and lessen the costs of petitioning are certainly welcome, as are recommendations that seek to provide a procedurally fair way of dealing with third-party challenges to proposed findings in favor of recognition. My concluding recommendation, though, is different. Rather than devise an independent commission, or increase bureaucratic structure at the BAR in an effort to remove politics from federal acknowledgment, I propose quite simply that all involved should acknowledge that politics are part of the process. Quite simply, fairness in acknowledgment processes will not be achieved by pretending that there is no colonial past with continuing racial and economic repercussions.

Let me be clear; I am not arguing or alleging that decision making at the BAR is influenced by political considerations. Rather, I argue that there are political, racial, colonial, and economic reasons why groups have not been acknowledged. There are also political, racial, and economic reasons why third parties oppose recognition petitions. Effort must be focused on understanding these aspects of federal acknowledgment—a colonial past, and a contentious present—even when they are particular and unique to only one region, or only one tribe.

It is not helpful to try to avoid "politics" in acknowledgment law. To do so is to deny that the intersections of cash, color, and colonialism have power in the lives of Indian people, recognized or not. Rather, in order that these factors might lose their ability to limit access to recognition for deserving groups, the intersections of cash, color, and colonialism must be specified, made clear; indeed, they must be acknowledged.

# Notes

CHAPTER 1

1. Novak and Thompson, "Lost Tribe?"
2. Barlett and Steele, "Look Who's Cashing In," 50.
3. How we name things is important, and a note about my use of the word "Indian" is appropriate. Unless speaking specifically about their tribal affiliation, most Indians refer to themselves using precisely that term—"Indian." They might add, for clarification, "American" Indian. I adopt the common usage in this manuscript. I respect the right of people to name themselves, and whenever possible, I will refer to the designation preferred by the community of which I am speaking (that is, the Mashantucket Pequot Tribe). As well, I will refer to individuals by the names they call themselves: only one of the people I interviewed for this project used the term "Native American" self-referentially, and I refer to her as such in this book. I also use the term "Indian tribe," though numerous authors have argued quite forcefully that to do so is to adopt an inappropriate colonial moniker. Critics of the term "tribe" note that tribal organizations were historically instruments of colonial administration; these scholars advocate instead for the use of the word "nation." I use "tribe" knowing that it may seem to place me at odds with some standard-bearers in this debate; I do so because "tribe" is the term of designation used by the federal government, and claims to federal tribal status are what I examine in this manuscript. To become an Indian tribe—a unit recognized by U.S. law—is, by definition, a goal of those groups seeking federal acknowledgment.
4. Several authors have offered excellent article-length treatments of specific tribal interactions with the BAR. I direct the reader to Field et al.,

"Ohlone Tribal Revitalization Movement;" Gunter, "Technology of Tribalism"; McCulloch, "Issues in Identity"; McCulloch and Wilkins, "Constructing Nations within States"; Miller, "After the F.A.P."; Paredes, "Federal Recognition"; Frank W. Porter, "In Search of Recognition"; Slagle, "Unfinished Justice." There are also several excellent examinations of BAR regulations in general. See Kim, "Administrative Procedures Act"; Paschal, "Imprimatur of Recognition"; Quinn, "Federal Acknowledgement"; and Starna, "Southeast Syndrome."

5. "Folk categories" are sets of words that describe normal, everyday experience as used by normal, everyday people. Many authors distinguish between "folk" and "expert" categories. Here, the "legal" term, "federal acknowledgment," would fall into the "expert" category. I use "legal" rather than "expert" because "normal, everyday people" (Indians) *are* experts in acknowledgment, or, as they may term it, "recognition." Their folk term signifies their own expertise; yet that expertise may not, strictly speaking, be *legal.*

6. Former Assistant Secretary of Indian Affairs Kevin Gover complicated the distinction between the two terms in congressional testimony in May 2000. Gover argued that the executive branch, through Interior, can only "acknowledge" an existing relationship. Congress, on the other hand, has the sole right of "recognizing" a new relationship. Gover's approach has not been standard in the Bureau of Indian Affairs, the Branch of Acknowledgement and Research (the arm of the BIA responsible for recognizing the trust relationship), Congress, or the courts (Gover, Testimony, 2000). For an intriguing discourse on the rights of the executive and legislative branches to recognize or acknowledge Indian tribes, see Ford, "Executive Prerogatives."

7. Hawaiian Islanders and Alaskan Natives, though not considered members of "tribes," are also parties to this relationship. They are governed under separate administrative regimes set up by acts of Congress. In 1999 and 2000, some Hawaiian activists pushed to be included in the federal trust relationship through congressional bills of recognition; those bills died in committee, and remain controversial among some Native Hawaiians who resist being called "Native American" or "American Indian." In February 2001, the governor of Alaska extended state recognition as tribes to all of the incorporated Alaskan Native Villages. It is unclear whether these tribes will seek federal status as anything other than Alaskan Native Villages.

8. The BIA administers over 43 million acres of tribally owned land, over 10 million acres of individually owned Indian land, and nearly 420,000 acres of federally owned land held in trust. The BIA is authorized to administer these programs through Code of Federal Regulations: 25, at various sections.

9. Indian Health Services are not provided under the auspices of the Department of the Interior through the BIA; rather, the Department of Health and Human Services administers them.

10. Both the circuit and district courts have found that the BIA grossly mismanaged the individual money accounts stemming from the trust relationship, failed woefully to discharge its fiduciary duties, and continues to be malfeasant in settling these accounts and claims. Litigation is ongoing in *Cobell v. Norton* (Civ. No. 96-1285), the largest class-action suit ever filed by Indians against the federal government. More than five hundred thousand Indian individuals seek billions of dollars in damages for unpaid revenue made from the land held in trust for them.

11. See Sandefur, "Economic Development," 1991.

12. *Native American Graves Protection and Repatriation Act.*

13. *Indian Arts and Crafts Act of 1990.*

14. For more detailed treatments, see Kupperman, *Settling with the Indians;* Prucha, *Great Father;* and Reid, *Law for the Elephant.*

15. A significant body of scholarship exists on tribes in this region. See Cotterrill, *Southern Indians;* Covington, *Seminoles of Florida;* Debo, *Rise and Fall of the Choctaw;* Paredes, "Federal Recognition"; and Weeks, *Farewell My Nation.*

16. For excellent information regarding treaties signed and made throughout the United States, see Deloria and DeMallie, *American Indian Diplomacy.* For more on the quest of landless tribes in particular, see Frank W. Porter, "Without Reservations."

17. The original name for what I write of as the Branch of Acknowledgment and Research (BAR) was the Federal Acknowledgment Project (FAP). As FAP, it was codified as Part 54 of Title 25 of the Code of Federal Regulations. The designation was officially changed to the BAR in 1982, when it was placed in Part 83 of Title 25 of the Code of Federal Regulations. As this manuscript goes to press, the name has been changed again, to the Office of Federal Acknowledgment (OFA). I continue to use "BAR" in this manuscript, as it is most readily identifiable to most readers; I use "FAPs" to indicate all federal acknowledgment processes available to hopeful groups, from judicial determination to administrative decision to congressional action.

18. 25 CFR 83.

19. Blu, "'Reading Back.'"

20. Campisi, "Trade and Intercourse Acts," 354.

## CHAPTER 2

1. Fitzpatrick, *Mythology of Modern Law,* 3 and 24.

2. *Cherokee Nation v. Georgia,* 30 U.S. (5 Pet.) 1 (1831); *Samuel A. Worcester v. The State of Georgia,* 31 U.S. (6 Pet.) 515 (1832).

3. Gonzalez and Cook-Lynn, *Politics of Hallowed Ground,* ix and 229; Carrillo, "Identity as Idiom," 10.

4. See Forbes, *Africans and Native Americans*.

5. See Deloria and DeMallie, *American Indian Diplomacy*. See also Churchill, "Implications of Treaty Relationships," 83.

6. See Williams, *American Indian*.

7. See Brosnan, "Indian Policy, Indian Gaming."

8. *Johnson v. M'Intosh*, U.S. 21 (8 Wheat) (1823).

9. *Fletcher v. Peck*, 10 U.S. (6 Cranch) 87 (1810).

10. Norgren, *Cherokee Cases*, 94. Wilkins and Lomawaima offer an important contribution to discussions of discovery and conquest. They note, in *Uneven Ground*, that Marshall's interpretation of these doctrines was not the only viable interpretation in circulation at the time of the consolidation of U.S. power. They offer a more "realistic and pragmatic definition of the discovery doctrine" (26) based on historical examples of treaty language and land policies. They argue that Marshall held a "distorted, historically inaccurate, and legally fictitious construction of the doctrine of discovery" (54). See also Wilkins, *American Indian Sovereignty*.

11. Gonzalez and Cook-Lynn, *Politics of Hallowed Ground*, xii.

12. Carrillo, 5.

13. Norgren, *Cherokee Cases*, 149.

14. Gonzalez and Cook-Lynn, *Politics of Hallowed Ground*, 229

15. Removal is most often spoken and written of as affecting primarily five tribes: the Creeks, Chickasaws, Choctaws, Seminoles, and Cherokees; however, it is important to note that many tribes suffered policies of removal at different points in their history. Tribal responses to Removal were also varied and diverse.

16. Kickingbird et al., "Pamphlet on Self-Determination," 6.

17. See, for example, the *Civilization Fund Act of March 3, 1819* (*U.S. Statutes at Large* 3: 516–17), reprinted in Prucha, *United States Indian Policy*.

18. *General Allotment Act, or Dawes Act of 1887*.

19. Prucha, *Great Father*, 650.

20. Ibid., 679.

21. Brosnan, "Indian Policy, Indian Gaming," 217. In 1919, Congress granted citizenship to all honorably discharged Indian veterans and passed the Indian Citizenship Act in 1924, extending citizenship and suffrage to all Indians.

22. Wilkinson, *American Indians, Time, and the Law*, 19.

23. Commissioner of Indian Affairs T. J. Morgan (1890), quoted in Frank W. Porter, "Without Reservations," 114.

24. Brosnan, "Indian Policy, Indian Gaming," 218.

25. Taylor, *New Deal*, 14. Prucha's *United States Indian Policy* reprints portions of the Meriam Report. It can be found in full at Lewis Meriam et al., *The Problem of Indian Administration* (Baltimore: Johns Hopkins University Press, 1928).

26. *Wheeler-Howard Act* (Indian Reorganization Act) 48 Stat. 984 (1934). Readers are encouraged to consult Deloria and Lytle, *Nations Within,* for an excellent treatment of this era in federal Indian law.

27. Three recent books are wonderful examinations of the consultative hearings in Indian Country that Collier organized prior to the passage of the IRA. See Rusco, *A Fateful Time* and Deloria, *Indian Reorganization Act.*

28. In his study of Lakota Sioux resistance to the IRA on the Rosebud Reservation, Tom Biolsi argues that this outcome rests in the IRA's roots in "earlier technologies of surveillance and control" (*Organizing the Lakota,* 83). At page 101, he points out that "the Indian New Deal in general and the IRA in particular were clearly not Indian ideas. The IRA was conceived and drafted by technical specialists in Washington who did their best to design a plan that would grant self-government to Indian people and would protect tribal resources." And, at page 150, he notes that because they required the approval of, and implementation by, the Department of the Interior, the tribal constitutions, for the Lakota, at least, "had the effect of creating *additional* government over [them]. Rather than transferring government from the Office of Indian Affairs to the Lakota, new levels of domination emerged with which Lakota people had to deal."

29. Philp, *Termination Revisited,* 4.

30. Ibid., 5.

31. Sider, *Lumbee Indian Histories,* 134.

32. This number does not include IRA elections held in Oklahoma and Alaska, which were covered and enumerated under separate parts of the act and were tallied differently.

33. Senator Morse held Progressive ideals that would lead him to be an effective labor arbitrator, a champion of civil rights, and an anti-Vietnam demonstrator. See Mason Drukman, *Wayne Morse: A Political Biography* (Portland: Oregon Historical Society Press, 1997).

34. During his first term in the Senate, Watkins endorsed the censure of Joe McCarthy; soon after, he lost his bid for reelection. He served for a short time as a consultant to the Department of the Interior, and President Eisenhower appointed him to the Indian Claims Commission in 1960. He eventually became chief commissioner of that body. See Arthur Vivian Watkins, *Enough Rope: The Inside Story of the Censure of Senator Joe McCarthy by His Colleagues; The Controversial Hearings That Signaled the End of a Turbulent Career and a Fearsome Era in American Public Life* (Englewood Cliffs, N.J.: Prentice-Hall, 1969).

35. Milwaukee Public Museum, "Menominee Termination and Restoration"; http://www.mpm.edu/wirp/ICW-97.html#political.

36. Philp, *Termination Revisited,* 2–3.

37. Ibid., 168.

38. Ibid., 132.

39. *Public Law 280 Act of August 15, 1953.*

40. Cornell, *Return of the Native,* 10.

41. Fixico, *Terminiation and Relocation,* 183.

42. Though pan-Indianism has been considered primarily an urban phenomenon, new histories of tribal activism show that there was considerable pan-Indian activism in previous eras, and in rural areas, as well. I mean the term here to include any American Indian groups or organizations in which the focus of action shifts from tribal governance to intertribal, or pan-tribal, politics. Pan-Indianism had been nascent due to a common history of oppression, and difficult to organize because of the diversities of tribes and individual Indians. As a result of anti-Termination efforts directed at the majority of the tribes, new constituencies in Indian politics developed; these new constituencies contributed to a rapid growth of political activity of various types. In addition to Cornell, *Return of the Native,* see Ablon, "Relocated American Indians"; Fixico, *Urban Indian Experience;* Hirabayashi, Willard, and Gemnitze, "Pan-Indianism"; Nagel, *American Indian Ethnic Renewal;* and Weibel-Orlando, *Indian Country, L. A.*

43. *United States v. Sandoval,* 231 U.S. 28 (1913).

44. Milwaukee Public Museum, "Menominee Termination and Restoration"; *http://www.mpm.edu/wirp/ICW-97.html#political.* See also, Deer, "Ada Deer (Menominee) Explains."

45. *Menominee Tribe of Indians v. United States,* 391 U.S. 404 (1968).

46. *Menominee Restoration Act.*

47. *United States v. John,* 437 U.S. 634 (1977).

48. For an excellent discussion of *Menominee* and *John,* see Wilkinson, *American Indians, Time, and the Law.*

49. *Indian Child Welfare Act.*

50. A number of other pan-Indian groups were formed during this time. They include the Council of Energy Recourse Tribes (CERT), which was formed in 1975 by tribes shaken by the Oil Producing and Exporting Countries (OPEC) oil embargo and resulting energy crisis. The CERT's goals included protecting tribal lands that were oil and mineral rich, which it did through the adoption of a capitalist monopoly strategy. Both the NCAI and the CERT are primarily liberal organizations; they hope to achieve a redistribution of economic and political power to Indians within existing structures of Indian-white relations.

51. Sider, *Lumbee Indian Histories,* 268.

52. Philp, *Termination Revisited,* 173.

53. *Alaskan Native Claims Settlement Act* (ANCSA) 43 USC 1604. Though many at the time viewed the ANCSA in a favorable light, time has shown its various deficiencies in adequately protecting the rights of Alaskan Native Villages.

54. *Indians, Pueblo de Taos Tribe, New Mexico, Lands in Trust,* 91 Public Law 550; 84 Stat. 1437 (1970).

55. *Indian Self-Determination and Education Assistance Act,* 25 USC 450, 95 Public Law 608; 92 Stat. 3069.

56. Even after President Johnson left office, pan-Indian lobbying groups like the NCAI were successful in getting pro-Indian legislation passed. Significant among these bills is the Indian Child Welfare Act (1978), which protected Native children from being adopted outside of their tribal community and reinforced the legitimacy of tribal government control over family and cultural issues in Indian Country.

57. See, for example, Bee, "Riding the Paper Tiger"; Deloria, *Custer Died;* and Deloria, *American Indian Policy.*

58. Cornell, *Return of the Native,* 123.

59. Ibid., 160 and 139.

60. Josephy, Nagel, and Johnson, *Red Power,* 170.

61. Leonard Peltier, imprisoned for allegedly shooting an FBI agent on the Pine Ridge Reservation, and a potent symbol of the continuing Red Power struggle, says this of the 1960s and 1970s: "[Red] Power wasn't the feeling with me. It was more a sense of [Red] Pride" (Josephy, Nagel, and Johnson, *Red Power,* 40). Red Power is used primarily in this text, as it is the more recognizable of the two terms (Red Power and Red Pride), and has useful resonance with the Black Power movement of the same era.

62. The faculty of American Indian Studies at the University of Michigan has put together an excellent website detailing the history of the American Indian Movement. Find it at http://www-personal.umich.edu/~jamarcus/aima.html.

63. It is important to note that the similarities between the AIM and black Nationalist movements extended to the ways in which the federal government tried to suppress them. The most radical Indians were targets of suppression through a variety of means—legal and illegal —including a media campaign against them, sensational trials, infiltration by the FBI, and even a campaign of terror and assassination. Ward Churchill has written extensively about this aspect of the joint movement. See also Matthiessen, *Spirit of Crazy Horse.*

64. Deloria, *Trail of Broken Treaties.*

65. *Puyallup Tribe v. Department of Game of Washington,* 391 U.S. 392 (1968).

66. *Department of Game of Washington v. Puyallup Tribe,* 414 U.S. 44 (1973).

67. *Puyallup Tribe v. Department of Game of Washington,* 422 U.S. 165 (1977).

68. *Trade and Intercourse Act of 1790,* 1 Stat. 137, Chap. 33; *Trade and Intercourse Act of 1802,* 2 Stat. 139, Chap. 13; and *Trade and Intercourse Act of 1934,* 4 Stat. 729, Chap. 161.

69. *Indian Claims Commission Act of 1946.*

70. Tureen and Margolin originally had worked only with the Passama-quoddy Tribe; the Penobscots approached them and asked if they would have a similar claim as the one being pursued by the Passamaquoddys. They soon joined the suit. See Brodeur, *Restitution.*

71. *Joint Tribal Council of Passamaquoddy v. Morton*, 528 F. 2nd 370 (1st Cir., 1975).

72. *Maine Land Claims Settlement Act.*

73. After the successful claims were paid out, the Maine tribes no longer qualified for foundation-funded legal services, and the for-profit law firm of Tureen and Margolin was formed. See Brodeur, *Restitution.*

74. Brodeur, *Restitution*, 145–46.

75. *Mashpee v. New Seabury et al.* , 427 F. Supp. 899 (1978). Intrepid readers will recognize the name: Judge Skinner also presided over the Grace and Beatrice Corporations trial, which was chronicled in Jonathan Harr's book, *A Civil Action.*

76. Jack Campisi, William Axtell, and William Sturtevant—two anthro-pologists and a historian, respectively—were witnesses for the tribe. Jean Guillemin, an anthropologist, and Francis Hutchins, a historian, testified for the New Seabury Corporation. At times, according to observers, it seemed as though the academic disciplines themselves were on trial: anthropology was pitted against history. New Seabury's attorney, St. Clair, parodied Campisi's fieldwork among the Mashpee as "twenty-four days and nights in Mashpee." There was occasional talk throughout the trial of issuing a subpoena for Campisi's field notes (see Clifford, *Predicament of Culture*, 318, and Campisi, *Mashpee Indians).*

77. Neither could scholarly witnesses agree on what constituted assimila-tion and acculturation (Clifford, *Predicament of Culture*, 319–25).

78. Since this was a federal case, it was litigated in district court in Boston, rather than in the town of Mashpee or in the surrounding areas of Cape Cod.

79. Clifford, *Predicament of Culture*, 286.

80. Ibid., 310–11.

81. *Montoya v. United States*, 180 U.S. 261 (1901).

82. *United States v. Joseph*, 94 U.S. 614 (1876).

83. Given the prevalence of incredibly high alcoholism rates on reserva-tions, many are sympathetic to the reasoning behind such a prohibition. However, principles of tribal sovereignty and self-determination would indi-cate that it is the right of the tribal or Pueblo council to determine com-mercial matters within tribal/Pueblo lands.

84. *United States v. Candelaria*, 271 U.S. 432 (1926).

85. The Mashpees submitted a petition to the BAR that entered the "ready active consideration" stage in 1996. It was still pending in early 2003.

86. See Medcalf, *Law and Identity*.

87. See Castile, "Commodification of Indian Identity."

## CHAPTER 3

1. Cornell, *Return of the Native*.

2. *Indian Civil Rights Act of 1968; Indian Self-Determination and Education Assistance Act of 1975; Indian Child Welfare Act of 1978*.

3. American Indian Policy Review Commission (AIPRC), *Task Force 10* and AIPRC, *Final Report of the American Indian Policy Review Commission*. See also Kim, "Administrative Procedures Act."

4. For a history of the federal acknowledgment process, see Quinn, "Federal Acknowledgment."

5. Locklear, Testimony.

6. *Montoya v. United States*, 180 U.S. 261 (1901).

7. *Title 25 CFR Chapter 83*. See also, U.S. Department of the Interior, Branch of Acknowledgment and Research, "Official Guidelines" (hereafter cited as "Guidelines").

8. "Guidelines."

9. U.S. Department of the Interior, Branch of Acknowledgment and Research, "Summary Conclusions."

10. The IBIA has discretion in determining which requests for review it will accommodate.

11. The BAR has made more recognition decisions since 2000. One such decision, to recognize the Eastern Pequot Tribe, is discussed in detail in chapter 8 of this book. These are not reported here, however, because several of these decisions are pending litigation, others have been reversed, and others have not been finalized. As a result of the *Cobell* litigation, no BIA information is accessible on-line, and the status of petitions is difficult to ascertain. I use the General Accounting Office's (GAO) report on problems with federal recognition, published in 2001, as the best source of information on pending and decided petitions. In addition, the cut-off of 2000 is appropriate because it signifies the end of the Clinton era in the BIA administration and the beginning of uncertainty attendant the Bush administration plans for the BAR.

12. The judicial option has been effectively foreclosed by the development of the BAR process. Groups can seek judicial review after an IBIA decision, but not prior to BAR action.

13. One *can* often discern congressional reasoning from the testimony and questions provided at hearings on specific bills of acknowledgement or bills to change the acknowledgment criteria and process found in the BAR.

14. Interview, April 26, 1999. Because recognition politics involve personal politics, as well as tribal, local, and national issues, and because I want to avoid personalizing these debates, I have not attributed these quotes. Each of the tribal members and leaders interviewed were knowledgeable about the tribal acknowledgment claim made by the tribe, and, in most cases, had direct experience with the petition or the congressional process. I also interviewed state-level elected leaders in Connecticut and Alabama (Indian and non-Indian), and those in charge of the states' Indian Offices. All of the interviews are coded by the month, day, and year they were conducted.

15. Interview, May 6, 1999.

16. Sheffield reports that BAR staff member George Roth and Cherokee tribal leader Wilma Mankiller are among the most outspoken advocates of keeping recognition within the BIA. They both see federal recognition as a protection for tribes. Sheffield, *Arbitrary Indian*, 80.

17. "Guidelines," 35.

18. Sider, *Lumbee Indian Histories*, 255.

19. For a great overview of even more views against acknowledgment processes and the BAR, see Beinart, "Lost Tribes."

20. Churchill, *From a Native Son*, 86–87.

21. Ibid., 87–91. But compare Kickingbird et al., "Pamphlet on Self-Determination," 20–25, for a treatment of IRA governments as schemes that recognize and protect the inherent sovereignty of tribes. Also, see Rusco, *A Fateful Time;* using transcripts of the consultative hearings, Rusco makes a compelling case for the argument that the IRA was not "imposed" and that tribes were able to construct governing documents suitable to their needs and traditions.

22. Barsh, "Political Recognition," 5.

23. Jaimes, *State of Native America*, 132.

24. Sockbeson, Testimony.

25. I was present at these hearings and recorded this exchange.

26. On the importance of oral histories for the petitioning process, and a critique of the BAR's handling of oral history evidence, see Slagle, "Native American Tradition."

27. Hearings on HR 4462 before the House Committee on Natural Resources, Office of Native American and Insular Affairs, 103rd Cong., 2nd sess., (1994).

28. Campisi, "New England Tribes," 184.

29. For a particularly good treatment of the political economy of reservations, see Terry Lee Anderson, *Sovereign Nations or Reservations?*

30. U.S. Bureau of Indian Affairs, Office of Tribal Statistics, "Indian Labor Force Report: Portrait 1997" (hereafter cited as "Portrait").

31. The most important employer for Indians is the government. According to the "Portrait" prepared by the BIA, only 34.5 percent of Indians on reservations work for a private employer, whereas 58.5 percent work for state or federal government, and 28.1 percent are employed by tribal governments.

32. Sandefur, "Economic Development," 208–11.

33. In contrast, non-Hispanic whites make up 84.5 percent of the population and experience 82.3 percent of the nation's violent crime; African Americans make up 12.0 percent of the population and experience 14.6 percent of crime (Greenfield and Smith, *American Indians and Crime,* 6 and 12).

34. In a 1997 Harvard study of mortality rates, published in part by the *New York Times,* Dr. Christopher Murray found that male Indians living on reservations in South Dakota have the lowest life expectancy rates of anyone else in the entire United States (56.5 years)—lower than mortality rates in some parts of Africa. The study shows that the five worst counties for mortality in the United States are Bennett, Jackson, Mellette, Shannon, and Todd—all five are reservation counties in South Dakota (*New York Times,* "Surprises in a Study").

35. Cornell and Kalt, *Pathways from Poverty,* 2.

36. Indian Health Services statistics.

37. Greenfield and Smith, *American Indians and Crime,* 35.

38. Shapard, Testimony.

39. Former assistant secretary of Indian Affairs Ada Deer (Menominee) calls the lack of proper funding for the BIA "a harmful trend that must be publicized and stopped," and notes that Senator Nighthorse Campbell, upon assuming the chair of the Senate's Committee on Indian Affairs, made reversing the downward spiral of funding a top priority (Deer, "Tribal Sovereignty," 18).

40. Shapard, Testimony.

41. Velky, Testimony. The BIA's yearly appropriation is $1.9 billion; Indian Health Services has an appropriation of $2.4 billion for fiscal year 2000.

42. Wilkins, "Intergovernmental Matrix," 122.

43. U.S. General Accounting Office, *Indian Issues,* 6.

44. The Lumbee Tribe is nearly three times the size of the next largest petitioning tribe, and is estimated to account for nearly 60 percent of the Indians in the United States seeking acknowledgment. If recognized, the Lumbee would still be significantly smaller than many long-recognized Tribal Nations, such as the Najavo (181,054 members) and the Sioux (74,253 in twenty different tribal designations). The Congressional Budget Office, in 1991, estimated that the cost to the federal government of recognizing the Lumbees would be $120 million annually. Though the per capita

cost of recognizing the Lumbees would still be less than the national aver-age appropriation of $3,000 per Indian annually, $120 million is an effec-tively enormous number when used against Lumbee recognition efforts. In efforts to appease both lawmakers and several recognized Indian tribes who feared a reduction in their own federal monies, several of the proposed Lumbee recognition bills have been written to make Lumbee access to fed-eral funds and services a difficult matter of yearly appropriations (Wilkins, "Intergovernmental Matrix," 132–39).

45. Wilkins, "Intergovernmental Matrix,"138, quoting AS-IA Swimmer's testimony on S 2672 (1988).

46. U.S. Department of the Interior, "Changes in the Internal Process-ing"; known as Directive 2000.

47. Leuthold, *Indigenous Aesthetics,* 25.

48. Goldberg, *Racial Subjects,* 208 and 48–73.

49. In this vein it is important to remember that all of the words used to describe Indian people are potentially essentializing, in that they tend to make unitary and essentialized what is actually a diverse and varied population.

50. See Berkhofer, *White Man's Indian,* and Jennings, *Invasion of America.*

51. Gossett, *Race,* 236, cited in Goldberg, *Racial Subjects,* at 103.

52. Bush and Mitchell, *Photograph and the American Indian,* xvi–xxi.

53. Spilde, "Rich Indian Racism."

54. "Indian Hunting Season" flier; text retrieved by author at http://www.h-net.msu.edu. Senator Ben Nighthorse Campbell (R-Colo.) report-edly requested that the Justice Department launch an inquiry into the ad's publication.

55. Krech, *Ecological Indian,* 15–30. See also Frank W. Porter, "Without Reservations."

56. Churchill, *From a Native Son,* 409.

57. Dippie, *Vanishing American.*

58. This is not to say that linguistic ability is inauthentic; in fact, recupera-tion or revitalization of the traditional language is often a pivotal step toward tribal self-determination. Deloria and Lytle argue that linguistic ability is often a marker of authenticity in Indian communities (*Nations Within,* 233).

59. From a 1991 speech by Robert Blye, quoted in Churchill, *From a Native Son,* 372.

60. The recent (mis)appropriation of the warrior-shaman archetype by New Age and Men's Movement groups has culminated in big business, with the financial success going to what some Indians call the "plastic shamans." There has been much harm done to Native culture and spirituality through the mass commercialization and the naïve use of powerful spiritual prac-tices outside of their intended cultural and social contexts. See Kehoe, "Pri-mal Gaia."

61. Roybal, Testimony, 2–8. Most important, Roybal goes on to acknowledge that "in our own case, we have pressed for protection of the privacy of our individual members and of our cultural heritage, and gradually negotiated with BAR to protect these materials, relying not only on 25 CFR, sec. 83 and the Privacy Act of 1974, but on such things as the limits imposed on the Tribe's use of sensitive materials by applicants for membership at the time they signed privacy waivers as part of the Tribe's membership application process" (8).

62. McCulloch and Wilkins, "Constructing Nations."

63. McCulloch and Wilkins write, "The social construction of the Aboriginal Indian has 'benefited' Western tribes more than the Eastern tribes. . . . Eastern tribes have often had a difficult time convincing the federal government (and their neighbors) that they remained 'indigenous' and were entitled to comparable recognition and benefits as their Western cousins" (168).

64. Paschal, "Imprimatur of Recognition."

65. Gunter, "Technology of Tribalism"; Richard Warren Perry, "Modern Nation-State."

66. Interviews, May 23, 1999 and June 9, 1999.

67. Ford, "Executive Prerogatives;" see also Gunter, "Technology of Tribalism" and Richard Warren Perry, "Modern Nation-State."

68. A discourse is an "interlinked set of histories, narratives, theories, ideas, notions, and images that together create a comprehensive story . . . a method of thinking about the objects of that discourse, a way of understanding, naming defining, and controlling them" (Gunter, "Technology of Tribalism," 98–99).

69. Fanon, *Wretched of the Earth.*

70. Bee and Gingerich briefly discuss acknowledgment in their article on colonialism and American Indians. They appear uncomfortable with the false consciousness argument, but are not yet able to refute its pull. Bee and Gingerich, "Colonialism, Classes, and Ethnic Identity."

71. Albers and James, "Dialectics of Ethnicity"; Bee and Gingerich, "Colonialism, Classes, and Ethnic Identity"; Forbes, "Envelopment,"; Lurie, "Menominee Termination"; and Roxanne Dunbar Ortiz, "Wounded Knee."

72. Churchill, *Struggle for the Land.*

73. Vizenor, *Cross Bloods.* The term "sub-altern" is used by post-colonial theorists to refer to southeast and southern Asia, including India.

74. Mohanty, "Under Western Eyes," 69.

75. See Pavlik, *A Good Cherokee,* for a compilation of scholarly papers by Cherokee anthropologist Robert K. Thomas, in the late 1960s, detailing the contributions to the theory of internal, or "hidden," colonialism in Indian Studies.

76. O'Brien, "Concept of Sovereignty," 71.

77. Barsh, "Indigenous Self-Determination," 169.
78. Ibid., 159–60.
79. Ibid., 169–70.
80. Churchill, *From a Native Son*, 40.
81. O'Brien, "Concept of Sovereignty," 46.
82. Tom Tureen, quoted in Barker, "Mapping New Territory," 94.
83. Wunder, *Recent Legal Issues*, xiii.
84. Wilkinson, *American Indians, Time and the Law*.
85. Pommersheim, *Braid of Feathers*.
86. Goldberg-Ambrose, "Of Native Americans," 509.

## CHAPTER 4

1. Paredes, "Federal Recognition," 122.
2. This is not uncommon. Blu discusses the importance of these desegregation activities to the Lumbee recognition claims, as well as the importance of churches and religious institutions, for the sense of community
they bring to unrecognized tribal peoples. See Blu, *Lumbee Problem*.
3. U.S. Department of the Interior, *Final Determination for Recognition of
Poarch Band of Creek Indians*, 10 (hereafter cited as *Poarch Creek Final Determination*).
4. Paredes, "Federal Recognition," 127.
5. Ibid., 131.
6. Ibid., 129.
7. *Atmore (Ala.) Advance*, "Poarch News," January 26, 1978.
8. Interview, May 10, 1999.
9. Kickingbird et al.
10. Interview, May 10, 1999.
11. Interviews, April 26, 1999, May 10, 1999, and May 18, 1999.
12. Interview, May 10, 1999.
13. *Atmore (Ala.) Advance*, "Creek Monies Being Questioned, " December
27, 1984.
14. Ibid.
15. *Atmore (Ala.) Advance*, "Poarch News," January 26, 1978.
16. Interview, May 10, 1999.
17. Patton, "Creeks Building More."
18. Patton, "Bingo Attracts Big Crowd."
19. Ibid.
20. Johanna Scogin, "Creek Bingo Palace Brings 1000s."
21. Patton, "Creeks Take Over Motel and Restaurant."
22. Ibid.

23. Mike Scogin, "Court Ruling Favors."

24. In my interviews, tribal leaders denied that Poarch Creeks had been much hurt by these casinos; state senators insisted that the Tribe had been very hard hit. The safest bet seems to be a happy medium, which would allow that the Class III facilities have diminished bingo profits, probably to a considerable, but not devastating, extent.

25. Everyone I interviewed in Alabama, and most of those whom I spoke with only casually, mentioned this battle and the Wetumpka site.

26. Eight percent of pari-mutuel profits wagering in Alabama goes to the state in the form of taxes and is used to fund public agencies. From 1981 to 1982, this amount reached $5.5 million. After 1988, the state legislature imposed a 1 percent privilege tax on pari-mutuel pools, and the finance office considers the proceeds of that tax a "major source of state revenue." The pari-mutuel tax represents a small but significant portion of the state's appropriations budget, which in FY2000 totaled $14,421,673,334, but funding for which fell short by 13 percent (State of Alabama Department of Finance website: http://www.budget.state.al.us/.)

27. Interview, May 18, 1999.

28. Interview, May 10, 1999.

29. Interview, May 18, 1999.

30. Readers should note that I would use the same words to describe the outstanding Mashantucket Pequot Museum and Research Center, adjacent to Foxwoods, as well as the Pequots' annual Feast of Green Corn and Dance (*Schemitzun*). It seems that whatever the Pequots do, they do it on a grand scale. The quote "For the wonder of it all—Foxwoods!" is used in the casino's television advertisements in the Northeast. Often confused for "Western," as in Western Pequot Tribe, "Mashantucket" actually translates into "much-wooded-land." Foxwoods, then, becomes a play on the Mashantucket Pequot name, since "Pequot" translates into "Fox People" or "People of the Fox." Therefore, the Mashantucket Pequots are the much-wooded-land fox people, and they operate Foxwoods.

31. Nearly everyone who writes about Foxwoods tries to describe the sight with some originality, and certainly I am no different. Most memorable of the accounts I have read include Brett Fromson's, who writes that the Grand Pequot Hotel "soars above the flat fields of southeastern Connecticut like a Hyatt on steroids," and Steve Kroft's, who calls it a "wampum wonderland." (Fromson, "Pequot Uprising"; Steve Kroft, "Wampum Wonderland," *60 Minutes,* CBS, September 18, 1994)

32. The *(Ledyard, Conn.) Pequot Times* is a tribal newspaper made widely available to tribal members, casino employees, and visitors. The Mashantucket Pequot Tribal Nation publishes it and maintains archived editions at the Research Center.

33. *(Ledyard, Conn.) Pequot Times,* March 2000, p. 12.

34. Quinn, "Federal Acknowledgement," 342.

35. In less than an hour, ninety English soldiers, backed by about two hundred Mohegan and Narragansett warriors, massacred nearly six hundred Pequot men, women, and children. The English sustained two casualties.

36. Pequots under the leadership of Mamoho lived on the Lantern Hill Reservation, which Connecticut purchased in 1683. Mamoho himself was the grandson of Uncas (sachem to the Mohegans) and the great-grandson of Sassacus (sachem to the Pequots). The descendants of the residents of the Lantern Hill Reservation make up petitioners for acknowledgement under the names of the Eastern Pequot and Paucatuck Eastern Pequot Tribes.

37. Even though some of the overseers might have wished to stop the encroachments of whites upon the Indians' land, it was impossible to do so. Often the overseers were elderly men, living at a distance from the reservations; both of these factors made efficacious action on behalf of the Indians unlikely. Despite its limitations, the overseer system remained in place for a century more, until 1936. Bureau of Indian Affairs, *Summary . . . Eastern Pequot,* 2000.

38. The story is related in a film, titled *Bringing the People Home,* shown at the MPMRC.

39. Russell, *Indian New England;* Hauptman and Wherry, *Pequots in Southern New England.*

40. Kroft, "Wampum Wonderland," *60 Minutes.*

41. As reported in the MPMRC's many exhibits on the history of the Tribe.

42. Captain Ahab's whaling vessel in *Moby Dick* (the *Pequod*) was named for the Tribe.

43. Fromson, "Pequot Uprising."

44. *Bringing the People Home.*

45. Ibid.

46. Eisler, "Revenge of the Indians."

47. *Western Pequot Tribe of Indians v. Holdridge Enterprises, Inc.,* Civil No. 76-193 (1976).

48. Mashantucket Pequot Museum and Research Center (MPMRC), *Bringing the People Home.*

49. Reagan , "Veto."

50. *Mashantucket Pequot Indian Claims Settlement Act of 1983,* 25 USC, sec. 1751.

51. Benedict, *Without Reservation.*

52. Eisler, *Revenge of the Pequots.*

53. Ibid., quoting tribal member Joey Carter.

54. MPMRC, *Bringing the People Home.*

55. To some extent, the tribe acknowledges that there remain those against the casino. In the Pequot museum's "Federal Acknowledgement Theater," Emmanuel Sebastian is shown on film saying, "I'm not going to gamble at the casino. I wish we could have made the money some other way. But I can see that society wouldn't let us."

56. Kroft, "Wampum Wonderland," *60 Minutes.*

57. *Mashantucket Pequot Tribe v. Connecticut,* 913 F. 2nd 1024 (1990).

58. As a senator, Weicker had been a staunch supporter of the Pequot recognition and land claims settlement. When he was elected to the governorship, however, he stunned the Pequots by remaining resolutely anti-gaming.

59. Baker, "Shays May Amend."

60. *California v. Cabazon Band of Mission Indians,* 480 U.S. 202 (1987).

61. With a cut of the Pequots' profit, Connecticut would not be compelled to institute the tax.

62. Eisler, *Revenge of the Pequots.*

63. Lim Goh Tong, a Malaysian investor who owns casinos in Malaysia, the Bahamas, and Australia, and was a pioneer of the "resort-destination" casino, marrying lavish accommodations, stellar recreational facilities, and high-stakes gambling, underwrote the casino. The figure of "over 60 million" comes from Kroft ("Wampum Wonderland," *60 Minutes*) and has also been reported by Eisler (*Revenge of the Pequots*).

64. The tribes and the state have Memorandums of Understanding (MOUs), which govern the payments in lieu of taxes made by each tribe.

65. Eisler, *Revenge of the Pequots,* 199.

66. Lightman and Jones, "Day 3: Identity Crisis."


## CHAPTER 5

1. Brosnan, "Indian Policy, Indian Gaming," 2.

2. See Brosnan, "Indian Policy, Indian Gaming"; Cornell and Kalt, *What Can Tribes Do?;* and Sandefur, "Economic Development."

3. Eisler, *Revenge of the Pequots,* 101.

4. *Seminole Tribe v. Butterworth,* 658 F. 2nd 310 (1981).

5. Mason, *Indian Gaming,* 54.

6. Ibid., 49.

7. *California v. Cabazon Band of Mission Indians,* 480 U.S. 202 (1987).

8. Mason, *Indian Gaming,* 53.

9. Tsosie, "Negotiating Economic Survival," 49.

10. The federal government has historically kept itself out of gaming

enterprises, leaving it, and other morality issues, to the states' police powers. Few commentators note this important aspect of the IGRA; Brosnan,
"Indian Policy, Indian Gaming," is a good source of discussion on the topic.

11. Eisler, *Revenge of the Pequots,* notes at 188, "Inouye had collected and
would continue to collect thousands of dollars in campaign contributions
from Indian tribes, even though his seat was one of the safest in Congress
and he was rarely even opposed for reelection. IGRA was Inouye's creation,
and he argued that the law 'balanced the need for strong enforcement of
gaming laws with strong federal interest in preserving the sovereignty rights
of the tribal governments.'"

12. Ibid., 118.

13. Ibid., 119.

14. O'Brien, *American Indians.*

15. Harris, Testimony.

16. Tsosie, "Negotiating Economic Survival," 49.

17. *Seminole Tribe of Florida v. Florida et al.,* 517 U.S. 44 (1996).

18. Since August 1996, tribes have been subject to Title 31, the Bank
Secrecy Act, and must monitor compliance to that act (National Indian
Gaming Association, "Fact Sheets and Folder").

19. Cornell et al., *American Indian Gaming,* 20.

20. See Mason, *Indian Gaming.*

21. For details regarding MIGA, see Klas and Robinson, *Economic Benefits.*
For details on WIGIA, see Nelson, Erickson, and Langan, *Indian Gaming.*

22. "Thousands" is based on my own web search through Lexis/Nexis
and periodic abstracts. The searches returned, literally, too much to read.

23. In 1982, gross gaming revenue in the United States was $10 billion; by
1996, gross gaming revenues (including, but not limited to, Indian gaming)
were $47 billion (Eadington, "Spread of Casinos," 128). The NIGA reports
that Indian gaming revenues in 1999 were $8.26 billion (10 percent of that
year's total gaming revenues). Tribal gaming revenues are not part of the
public domain; unlike businesses and charities, tribes are not required to
issue financial statements. These reports are all estimates; the NIGA's estimates rely upon self-reporting by tribes.

24. One hundred and eighty-three tribes offer Class III gaming; fifteen
offer Class II only.

25. Nolin, "Indian Tribe Waiting."

26. These profits are unusual, however; in fact, the NIGA noted in 1999
that only twenty-two tribes account for over half (56 percent) of all Indian
gaming revenue.

27. Kroft, "Wampum Wonderland," *60 Minutes.*

28. Robert Porter, "Akwe:kon Forum," 55.

29. Brosnan, "Indian Policy, Indian Gaming," 214.

30. Novak and Thompson, "Lost Tribe?"

31. U.S. Department of the Interior, "Draft Technical Report . . . Paucatuck Eastern Pequot,"149, citing Hayward to Deer, October 17, 1996; Hayward to Babbitt, October 2, 1998.

32. "Cultural Celebration," WTNH-TV, September 15, 1998.

33. "Connecticut News," WVIT-TV, January 15, 1997.

34. Foster, "Golden Hill Tribe."

35. Four of the nine tribes recognized or restored by Congress since 1978 were post-1988 petitioners at the BAR. Five of the nine have signed gaming compacts.

36. Norgren, *Cherokee Cases*, 138.

37. Barker, "Mapping New Territory."

38. Bee, "American Indian Policy."

39. The American Indian Equal Justice Act attempted to void the sovereign immunity of tribes and make them subject to tort law.

40. Goren, Testimony.

41. Ferdon, Testimony.

42. A Bill to Amend the Indian Gaming Regulatory Act (S 1077) sought both taxation of tribal gaming enterprises and a moratorium on new Indian casinos.

43. Eadington, "Spread of Casinos," 135.

44. Quoted in Kirk Johnson, "Weicker to Veto."

45. Eadington, "Spread of Casinos," 136.

46. Nelson, Erickson, and Langan, *Indian Gaming*, 2.

47. Ibid., 12.

48. Ibid., 12–14.

49. Interview, April 26, 1999.

50. Klas and Robinson, *Economic Benefits*, 4. The heading for this section of the chapter comes from Republican Connecticut State senator William H. Nickerson, who is quoted in a news report titled "All Bets Are Now off for Bridgeport Casino" ([Hackensack, N.J.] *The Record*, November 18, 1995).

51. See Eadington, "Spread of Casinos" and Klas and Robinson, *Economic Benefits*.

52. Klas and Robinson, *Economic Benefits*, 5–11.

53. Ibid., 5.

54. Evans Group, *Economic Impact*.

55. The White Buffalo Woman is considered a sacred sign of good fortune by several Plains peoples.

56. Spilde's 1999 article for *International Gaming and Wagering Business* notes that "22 of the 250 tribal casinos and bingo halls generate 56% of the nation's Indian gaming revenue" (Spilde, "Rich Indian Racism," 13).

57. Mason, *Indian Gaming*, 44.

58. The Yuchi Tribal Organization failed at the BAR effective March 21, 2000 (petitioner no. 121, letter of intent filed in 1990). The BAR does have two post-IGRA petitioners on "Ready, Waiting" status—the Meherrin Tribe of North Carolina, which filed a letter of intent in 1990, and the Muwekma Indian Tribe (Ohlone / Costanoan Muwekma Tribe) of California, which filed in 1989. A Final Determination to recognize the Paucatuck Eastern Pequots (petitioner no. 113, filed in 1989) is being litigated.

## CHAPTER 6

1. Sheffield, *Arbitrary Indian*, 134.

2. Interview, June 8, 1999.

3. Spilde notes that this notion of need was a key argument against the Mille Lacs Band of Ojibwe in its recent treaty-rights case. "Rich Indian Racism" was successfully used to deny land-in-trust for the Shakopee Mdewakanton Sioux just last year. Both have successful gaming operations.

4. The individual who made this statement was a staff member for a U.S. congressman. The representative has supported Mowa Choctaw recognition in the past, but has recently declined to do so. The statement was made as a way of explaining that the representative felt that the Mowas, though Indian, should not be recognized until they could meet the *tribal* criteria set by the BAR. The comment "on visual" is a reminder of the subjective and racialized nature of these types of decisions.

5. Forbes, *Africans and Native Americans*.

6. Heffernan, "Creeks Stay on War Path."

7. *Mobile (Ala.) Press Register*, "Shards of Choctaw."

8. Benedict, *Without Reservation*.

9. Trump, Testimony. Trump has since reversed his stance on Indian gaming, and has entered into a number of discussions, hoping to finance, manage, and profit from tribal casinos in the Northeast.

10. These jokes are double racial puns: they question the Pequots' authenticity while reinforcing the assumption that all Italians are mobsters (and all mobsters are Italian, and all casinos are really mobster fronts).

11. First aired on ABC, December 18, 2002. I must note that this sitcom is actually much more subtle in its presentation than the excerpted portion; there is an underdeveloped, though present, critique of the jokes as they are delivered. Interestingly, the critique is delivered by the only white character on the episode, a nine-year-old, freckled redhead attending the sleepover.

12. "Saturday Night Live 25th Anniversary Special," *Saturday Night Live*, NBC, September 25, 1999.

13. This episode of *The Family Guy* was titled "The Son Also Draws," and first aired on the Fox Television network on May 5, 1999.

14. *New York Times*, "New Means for Recognizing Tribes."

15. Fromson, "Pequot Uprising."

16. Gene Randall and Maria Hinojosa, "Casinos Become a Matter of Survival on the Mashantucket Pequot Reservation," CNN, June 16, 1999.

17. *Mobile (Ala.) Press Register*, "Shards of Choctaw."

18. Brooks, "Tribal Leader May Surrender."

19. Eisler, "Revenge of the Indians."

20. Scott Simon, "Kickapoo Tribe," National Public Radio.

21. Kirsch, "Lost Tribes, Imaginary Indians," 1.

22. Eadington, "Spread of Casinos," 140.

23. Jansen-Verbeke and Lievois, "Heritage Resources," 89.

24. Ibid.

25. Richter, "Heritage Tourism."

## CHAPTER 7

1. Quinn, "Southeast Syndrome."

2. "Wannabes" are non-Indians who claim Native identity for a variety of reasons, often attaching themselves to a tribal or intertribal community, and occasionally seeking benefits from government programs meant for Indians (Tomas, "A Look at Wannabe-ism," 12).

3. Starna, "Southeast Syndrome."

4. *(Citronelle, Ala.) Call-News Dispatch*, "Chief River Rat." I include this story not to question whether Chief River Rat was indeed Indian, or Choctaw Indian, but to exemplify the presence of "Indian organizations" that were not aspiring to "tribal status," and never sought recognition from either the state or the federal government.

5. Mrs. Cecil Brown, letter to the editor, *(Citronelle, Ala.) Call-News Dispatch*.

6. Mrs. Mary Skipper to Alabama Indian Affairs commissioner, 1981, Indian Affairs Commission Correspondence, 1980–1982 Correspondence—General (N–Z), Alabama Department of Archives and History.

7. Paredes and Joos, "Economics, Optimism," 150.

8. Interview, June 8, 1999. The 2000 census showed Alabama's population to be 0.5 percent American Indian, 0.7 percent Asian, 1.7 percent Hispanic, 26 percent black, and 71 percent white. One percent of the population chose the "Mixed Race" category.

9. Roth, "Overview," 92.

10. Forbes, "Envelopment," 106–107.

11. Churchill, "Crucible," 46. See also Forbes, *Africans and Native Americans* and Forbes, "Manipulation of Race."

12. Rountree, "'Citizen' Indians," 183.

13. Which category one was placed into often wasn't a matter of choice. And even when a choice was given, such as in Virginia, where Indians could register as mixed-bloods, "those chances for choosing ones' identity were missed due to illiteracy, not being able to find the (White) witnesses to their identity, or under-publicization of the opportunity." Rountree, "'Citizen' Indians," 184.

14. Forbes, *Africans and Native Americans*.

15. Although these privileges depended upon time and place, and changed from state to state, even from county to county, after the Civil War, "Free Persons of Color" held, in general, more privileges than "Mixed Bloods" or "Mulattoes"; they were usually able to cross county and state lines freely, and even hold property. See Forbes, "Manipulation of Race."

16. Churchill, "Crucible," 46.

17. Rountree, "'Citizen' Indians," 185. Most tribal groups did maintain internal (private) ethnic boundaries that were visible to members, but invisible to whites and other outsiders.

18. Ibid., 178.

19. Ibid., 191.

20. It is clear that many Indians did, repeatedly, challenge the white community's perceptions of them and actions toward them; the recent history of the Lumbees of North Carolina provides one excellent example of this type of contestation. See Blu, *Lumbee Problem*.

21. Reed, "People Whom Time Forgot," pt. 1.

22. The Mowas take their name from these two counties: M-O-bile and W-A-shington counties—Mowa. See Blu, "Where Do You Stay At?" for more on the importance of place and place-names in the life of unrecognized groups.

23. Matte, *Response to the Proposed Finding*.

24. Ibid.

25. Matte et al., *Papers*, 92.

26. Matte, *Response to the Proposed Finding*, 111.

27. Ibid.

28. For an excellent treatment of these issues see LaVelle.

29. See, generally, May, *African Americans*.

30. Matte et al., *Papers*, 113–15.

31. Matte, *Response to the Proposed Finding*, 123.

32. See Blu, "'Reading Back,'" regarding the importance of churches in the lives of unrecognized southern Indian tribes.

33. Benn, "State Pow-Wow."

34. Ibid.

35. *(Citronelle, Ala.) Call-News Dispatch,* "Mowa Elect Tribal Council."

36. The state had no extra resources to bring medical care directly to the afflicted communities, but the Red Cross was able to facilitate emergency vaccinations (*[Citronelle, Ala.] Call-News Dispatch,* "Hepatitis Outbreak").

37. The AIAC also provided technical assistance to the Cherokee Indians of Jackson County and the Star Clan of Muskogee ("AIAC Progress Report of Activities and Financial Records, Month of June," A. D. Price Folder, AIAC Correspondence—General (N–Z), Informal Files 80-2, SG4991, Alabama Department of Archives and History).

38. *Linton v. State,* 88 Ala. 216, Ala. State Supreme Court (1889).

39. It is extraordinary for an American Indian community to have such disciplined and regular voters. Most analysts agree that the Indian population in the United States is most unlikely to vote in national elections. See Geoff Peterson, "Native American Turnout." However, Corntassel and Witmer, "American Indian Tribal Government," note that, since 1988, tribes have become increasingly and successfully active in electoral politics.

40. *(Citronelle, Ala.) Call-News Dispatch,* November 3, 1986.

41. Interview, June 19, 1999.

42. Ibid.

43. Letter of obvious deficiency from Hazel Elber to Mowas (February 15, 1990), reprinted in Matte, *Response to the Proposed Finding.*

44. U.S. Department of the Interior, *Final Determination against Recognition of the Mowa Choctaw Band of Indians of Alabama* (hereafter cited as *Mowa Final Determination*).

45. Expedited review shifts the burden from the BAR to the petitioner, and requires that the petitioner show a likelihood of providing required proof of the criteria, in order for a full review to take place. The Mowas appealed the grounds of expedited review to the IBIA, which found in spring 2000 that the expedited review had been well founded, and ordered an affirmation of the BIA's proposed determination against recognition.

46. U.S. Department of the Interior, *Proposed Finding against the Recognition of the Mowa Choctaw Band of Indians of Alabama* (hereafter cited as *Mowa Proposed Finding*).

47. From 1830 to 1852, "mulatto" extended only to a third-generation descendant; the Alabama State legislature changed its code in 1852 to extend to fourth-generation African American descendants (*Mowa Proposed Finding*). It should be noted that Alabama's antimiscegenation law was on the books until a referendum in November 2000. At that time, the ban on interracial marriage was eradicated by a vote of 60 percent to 40 percent in favor of ending the ban.

48. Donelson, "Creeks Object," 1991.

49. I located this document, uncatalogued, in the Alabama Department of Archives and History, Governor's Papers for Governor Hunt, in the 1991–93 Administrative Files—Indian Affairs, box SG17980.

50. My examination of county voting records for the last three decades confirms state officials' and tribal leaders' assertions that the Mowas, who are geographically localized in two primary communities within the district, tend to be a disciplined, active, and unitary voting block. However, in their congressional district, Sonny Callahan has run unopposed, leaving them little choice but to vote for him.

51. Interview, May 18, 1999.

52. This representative attributes pure economics to Tullis's motivation against the Mowas; he further points out that Callahan is a close associate of former Alabama governor Fob James, who is also a close associate and friend of Tullis.

53. Interview, May 12, 1999.

54. Interview, May 5, 1999.

55. (Citronelle, Ala.) Call-News Dispatch, "Senate Passes Bill."

56. Interview, May 10, 1999.

57. Jones, Testimony.

58. Interview, May 10, 1999.

59. Interview, April 26, 1999.

60. Two of those three denied are the exceedingly large Houma and Lumbee Nations. One tribal leader from a recently recognized tribe told me that he considers the Lumbees a "prime example" of a political mistake. They are, in his words, "a people who definitely have Indian history, but they made a bad political decision when they decided they numbered fifteen thousand people and all of a sudden, they wanted to be number two in the nation, and got a lot of adverse reaction" (interview, May 10, 1999).

61. Interview, May 18, 1999.

62. As an example of this I offer a recent conversation I had with a local historian, who had written an article on Indian Removal from Alabama. He was unaware that there were any state-recognized tribes in Alabama, though he had interviewed Poarch leaders and members of the AIAC. Other tribal groups apparently did not make it into their conversations.

63. Patton, "Bingo Attracts Big Crowd."

64. Patton, "Creeks Take Over Motel and Restaurant."

65. For example, BIA Representative Carl Shaw was quoted as saying that the Poarch are "on the right track" toward becoming less dependent on the federal government, for sustaining themselves. He praised their bingo and hotel, and said their "efforts have not gone without notice at the national level" and stated that "their enterprises will reap them better rewards in the years to come" (Atmore (Ala.) News Journal, "Shaw Praises Creeks").

66. Paschal notes that the intermarriage of non-Indian settlers and Indian women in the Poarch community was not a problem for the BAR, but did constitute a recognition problem for the Snohomish and the Tchinouk. It was not addressed for a similar group, the Jamestown Klallam, who did receive recognition. I can only note this inconsistency, and not develop it further here. It is clear the Poarch have been able to transcend identity controversy not only in the region, but also at the BAR (Paschal, "Imprimatur of Recognition," 222n120).

67. Tribal member Cielo Gibson, quoted in Johanna Scogin, "Years of Work Pay Off."

68. Patton, "Poarch Pow-wow" and "Another Celebration."

69. Roth, "Overview," 187. The powwow is often mentioned in the BAR's *Final Determination for Recognition of Poarch Band of Creek Indians.*

70. Paredes, "Federal Recognition," 126. Paredes notes that the Poarch have been very "savvy" in the invitations they extend to intertribal figures.

71. In 1982, joblessness in Alabama was at 14.8 percent, the second highest joblessness rate in the nation. Coverage from this period focuses on the poor economy and rising crime in the county, especially the proliferation of "marijuana hauls" and the arrests of locals growing the cash crop, which always made the front page.

72. *Atmore (Ala.) Advance,* "Creeks Awarded Federal Grant."

73. Patton, "Creeks Take Over Motel and Restaurant."

74. *Atmore (Ala.) Advance,* "Poarch Creeks Buy Building."

75. Mike Scogin, "Top 10."

76. *Atmore (Ala.) Advance,* "Construction of Spec."

77. Radalet, "Congressmen Renew Push."


## CHAPTER 8

1. Giselle Fernandez, "Golden Hill Paugussett Indians Press Claim for Land and Gambling Rights," *Evening News,* CBS, August 8, 1993.

2. Liberman, "Connecticut Casino Neighbors."

3. Ibid.

4. Eisler, *Revenge of the Pequots,* 14.

5. Kirk Johnson, "Weicker to Veto."

6. Lord, "Six Flags Plan."

7. "Connecticut News," WVIT-TV, January 15, 1997. Significantly, the nearby Mohegan Sun Casino generates much less public outrage. The Mohegan Tribe, recognized by the BAR in 1994, has not engendered the hostility of Connecticut landowners to the extent that the Mashantucket Pequots have.

8. Eisler, *Revenge of the Pequots*, 197. Elsewhere, he writes, "Weicker's negotiations with the Pequots were kept so secret that in late September, when Weicker suddenly announced that he had unilaterally reached an agreement with the Pequot Nation to allow them to install slot machines, the reaction in Hartford was one of utter shock" ("Revenge of the Indians."). He also writes, "The transactions were handled with such discretion . . . that few of the Yankee residents from the towns of Ledyard or North Stonington or Preston knew that anything unusual was taking place" (*Revenge of the Pequots*, 195).

9. A Connecticut citizen-action group, Homeowners Held Hostage, or HHH, is against any Indian casino expansion, but is particularly outspoken against the recognition of the Golden Hill Paugussetts.

10. Kroft, "Wampum Wonderland," *60 Minutes*.

11. Scott Simon, "Kickapoo Tribe," National Public Radio.

12. Fromson, "Pequot Uprising."

13. Kroft, "Wampum Wonderland," *60 Minutes*.

14. Ibid.; Fromson, "Pequot Uprising."

15. Kroft, "Wampum Wonderland," *60 Minutes*.

16. The BIA issued a Final Determination for recognition of the Schaghti-coke Tribe (Conn.) in February 2004. The state of Connecticut will join suit with several towns to block the Tribe's recognition, and to stop land from being put into trust for it.

17. The BAR has accepted the overseer's lists, which report the "direct ancestors of both current petitioners as members of the Eastern Pequot tribe." (U. S. Department of the Interior, *Draft Technical Report: Historical and Genealogical Portions; Paucatuck Eastern Pequot Petitioners*, 4, hereafter cited as *PEP Draft Technical Report*).

18. The state does this through documentation known as the Lynch Report. The BAR and many independent scholars have thoroughly discred-ited the Lynch Report (formal technical assistance hearings notes, on file with author; *PEP Draft Technical Report*).

19. *PEP Draft Technical Report*.

20. Statement of Gilbert S. Raymond, appearing in the *Norwich Bulletin*, June 10, 1937, cited in *PEP Draft Technical Report*, 58–.

21. Grasso had a history of friendship with Connecticut's Indians; as a member of the U.S. House of Representatives, she kept records of Indian requests and problems, and was considered favorably disposed to resolving Indian issues (Grasso, meeting minutes, Connecticut State Archives).

22. Originally, the Golden Hill Paugussett Tribe, though state-recog-nized, was not afforded a seat on the CIAC; that oversight was rectified before the first official meeting of that body, by Public Act 74-168.

23. LeGault claimed Eastern Pequot heritage.

24. Testimony of Helen LeGault, March 23, 1961, before the state of Connecticut's general assembly (Joint Standing Committee, *Hearings on Public Welfare and Humane Institutions*, reprinted in *PEP Draft Technical Report*, 91).

25. The BIA found that Marlboro[ugh] Gardner was a whaler of Narragansett descent. His wife, Eunice (Wheeler) Gardner, was also of Narragansett ancestry. The Gardner-Wheeler-Potter family line was identified as Narragansett throughout the 1880s and early 1900s, at least. See *PEP Draft Technical Report*, 17–19. Eunice was married four times prior to her marriage to Marlboro[ugh] Gardner, and some of her children's descendants (through husbands Amos and Austin George) identify now as Western Pequot. Some of these George children married Sebastians, and are also Mashantucket Pequot tribal members. Elizabeth Plouffe George, the matriarch of the Mashantucket Pequot Tribe, was wife to one of the George brothers.

26. Though such issues of tribal sovereignty were at stake in the case, the Native American Rights Fund (NARF) declined to assist the Paucatuck Eastern Pequots in their litigation; the unresolved issue of Sebastian family membership precluded the NARF from being of any help subsequently, as well (*Summary under the Criteria and Evidence for Proposed Finding, Eastern Pequot Indians of Connecticut* [hereafter cited as *EP Summary Finding*] 151n124, citing February 5, 1986 letter from Richard Dauphinais [NARF attorney] to Raymond Greer).

27. *EP Summary Finding*, 151.

28. Ibid., 130, citing Cunha to Blumenthal, June 11, 1991; Cunha to Mullane, August 10, 1993; and Cunha to Reckord, August 10, 1993. The BAR staff did find that a birth certificate from 1917 had been altered, but since the person it affects is already an enrolled member of the Mashantucket Pequot Tribe, it is "unclear what advantages could be gained from the changes made on the certificate," and they appear inconsequential in the present acknowledgment case. The BAR staff also wrote, in the *EP Summary Finding*, 23, that there is no "data in the record to substantiate the allegation that EP had falsified the wedding and death certificates of Tamar (Brushell) Sebastian," though Cunha had made this claim to the press.

29. *PEP Draft Technical Report*, 137n183, citing the *Middletown Press*, August 26, 1989.

30. *PEP Draft Technical Report*, 138n184, citing Libby article from December 8, 1991.

31. *PEP Draft Technical Report*, 146, citing letter from Cunha to Babbitt, March 30,1996.

32. AS-IA Gover's February 2000 directive complicated the BAR staff's evaluation of PEP and EP claims. Under the directive, BAR staff members

were not permitted to complete work on the genealogical, anthropological, or historical technical reports; they were not able to analyze interviews or oral history data to evaluate the PEP or EP petitions for the presence of political leadership and continuity after 1960.

33. The magnitude of Gover's decision cannot be overstated. Although Gover's decision in the Paucatuck and Eastern Pequot cases *was* thought to be unprecedented at the time, it has been revealed, subsequent to Gover's leaving the BIA, that he also disregarded the BAR staff recommendations on the Nipmuc and Chinook Tribes. The Chinook had received a negative proposed finding in 1997, but successfully appealed the decision at the IBIA, after proving that the BAR staff had mislaid important documentation regarding their claims. Though the BAR staff did not recommend recognition for those two groups, Gover signed positive proposed findings in his final days in office. There have been subsequent reports that Gover took "payoffs" for this action; he vehemently denies this, and absolutely no evidence has come to light to suggest anything dishonest. Gover left the BIA when the Bush administration took office; he first worked for the Washington, D.C., law firm of Steptoe and Johnson, handling Indian litigation. One of his clients was the Chinook Tribe, which is still awaiting a Final Determination on their acknowledgment case. The Chinook have issued statements that they are not prioritizing gaming as an option for the Tribe; one faction of the Nipmuc Tribe has announced that it already has plans to open a Class III facility. See *Minneapolis Star Tribune,* "Government Recognizes Tribe."

34. DeMarce appeared exasperated through much of the hearings—by Connecticut's refusal to acknowledge the tribal status of pre-1960s Eastern (Paucatuck Pequots), and by Connecticut's claim that the tribes hadn't maintained social relations. At one point she said, "Generally, the assumption that we make is that people who marry each other maintain social relationships!" She was, as well, exasperated by Gover's thwarting of BAR recommendations and her subsequent need to defend his actions; exasperated that the two groups couldn't find common ground; exasperated even by the "no eating" rule, which she flouted each day with a bag of pecan sandies.

35. Those Sebastians who became Mashantucket Pequots include all of the descendants of one of Tamar's children, and some of the descendants of two others. The Narragansetts had already successfully defended their Indian identity against charges that intermarriage with blacks had made them less "Indian" and justified dissolution of the tribe (see U.S. Department of the Interior, *Proposed Finding . . . Narragansett,* 3).

36. Fromson, "Pequot Uprising."

37. Eisler, *Revenge of the Pequots.*

38. Fromson, "Pequot Uprising."

39. See Eisler, *Revenge of the Pequots;* Benedict, *Without Reservation;* and *EP Summary Finding* and *PEP Draft Technical Report* for details on Elizabeth George's racial attitudes in the 1940s and 1950s.

40. *EP Summary Finding,* 64nn96–97, citing *Williams Notebook,* ca. 1941.

41. I attended this workshop in 1998.

42. And, just as Helen LeGault had opposed any representation of the Sebastian side of the Eastern Pequot family on the CIAC, she also did much to discredit Moonface Bear to the committee. She not only attacked his racial identity, but she also accused him of "leading the Sebastian people in drug trafficking and homosexual activity" (minutes of the Connecticut Indian Affairs Commission, Connecticut State Archives).

43. I reached at that number, instead, an incredibly irritated man who said he'd been getting calls every day for the past few months; he told me that he'd never had an opinion on Golden Hill recognition one way or the other until now; now he hoped they lost, the calls had annoyed him so much.

44. The Golden Hill Tribe also holds the first, and smallest, state reservation on a quarter-acre of land in Trumbull, Conn. That reservation is uninhabited.

45. In late winter 2000, they traveled to the BIA, accompanied by *New York Times* reporter Sam Libby, and reviewed the file.

46. *Hartford (Conn.) Courant,* May 22, 1986.

47. Letter from Moonface Bear to the Connecticut Indian Affairs Commission, March 12, 1986 (Connecticut State Archives).

48. *Golden Hill Paugussett Tribe v. Weicker,* 837 F. Supp. 130 (1993).

49. Brooks, "Tribal Leader May Surrender."

50. Fox News, WTIC-TV, October 18, 1993.

51. He was only thirty-eight.

52. They received special permission from the Environmental Protection Agency to designate a burial plot in the residential area that holds the Colchester Reservation.

53. The doorman/bouncer asked for their tribal identification cards, with federal enrollment numbers. It is extremely rare for Indian participants in intertribal social events to be "carded," though rumors fly that some recently recognized tribes are abusing their privilege by asking for federal enrollment information at the gates of their powwows.

54. U.S. Department of the Interior, *Genealogical Technical Report: Golden Hill Paugussett Indian Tribe* (hereafter cited as *GHP Technical Report*); U.S. Department of the Interior, *Final Determination against Federal Acknowledgment of the Golden Hill Paugussett Tribe* (hereafter cited as *GHP Final Determination*).

55. *EP Summary Finding,* 122.

56. The Mowa Choctaws of Alabama are in a similar administrative, legal, and cultural situation.

57. Although an extended discussion of Mohegan politics, government, and gaming might be appropriate here, I have not endeavored to provide one. I did no field research on Mohegan land, in large part because I was unable to gain tribal permission to do so. I also decided, early in this project, to focus on one recognized tribe per state, in order to have a symmetry between the Alabama and Connecticut examples. Also of import, Mohegan recognition and gaming have been *much less* controversial than Pequot recognition and gaming.

58. Cornell et al., *American Indian Gaming*, 3.

59. The separation isn't always clear; for the Poarch, for instance, Eddie Tullis was tribal chair and the head of the corporation.

60. Kroft, "Wampum Wonderland," *60 Minutes*.

61. Castile, in "Indian Sign ," attributes this lack of clout to lack of "scale," or sheer numbers.

62. Martin, "Under His Authority."

63. Paul E. Peterson, "Politically Correct Solution."

64. Corntassel and Witmer, "Battlelines of Sovereignty," 13.

65. PACs have fewer restrictions than those that cover so-called soft money, or party contributions. They are limited to donating five thousand dollars per candidate, per election.

66. Sack, "Legalized Gambling Spreads."

67. Larrabee, "Pequots Wield the Power."

68. Drinkard, "Winning Combination."

69. The gaming industry has long been a significant contributor to congressional candidates and national parties; however, gambling-financed PACs gave three times as much money in 1993–94 as they had the previous two years. This growth is widely attributed to a combination of Indian-backed giving and donations by non-Indian enterprises hoping to receive some restrictions on the IGRA in exchange for their largess. The gaming PACs contributed $2 million that year, comparable to the United Automobile Workers ($2.4 million) and the National Rifle Association ($2.2 million). See Sack, "Legalized Gambling Spreads."

70. Fox News, WTIC-TV, March 20, 1997.

71. Larrabee ("Pequots Wield the Power) argues that this philanthropic gesture "was made at the suggestion of museum trustee Senator Daniel Inouye," the head of the Senate Indian Affairs Committee, and a good friend of Skip Hayward.

72. O'Brien, *American Indians*, 120.

73. Brosnan, "Indian Policy, Indian Gaming," 226.

74. Drinkard, "Winning Combination."

75. Brooks, "Gambling Means Wealth."

76. In *Revenge of the Pequots,* Eisler reports that President Clinton called the Pequots from the White House on at least one occasion; Skip Hayward was an occasional guest at White House activities, and, when in attendance at these functions, was always seated with the President, or in the front row when the president gave a speech.

77. Ibid.

78. The library holds more than thirty-five thousand titles that specialize in twentieth-century materials and span the histories and cultures of indigenous people in North America.

79. Kroft, "Wampum Wonderland," *60 Minutes.*

80. The MPMRC's mission states that the museum is "devoted to preserving and reclaiming the cultural heritage of the Mashantucket Pequot tribal Nation as well as preserving the histories and cultures of other Native North Americans" (MPMRC, "Our Legacy").

81. MPMRC, "Pequot Village" promotional brochures, 2000.

82. Kroft, "Wampum Wonderland," *60 Minutes.*

83. Ibid.

84. Eisler, *Revenge of the Pequots.*

85. Ibid.

86. Scott Simon, "Kickapoo Tribe," 1992.

87. Blumenthal, "Attorney General Files Brief Supporting Denial of Federal Recognition for Nipmuc Indians," October 1, 2002 (Indian Issues: Correspondence, Connecticut State Archives; http://www.cslib.org/attygenl/mainlnks/tabindez2htm).

88. Washington State Gambling Commission.

89. Ibid.

90. Blumenthal, "Statement of the Attorney General on BIA's Proposed Denial of Recognition for Schaghticokes," December 5, 2002 (Indian Issues: Correspondence, Connecticut State Archives; http://www.cslib.org/attygenl/mainlnks/tabindez2htm).

91. Blumenthal, "Attorney General's Statement Regarding BIA's Release of Strategic Plan to Improve Acknowledgment Process," October 3, 2002 (Indian Issues: Correspondence, Connecticut State Archives; http://www.cslib.org/attygenl/mainlnks/tabindez2htm).

92. Blumenthal, "Attorney General, Towns, Appeal BIA's Recognition of the Eastern Pequot Tribe," September 26, 2002 (Indian Issues: Correspondence, Connecticut State Archives; http://www.cslib.org/attygenl/mainlnks/tabindez2htm).

93. Blumenthal, Testimony.

## CONCLUSION

1. For an excellent discussion of the ideology of legalism, see Delaney, *Race, Place.*

2. U.S. Congress, *Reform Act of 2003.*

# Bibliography

ARCHIVES

*Mashantucket Pequot Museum and Research Center*

Clippings and Scrapbooks. Ser. 31., 1960–1998. Mashantucket Pequot Tribal Nation. Mashantucket Pequot Museum and Research Center (MPMRC) Archives.
*Pequot Times.* Ser. 30, 1992–1999. Mashantucket Pequot Tribal Nation. MPMRC Archives.
Schemitzun Materials. Ser. 16, 1993–1999. Mashantucket Pequot Tribal Nation. MPMRC Archives.

*State of Alabama*

Governor's Papers. Guy Hunt. Alabama Department of Archives and History.
Indian Affairs Commission Correspondence. Mrs. Mary Skipper. Alabama Department of Archives and History.
———. A. D. Price Folder. Alabama Department of Archives and History.
Special Collections/Private Records. Papers Concerning the Origins of the Mowa Band of Choctaw. Jacqueline A.Matte, Susan Greenbaum, Doris Brown, and Peter A. Rivers. Alabama Department of Archives and History.
Vertical File: Indians. City of Mobile Archives.

*State of Connecticut*

Connecticut Department of Welfare. Abraham Ribicoff. Connecticut State Archives.

Connecticut Governor's Papers. Ella Grasso. Connecticut State Archives.
Connecticut Indian Affairs Commission Correspondence. Connecticut State
    Archives.
Correspondence and Genealogy. Pequot Tribes. Connecticut State Archives.
Indian Issues: Correspondence. Richard Blumenthal. Connecticut State Archives.


## AUDIOVISUAL

Brooks, Anthony. "Gambling Means Wealth, Political Access for One Tribe."
    *All Things Considered,* National Public Radio, August 24, 1994.
————. "Paugussett Tribal Leader May Surrender to Authorities." *Morning
    Edition,* National Public Radio, October 21, 1993.
"Connecticut News." WVIT-TV, January 15, 1997.
"Cultural Celebration: Mashantucket Pequots Get Ready for Schimitzun."
    WTNH-TV, September 15, 1998.
Fernandez, Giselle. "Golden Hill Paugussett Indians Press Claim for Land
    and Gambling Rights." *Evening News,* CBS, August 8, 1993.
Fox News. WTIC-TV, October 18, 1993.
————. March 20, 1997.
Kroft, Steve. "Wampum Wonderland." *60 Minutes,* CBS, September 18, 1994.
Mashantucket Pequot Museum and Research Center. *Bringing the People
    Home.* Film, ca. 2000.
Randall, Gene, and Maria Hinojosa. "Casinos Become a Matter of Survival
    on the Mashantucket Pequot Reservation." CNN, June 16, 1999.
"Saturday Night Live 25th Anniversary Special." *Saturday Night Live.* NBC,
    September 25, 1999.
Simon, Ken. *The New Pequot: A Tribal Portrait.* Videocassette. Connecticut
    Public Television, 1988 (viewed at MPMRC, call no. 999).
Simon, Scott. "Kickapoo Tribe Seeks Casino Gambling." *Weekend Edition,*
    National Public Radio, July 11, 1992.
"The Son Also Draws." *The Family Guy.* Fox Television, May 5, 1999.
Wilder, Tandaleya, and Bob Edwards. "Native American Museum." *Morning
    Edition,* National Public Radio, August 11, 1998.


## BILLS

U.S. Congress. Senate. *American Indian Equal Justice Act of 1998.* S 1691.
    105th Cong., 2nd sess., 1998.
————. *Federal Acknowledgement Administrative Procedures Act of 1989.* S 611.
    101st Cong., 1st sess., 1989.

————. *Federal Acknowledgement Reform Act of 2003.* S 297. 108th Cong., 1st sess., 2003.

————. *Federal Recognition of the Lumbee Indian Tribe of North Carolina.* S 2672. 100th Cong., 2nd sess., 1988.

————. *Indian Federal Recognition Administrative Procedures Act of 1991.* S 1315. 102nd Cong., 1st sess., 1991.

————. *Indian Federal Recognition Administrative Procedures Act of 1995.* S.479. 104th Cong., 1st sess., 1995.


## CONGRESSIONAL HEARINGS

Blumenthal, Richard. Senate. Testimony before Committee on Indian Affairs. *Trial Recognition and Indian Bureau Enhancement Act of 2001: Hearings on S 1392 and S 1393.* 107th Cong., 2nd sess.

Ferdon, Dennis A. Senate. Testimony before Committee on Indian Affairs. *American Indian Equal Justice Act: Hearings on S 1691.* 105th Cong., 2nd sess., May 6, 1998.

Goren, Richard A. Senate. Testimony before Committee on Indian Affairs. *American Indian Equal Justice Act: Hearings on S 1691.* 105th Cong., 2nd sess., May 6, 1998.

Gover, Kevin (assistant secretary of Indian Affairs). Senate. Testimony before Committee on Indian Affairs. *Federal Acknowledgment Reform Act of 2003: Hearings on S 297.* 108th Cong., 2nd sess., April 21, 2004

————. *Indian Federal Recognition Administrative Procedures Act of 1999: Hearings on S 611.* 106th Cong., 2nd sess., May 24, 2000.

Grabowski, Christine Tracey. Senate. Testimony before Committee on Indian Affairs. *Indian Federal Recognition Administrative Procedures Act of 1999: Hearings on S 611.* 106th Cong., 2nd sess., May 24, 2000.

Halloran, Lawrence J. (counsel for the state of Connecticut). Senate. Testimony before Committee on Indian Affairs. *Mohegan Land Claim Settlement Act of 1994: Hearings on S2329.* 103rd Cong., 2nd sess., August 1, 1994.

Harris, Roland (chair, Mohegan Tribe). Senate. Testimony before Committee on Indian Affairs. *A Bill to Amend the Indian Gaming Regulatory Act: Hearings on S 1077.* 105th Cong., 1st sess., October 29, 1997.

Hayes, Patrick (acting deputy commissioner of Indian Affairs, Department of the Interior). House. Testimony before House Committee on Natural Resources, Office of Native American and Insular Affairs. *Indian Federal Recognition Administration Procedures Act of 1994: Hearings on HR 4462 and A Bill To Establish Administrative Procedures to Extend Federal Recognition to Certain Indian Groups: Hearings on HR 2549.* 103rd Cong., 2nd sess., July 22, 1994.

Johnson, Pedro (treasurer, Mashantucket Pequot Tribal Nation). Senate. Testimony before Committee on Indian Affairs. *Trial Sovereign Immunity.* 105th Cong., 2nd sess., May 6, 1998.

Jones, Stan (chair, Tulalip Tribe). House. Testimony before Natural Resources Sub-Committee on Native American Affairs. *Hearings on HR 2549 and HR 4462.* 103rd Cong., 2nd sess., July 22, 1994.

Locklear, Arlinda (lawyer on behalf of Miami Nation of Indiana). Senate. Testimony before Committee on Indian Affairs. *Indian Federal Recognition Administrative Procedures Act of 1999: S 611.* 106th Cong., 2nd sess., May 24, 2000.

Rasmussen, James (tribal councilman, Duwamish Indian Tribe). House. Testimony before Natural Resources Sub-Committee on Native American Affairs. *Hearings on HR 4462 and HR 2549.* 103rd Cong., 2nd sess., July 22, 1994.

Roybal, Louis (governor, Piro/Manso/Tiwa Indian Tribe; Pueblo of San Juan de Guadalupe; Las Cruces, N.Mex.). Senate. Testimony before Committee on Indian Affairs. *Indian Federal Recognition Administrative Procedures Act: Hearings on S 611.* 106th Cong., 2nd sess., May 24, 2000.

Shapard, John (former chief of the Branch of Acknowledgment and Research). House. Testimony before Natural Resources Sub-Committee on Native American Affairs. *Hearings on HR 2549 and HR 4462.* 103rd Cong., 2nd sess., July 22, 1994.

Shibles, Jill E. (tribal member, Penobscot Tribe; president, National American Indian Court Judges Association; chief judge, Mashantucket Pequot Tribal Court). Senate. Testimony before Committee on Indian Affairs. *Tribal Justice Issues.* 105th Cong., 2nd sess., June 3, 1998.

Sturges, Ralph W. (chief, Mohegan Nation of Connecticut). House. Testimony before Natural Resources Sub-Committee on Native American Affairs. *Mohegan Nation of Connecticut Land Claim Settlement Act of 1994: Hearings on HR 4653.* 103rd Cong., 2nd sess., June 30, 1994.

Tilden, Mark (staff counsel for Native American Rights Fund on behalf of Mashpee Wampanoag Indian Tribal Council, the United Houma Nation, the Shinnecock Indian Nation, the Pawmunkey Tribe, and the Miami Nation of Indiana). Senate. Testimony before Committee on Indian Affairs. *Indian Federal Recognition Administrative Procedures Act of 1999: Hearings on S 611.* 106th Cong., 2nd sess., May 24, 2000.

Trump, Donald. Senate. Testimony before Committee on Indian Affairs. *Proposed Changes to the Indian Gaming Regulatory Act.* 102nd Cong., 1st sess., March 18, 1992.

U. S. Congress. House. Committee on Interior and Insular Affairs. *To Establish Administrative Procedures to Extend Federal Recognition to Certain Indian Groups: Hearings on H.R. 3430,* 102nd Cong., 1st sess., September 15, 1992.

————. House. Subcommittee on Indian Affairs and Public Lands of the Committee on Interior and Insular Affairs. *Federal Recognition of Indian Tribes: Hearings on H.R. 13773 and H.R. 12996,* 88th Cong., 1st sess., August 10, 1978.

————. House. Subcommittee on Native American Affairs of the Committee on Natural Resources. *Federal Recognition of Indian Tribes: Hearings on H.R. 2549, H.R. 4462, and H.R. 4709,* 103rd Cong., 2nd sess., July 22, 1994.

————. Senate. Committee on Indian Affairs. *The Federal Recognition Administrative Procedures Act: To Provide for Administrative Procedures to Extend Federal Recognition to Certain Indian Groups; Hearings on S. 479,* 104th Cong., 1st sess., July 13, 1995.

————. Senate. Select Committee on Indian Affairs. *Federal Recognition of Certain Indian Tribes: Hearings on S. 661,* 87th Cong., 1st sess., September 27, 1977.

————. Senate. Select Committee on Indian Affairs. *Indian Federal Recognition Administrative Procedures Act of 1991: A Bill to Transfer Administrative Consideration of Applications for Federal Recognition of an Indian Tribe to an Independent Commission; Hearings on R.E. S. 1315,* 101st Cong., 1st sess., October 22, 1991.

Velky, Richard (Schaghticoke Tribal Nation). Senate. Testimony before Committee on Indian Affairs. *A Bill to Provide Administrative Procedures to Extend Federal Recognition to Certain Indian Groups: Hearings on S 611.* 106th Cong., 2nd sess., May 24, 2000.

## COURT CASES

*California v. Cabazon Band of Mission Indians,* 480 U.S. 202 (1987).

*Cherokee Nation v. Georgia,* 30 U.S. (5 Pet.) 1 (1831).

*Department of Game of Washington v. Puyallup Tribe,* 414 U.S. 44 (1973).

*Fletcher v. Peck,* 10 U.S. (6 Cranch) 87 (1810).

*Golden Hill Paugussett Tribe v. Weicker,* 837 F. Supp. 130 (1993).

*Johnson v. M'Intosh,* U.S. 21 (8 Wheat) (1823).

*Joint Tribal Council of Passamaquoddy v. Morton,* 528 F. 2nd 370 (1st Cir., 1975).

*Joseph v. United States,* 94 U.S. 614 (1876).

*Linton v. State,* 88 Ala. 216, Ala. State Supreme Court (1889).

*Mashantucket Pequot Tribe v. Connecticut,* 913 F. 2nd 1024 (1990).

*Mashpee v. New Seabury et al.,* 427 F. Supp. 899 (1978).

*Menominee Tribe of Indians v. United States,* 391 U.S. 404 (1968).

*Montoya v. United States,* 180 U.S. 261 (1901).

*Morton v. Mancari,* 417 U.S. 535 (1974).

*Puyallup Tribe v. Department of Game of Washington,* 391 U.S. 392 (1968).

*Puyallup Tribe v. Department of Game of Washington*, 422 U.S. 165 (1977).

*Samuel A. Worcester v. The State of Georgia*, 31 U.S. (6 Pet.) 515 (1832).

*Schaghticoke Tribe v. Kent School Corp*, 423 Fed. Supp. 780 (D. Conn., 1976).

*Seminole Tribe v. Butterworth*, 658 F. 2nd 310 (1981).

*Seminole Tribe of Florida v. Florida et al.*, 517 U.S. 44 (1996).

*Skeem v. United States*, 273 F. 93 (9th Cir., 1921).

*State v. Spears*, 15117 Supreme Court of Conn. (1995).

*Tee-Hit-Ton v. United States*, 348 U.S. 272 (1955).

*United States v. Candelaria*, 271 U.S. 432 (1926).

*United States v. John*, 437 U.S. 634 (1977).

*United States v. Joseph*, 94 U.S. 614 (1876).

*United States v. Kagama1*, 18 U.S. 375 (1886).

*United States v. Mazurie*, 95 U.S. 692 (1975).

*United States v. Sandoval*, 231 U.S. 28 (1913).

*United States v. Washington*, 384 F. Supp. 312 (1974).

*Western Pequot Tribe of Indians v. Holdridge Enterprises, Inc.*, Civil No. 76-193 (1976).

*Winters v. United States*, U.S. 207 (1908) 564.

## EXECUTIVE DOCUMENTS

Reagan, Ronald. "Veto of Mashantucket Pequot Indian Claims Settlement Bill" (S 366), *Weekly Compilation of Presidential Documents* 19, no. 503.Washington, D.C.: GPO, April 5, 1983.

U. S. Department of the Interior. Branch of Acknowledgment and Research. "Decision-Making Structure." Undated mimeograph.

———. "Formal Technical Assistance Meetings, Section 83.10." Undated mimeograph.

———. "Official Guidelines of the Federal Acknowledgment Regulations, 35 CFR 83." Undated mimeograph.

———. "Process." Undated mimeograph.

———. "Summary Conclusions under the Criteria (25 CFR 83.7 a–g), Proposed Finding against Recognition of the Ramapough Mountain Indians."

U.S. Department of the Interior. Bureau of Indian Affairs. *Anthropological Report: Mowa Choctaw of Alabama*, 1998.

———. *Anthropological Report: Poarch Band of Creek Indians*, 1983.

———. *Anthropological Technical Report: Golden Hill Paugussett Indian Tribe.*

———. "Brief Overview: Branch of Acknowledgment and Research." Undated mimeograph.

———. "Changes in the Internal Processing of Federal Acknowledgment Petitions." *Federal Register* 65, no. 29 (February 11, 2000): 7052–53.

————. *Draft Geneaological Report: Paucatuck Eastern Pequot,* February 2000.

————. *Draft Historical Report: Paucatuck Eastern Pequot,* February 2000.

————. *Draft Technical Report: Historical and Genealogical Portions; Eastern Pequot Petitioners,* February 2000.

————. *Draft Technical Report: Historical and Genealogical Portions; Paucatuck Eastern Pequot Petitioners,* February 14, 2000.

————. *Final Determination against Federal Acknowledgment of the Golden Hill Paugussett Tribe,* 1996.

————. *Final Determination against Recognition: Creek Nation East of the Mississippi,* 1981.

————. *Final Determination against Recognition of the Mowa Choctaw Band of Indians of Alabama,* 1999.

————. *Final Determination against Recognition of the Principal Creek Nation of Alabama,* 1985.

————. *Final Determination against Recognition of the Ramapough Mountain Indians of New Jersey,* 1998.

————. *Final Determination for Recognition of Poarch Band of Creek Indians,* 1984.

————. *Genealogical Report: Mowa Choctaw of Alabama,* 1999.

————. *Genealogical Report: Poarch Band of Creek Indians,* 1984.

————. *Genealogical Technical Report: Golden Hill Paugussett Indian Tribe,* 1995.

————. *Historical Report: Mowa Choctaw of Alabama,* 1999.

————. *Historical Report: Poarch Band of Creek Indians,* 1984.

————. *Historical Technical Report: Golden Hill Paugussett Indian Tribe,* 1995.

————. "Official Guidelines of the Federal Acknowledgment Regulations, 25 CFR 83," September 1997.

————. *Proposed Finding against the Recognition of the Mowa Choctaw Band of Indians of Alabama.* Undated mimeograph.

————. *Proposed Finding for Federal Acknowledgment of the Eastern Pequot Indians of Connecticut,* March 31, 2000.

————. *Proposed Finding for Federal Acknowledgment of the Narragansett Indian Tribe of Rhode Island,* 1983.

————. *Proposed Finding for Federal Acknowledgment of the Paucatuck Eastern Pequot Indians of Connecticut,* March 21, 2000.

————. *Proposed Finding for Federal Acknowledgement of the Paucatuck Eastern Pequot Indians of Connecticut,* March 31, 2000.

————. *Summary under the Criteria and Evidence for Proposed Finding, Eastern Pequot Indians of Connecticut,* May 24, 2000.

————. *Summary under the Criteria and Evidence for Proposed Finding for Federal Acknowledgment for the Snoqualmie,* 1999.

————. Office of Tribal Statistics. "Indian Labor Force Report: Portrait 1997." Washington, D.C.: GPO, 1998.

U.S. General Accounting Office. *Indian Issues: Basis for BIA's Tribal Recognition Decisions Not Always Clear.* GAO-02-49. Washington, D.C.: General Accounting Office, 2001.

————. *Indian Issues: Improvements Needed in Tribal Recognition Process.* GAO-02-49. Washington, D.C.: General Accounting Office, 2002.


STATUTES


*Alabama Indian Affairs Commission Administrative Code.* Chap. 475-X-3. "Procedures and Criteria for the Recognition of Indian Tribes, Bands, Groups and Associations." Codified June 30, 1995.

*General Allotment Act, or Dawes Act of 1887.* 25 USC (1982) secs. 331–81.

*Indian Arts and Crafts Act of 1990.* 25 USC sec. 305.

*Indian Child Welfare Act.* 25 USC (1902).

*Indian Citizenship Act.* 8 USC (1924) sec. 1401.

*Indian Civil Rights Act.* 25 USC sec. 1301(1).

*Indian Claims Commission Act of 1946.* Public Law 79-726, Stat. 60, 1049.

*Indian Economic Development Act.* 25 USC sec. 1452(c).

*Indian Health Care Act.* 25 USC sec. 1603(d).

*Indian Reorganization Act (Wheeler-Howard Act).* 48 Stat. 984 (1934).

*Indian Self-Determination and Education Assistance Act of 1975.* Public Law 93-638, Stat. 88 (1976), part 2, 2203–04.

*Klamath Restoration Act.* 100 Stat. 849 (1986).

*Maine Land Claims Settlement Act.* Public Law 96-420, Stat. 94, 1785 (codified 25 USC, 1721–35).

*Mashantucket Pequot Indian Claims Settlement Act of 1983.* 25 USC sec. 1751.

*Mashantucket Pequot Land Claims Settlement Act.* Public Law 98-134, 25 USC, 1751–60.

*Menominee Restoration Act.* Public Law 93-197, 25 USC (1973).

*Mohegan Nation of Connecticut Land Claims Settlement Act of 1994.* HR 4653.

*Native American Graves Protection and Repatriation Act.* 25 USC (1990) sec. 3001; 43 CFR, part 10, fully revised and updated, 1997.

*Paiute Restoration Act.* 94 Stat. 317 (1980).

*Public Law 280 Act of August 15, 1953.* Chap. 505, 67 Stat. 588–90 (now codified as 18 USC 1162, 28 USC 1360, and other scattered sections in 18 and 28 USC).

*Rhode Island Claims Settlement Act of 1978.* 94 Stat., 3498.

*Siletz Restoration Act.* 91 Stat. 1415 (1977).

*Termination Resolution.* H.R. Res. 108 (1953).

*Title 25 CFR Chapter 83.* "Procedures for Establishing That an American

Indian Group Exists as an Indian Tribe." Subsec. 7. "Mandatory Criterion for Federal Acknowledgment." *Federal Register.* Washington, D.C.: GPO.

*Trade and Intercourse Act of 1790.* 1 Stat. 137, Chap. 33.

*Trade and Intercourse Act of 1802.* 2 Stat. 139, Chap. 13.

*Trade and Intercourse Act of 1934.* 4 Stat. 729, Chap. 161.


## BOOKS AND ARTICLES


Ablon, Joan. "Relocated American Indians in the San Francisco Bay Area: Social Interaction and Indian Identity." *Human Organization* 23 (1962): 296–304.

Alabama Indian Affairs Commission. "Year of the American Indian in Alabama, 1998." Brochure.

Albers, Patricia C., and William R. James. "On the Dialectics of Ethnicity: To Be or Not to Be Santee (Sioux)." *Journal of Ethnic Studies* 14, no. 1 (1986): 1–29.

American Indian Policy Review Commission. *Final Report of the American Indian Policy Review Commission.* Washington, D.C.: GPO, 1977.

———. *Final Report: Report on Terminated and Non-Federally Recognized Indians (Task Force 10).* Washington, D.C.: GPO, 1976.

Anderson, Terry H. *The Movement and the Sixties: Protest in America from Greensboro to Wounded Knee.* New York: Oxford University Press, 1995.

Anderson, Terry Lee. *Sovereign Nations or Reservations? An Economic History of American Indians.* San Francisco: Pacific Research Institute for Public Policy, 1995.

*Atmore (Ala.) Advance.* "Construction of Spec. Building Is a Move Forward for Atmore," February 17, 1988.

———. "Creek Celebration Looks Like Biggest Yet," November 19, 1981.

———. "Creek Monies Being Questioned," December 27, 1984.

———. "Creek Nation Acquires Historic Lands," August 16, 1980.

———. "Creek Pow-wow Filled with Color, Food, Tradition," November 28, 1987.

———. "Creeks Awarded Federal Grant," July 31, 1995.

———. "Creeks: Not Just Bingo Anymore," March 10, 1991.

———. "Creeks Receive Grant," October 8, 1986.

———. "Dog Racing Taxes Total $5.5 Million in 9 Years," January 17, 1982.

———. "History of the Poarch Band of Creek Indians," January 14, 1985 (entire sec. B insert).

———. "Indian Bureau Issues Reminder," July 26, 1979.

———. "Mega-Bingo Underway for Creek Bingo," November 20, 1988.

———. "Planning and Development Helps Creeks Prepare for Future," April 15, 1990.

———. "Poarch Creeks Begin Sewing, Design Center," March 20, 1980.

———. "Poarch Creeks Buy Building, Woo Industry," June 7, 1987.

———. "Poarch Creeks Featured on ATP," July 15, 1987.

———. "Poarch Creeks Receive Grant," May 20, 1987.

———. "Poarch News," January 26, 1978.

———. "Poarch News," June 1, 1978.

———. "Poarch News," June 15, 1978.

———. "Poarch News," June 22, 1978.

———. "Poarch Plans Media Program," October 11, 1979.

———. "President Names Tullis," February 23, 1982.

———. "Property, Business Owners Celebrate Grant Award," October 23, 1988.

———. "Strader Manufacturing Purchased by Creeks," February 14, 1988.

———. "Thanksgiving Powwow Event Scheduled," November 16, 1978.

*Atmore (Ala.) News Journal.* "Shaw Praises Creeks," March 6, 1986.

Baker, Amy Brooke. "Shays May Amend Federal Law That Requires Pequot Casino in Ledyard." States News Service, May 7, 1991. www.lexisnexis.com.

Balu, Rekha. "Indian Identity: Who's Drawing the Boundaries?" Chicago: American Bar Association, 1995. *http://www.abanet.org/genpractice/lawyer/complete/f95identity.html.*

Barker, Emily. "Mapping New Territory for Native Americans." *American Lawyer* (November 1991).

Barlett, Donald L., and James B. Steele. "Look Who's Cashing In at Indian Casinos: Hint: It's Not the People Who Are Supposed to Benefit." *Time* 160, no. 25 (December 16, 2002).

Barsh, Russel Lawrence. "The Challenge of Indigenous Self-Determination." In Wunder, *Native American Sovereignty,* 143–78.

———. "Political Recognition: An Assessment of American Practice." Unpublished paper (on file with author).

Barsh, Russel Lawrence, and James Youngblood Henderson. *The Road: Indian Tribes and Political Liberty.* Berkeley: University of California Press, 1980.

Barth, Fredrik. *Ethnic Groups and Boundaries.* Boston: Little, Brown, 1969.

Bayes, Jane H. *Minority Politics and Ideologies in the United States.* Novato, Calif.: Chandler and Sharp, 1982.

Bee, Robert L. "To Get Something for the People: The Predicament of the Native American Leaders." *Human Organization* 38, no. 3 (1979): 239–47.

———. *The Politics of American Indian Policy.* Cambridge, Mass.: Schenkman, 1982.

———. "Politics of American Indian Policy." Presentation, Mashantucket Pequot Museum and Research Center, Ledyard, Conn., 1999 (notes on file with author).

———. "The Predicament of Native American Leader: A Second Look." *Human Organization* 49, no. 1 (1990): 56–63.

———. "Riding the Paper Tiger." In Castile and Bee, *State and Reservation*, 139–64.

Bee, Robert L., and Donald Gingerich. "Colonialism, Classes, and Ethnic Identity: Native Americans and the National Political Economy." *Studies in Comparative International Development* 12, no. 2 (1977): 70–94.

Beinart, Peter. "Lost Tribes: Native Americans and Government Anthropologists Feud over Indian Identity." *Lingua Franca*, May/June, 1999.

Benedict, Jeff. *Without Reservation: The Making of America's Most Powerful Indian Tribe and Foxwoods, the World's Largest Casino*. New York: Harper-Collins, 2000.

Benn, Alvin. "State Pow-Wow to Demonstrate Choctaw Identity." *(Citronelle, Ala.) Call-News Dispatch*, June 19, 1981.

Berkhofer, Robert F. *The White Man's Indian: Images of the American Indian from Columbus to the Present*. New York: Knopf, 1978.

Bernstein, Alison. *American Indians and World War II: Toward a New Era in Indian Affairs*. Norman: University of Oklahoma Press, 1991.

———. "A Mixed Record: The Political Enfranchisement of American Indian Women during the Indian New Deal." *Journal of the West* 23, no. 3 (July 1986).

Biolsi, Thomas. "The Birth of the Reservation: Making the Modern Individual among the Lakota." *American Ethnologist* 22, no. 1 (1995): 28–53.

———. *Organizing the Lakota: The Political Economy of the New Deal on the Pine Ridge and Rosebud Reservations*. Tucson: University of Arizona Press, 1992.

Blu, Karen I. *The Lumbee Problem: The Making of an American Indian People*. Cambridge: Cambridge University Press, 1980.

———. "'Reading Back' to Find Community: Lumbee Ethnohistory." In *North American Indian Anthropology*, edited by Raymond J. DeMallie and Alfonso Ortiz, 278–95. Norman: University of Oklahoma Press, 1994.

———. "Where Do You Stay At?" In *Senses of Place*, edited by Steven Feld and Keith H. Basso, 197–228. Santa Fe, N.Mex.: School of American Research Press, 1995.

*Boston Globe*. "Two Quit Foxwoods Gaming Panel: Tribe Probing Eavesdropping of Commission Employees," November 24, 1996.

Bourdieu, Pierre. *Outlining a Theory of Practice*. Cambridge: Cambridge University Press, 1977.

Brodeur, Paul. *Restitution: The Land Claims of the Mashpee, Passamaquoddy, and Penobscot Indians of New England*. Boston: Northeastern University Press, 1985.

Brophy, William A., and Sophie D. Aberle. *The Indian: America's Unfinished Business*. Norman: University of Oklahoma Press, 1966.

Brosnan, Dolores. "Indian Policy, Indian Gaming, and the Future of Tribal Economic Development." *American Review of Public Administration* 26, no. 2 (June 1996).

Brown, Barbara W., and James M. Rose. *Black Roots in Southeastern Connecticut, 1650–1900*. Detroit: Gale Research, 1980.

Brown, Mrs. Cecil. Letter to the editor. *(Citronelle, Ala.) Call-News Dispatch,* May 15, 1986.

Bruce, Louis. "The Bureau of Indian Affairs, 1972." In *Indian-White Relations: A Persistent Paradox,* edited by Jane F. Smith and Robert M. Kvasnicka, 242–50. Washington, D.C.: Howard University Press, 1976.

Bush, Alfred L., and Lee Clark Mitchell. *The Photograph and the American Indian.* Princeton: Princeton University Press, 1994.

Campisi, Jack. *The Mashpee Indians: Tribe on Trial.* Syracuse, N.Y.: Syracuse University Press, 1991.

———. "New England Tribes and Their Quest for Justice." In Hauptman and Wherry, *The Pequots in Southern New England,* 117–40.

———. "The Trade and Intercourse Acts: Land Claims on the Eastern Seaboard." In Sutton, *Irredeemable America,* 337–62.

Carelli, Richard. "Ruling Requires Connecticut to Negotiate with Indians on Gambling." Associated Press, April 21, 1991.

Carlson, Leonard A. *Indians and the Land: The Dawes Act and the Decline of Indian Farming.* Westport, Conn.: Greenwood University Press, 1981.

Carrillo, Jo. "Identity as Idiom: Mashpee Reconsidered." *Indiana Law Review* 28, no. 3 (1995): 511–47.

Castile, George Pierre. "The Commodification of Indian Identity." *American Anthropologist* 98, no. 4 (1996): 21–28.

———. "Federal Indian Policy and the Sustained Enclave." *Human Organization* 3, no. 3 (1994): 219–28.

———. "Indian Sign: Hegemony and Symbolism in Federal Indian Policy." In Castile and Bee, *State and Reservation,* 165–86.

———. "Native North Americans and the National Question." In *The Political Economy of North American Indians,* edited by John H. Moore, 270–87. Norman: University of Oklahoma Press, 1993.

Castile, George Pierre, and Robert L. Bee, eds. *State and Reservation: New Perspectives on Federal Indian Policy.* Tucson: University of Arizona Press, 1992.

*CBS Newsworld Online,* "Landless MicMac Sign Deal for Self-Government," May 19, 1999.

Champagne, Duane. "Organization Change and Conflict: A Case Study of the Bureau of Indian Affairs." In Letgers and Lyden, *Native Americans and Public Policy,* 33–62.

Churchill, Ward. "The Crucible of American Indian Identity: Native Tradition Versus Colonial Imposition in Postconquest North America." *American Indian Culture and Research Journal* 23, no. 1 (1999): 39–67.

———. *From a Native Son: Selected Essays on Indigenism, 1985–1995.* Boston: South End Press, 1996.

———. "Implications of Treaty Relationships between the United States and Various American Indian Nations." In Wunder, *Native American Sovereignty*, 81–96.

———. *Struggle for the Land: Indigenous Resistance to Genocide, Ecocide, and Expropriation in Contemporary North America.* Monroe, Wash.: Common Courage Press, 1993.

*(Citronelle, Ala.) Call-News Dispatch.* "Chief River Rat," September 23, 1982.

———. "Choctaw Indian Festival Begins Today at McIntosh," June 7, 1982.

———. "Choctaw Indians Slate 2nd Annual Pow-wow," June 11, 1981.

———. "Choctaw Tribal Elections Held," May 22, 1984.

———. "Governor Signs Indian Commission Bill Into Law," June 12, 1978.

———. "Hepatitis Outbreak," February 1, 1979.

———. "Hunger-Poverty Tour Slated in 2 Counties," September 6, 1979.

———. "Industries Plan 4.2 Billion Worth of Expansion in Alabama," March 4, 1982.

———. "Mowa Elect Tribal Council," May 10, 1984.

———. "Mowa Indians to Meet Sunday," January 10, 1990.

———. "Senate Passes Bill to Recognize Choctaws," October 8, 1992.

———. "Washington County Scalps Silas Indians," September 14, 1989.

———. "Youth Pow-wow This Weekend," March 13, 1986.

Clapp, John M., Dennis R. Heffley, Subhash C. Fay, John Vilasusa, and Arthur W. Wright. *The Economic Impacts of the Foxwoods High Stakes Bingo and Casino On New London County and Surrounding Areas.* Hartford, Conn.: Arthur W. Wright and Associates, 1993.

Clifford, James. *The Predicament of Culture: Twentieth-Century Ethnography, Literature, and Art.* Cambridge, Mass.: Harvard University Press, 1988.

Clines, Francis X. "The Pequots." *New York Times Magazine,* February 27, 1994.

Cohen, Fay G. *Treaties on Trial: The Continuing Controversy over Northwest Indian Fishing Rights.* Seattle: University of Washington Press, 1986.

Cohen, Felix. "The Erosion of Indian Rights, 1950–1953: A Case Study in Bureaucracy." *Yale Law Review* 62 (1953): 348–90.

———. *The Handbook of Federal Indian Law.* Washington, D.C.: GPO, 1942.

Colquitt, Ron. "Poarch Boss: Mowas Not Going by the Rules." *Mobile (Ala.) Press Register,* March 22, 1991.

*Connecticut Law Tribune.* "Native American Law," July 19, 1999.

Coombe, Rosemary J. "The Properties of Culture and the Politics of Possessing Identity: Native Claims in the Cultural Appropriation Controversy." *Canadian Journal of Law and Jurisprudence* 6, no. 2 (1991).

———. "Tactics of Appropriation and the Politics of Recognition in Late Modern Democracies." *Political Theory* 21, no. 3 (August 1993): 411–33.

Cornell, Stephen. *The Return of the Native: American Indian Political Resurgence.* New York: Oxford University Press, 1988.

Cornell, Stephen, and Joseph P. Kalt. "Pathways from Poverty: Development and Institution Building on American Indian Reservations"; http://www.ksg .harvard.edu/hpaied/docs/PRS89-5.pdf.

———, eds. *What Can Tribes Do? Strategies and Institutions in American Indian Economic Development.* Los Angeles: American Indian Studies Center, University of California, Los Angeles, 1992.

Cornell, Stephen, Joseph P. Kalt, Matthew Krepps, and Jonathan Taylor. *American Indian Gaming Policy and Its Socio-Economic Effects: A Report to the National Gambling Impact Study Commission.* Cambridge, Mass.: Economics Resource Group, 1998.

Corntassel, Jeff J., and Richard C. Witmer. "American Indian Tribal Government Support of Office-Seekers: Findings from the 1994 Election." *Social Science Journal* 34, no. 4 (1997): 511–25.

———. "Battlelines of Sovereignty: Forced Federalism and American Indian Mobilization in the 1990s." Paper presented at the annual meeting of the American Political Science Association, Marriott Wardman Park, Washington, D.C., August 31–September 3, 2000 (on file with author).

Cotterill, R. S. *The Southern Indians: The Story of the Civilized Tribes before Removal.* Norman: University of Oklahoma Press, 1954.

Covington, James W. *The Seminoles of Florida.* Gainesville: University of Florida Press, 1993.

Cowger, Thomas W. "The Crossroads of Destiny: The NCAI's Landmark Struggle to Thwart Coercive Termination." *American Indian Culture and Research Journal* 20, no. 4 (1996): 121–44.

Cox, Michael. "At Stake: Expanded Gaming Activities—Petition Opposes Gaming Expansion." *Atmore (Ala.) Advance,* March 10, 2001.

———. "Atmore Operates in Black for '89–'90." *Atmore (Ala.) Advance,* October 13, 1990.

———. "Creek Gaming Negotiations Are Confirmed." *Atmore (Ala.) Advance,* March 13, 1991.

———. "Creek Museum Planned." *Atmore (Ala.) Advance,* August 19, 1990.

———. "New Spec Buildings Planned for City." *Atmore (Ala.) Advance,* August 29, 1990.

Crazy Bull, Cheryl. "A Native Conversation about Research and Scholarship." *Tribal College: Journal of American Indian Higher Education* 9, no. 1 (Summer 1997):16–30.

Croner, Marie. "Echota Tribe Seeks Land Base." *St. Clair (Ala.) News-Aegis,* December 31, 1981.

Dahl, Dick. "The Gamble That Paid Off." *American Bar Association Journal* 81, no. 86 (1995).

Debo, Angie. *The Rise and Fall of the Choctaw Republic.* Norman: University of Oklahoma Press, 1961.

Deer, Ada. "Ada Deer (Menominee) Explains How Her People Overturned Termination, 1974." In *Major Problems in American Indian History: Documents and Essays,* edited by Albert L. Hurtado and Peter Iverson, 524–26. Lexington, Mass.: D. C. Heath, 1996.

———. "Tribal Sovereignty in the Twenty-First Century." *St. Thomas Law Review* 10 (1997): 17–24.

Delaney, David. *Race, Place and the Law: 1836–1948.* Austin: University of Texas Press, 1998.

Deloria, Vine, Jr. *American Indian Policy in the Twentieth Century.* Norman: University of Oklahoma Press, 1985.

———. *Behind the Trail of Broken Treaties: An Indian Declaration of Independence.* Austin: University of Texas Press, 1974.

———. *Custer Died for Your Sins: An Indian Manifesto.* New York: Macmillan, 1969.

———. *The Indian Reorganization Act: Congresses and Bills.* Norman: University of Oklahoma Press, 2000.

———. *Of Utmost Good Faith.* San Francisco: Straight Arrow Books, 1971.

———. *We Talk, You Listen: New Tribes, New Turf.* New York: Macmillan, 1970.

Deloria, Vine, Jr., and Raymond J. DeMallie, eds. *Documents of American Indian Diplomacy: Treaties, Agreements, and Conventions, 1775–1979.* Norman: University of Oklahoma Press, 1999.

Deloria, Vine, Jr., and Clifford Lytle. *The Nations Within: The Past and Future of American Indian Sovereignty.* New York: Pantheon Books, 1984.

Deloria, Vine, Jr., and David E. Wilkins. *Tribes, Treaties and Constitutional Tribulations.* Austin: University of Texas Press, 1999.

Dignam, Jim. "Decision on Nipmuc Recognition Postponed." *(Worcester, Mass.) Telegram and Gazette,* November 30, 2000.

Dippie, Brian. *The Vanishing American: White Attitudes and U.S. Indian Policy.* Lawrence: University of Kansas Press, 1991.

Donelson, Cathy. "Creeks Object to Mowa Recognition." *Mobile (Ala.) Press Register,* ca. 1991 (City of Mobile Archives; "Indians" vertical file [precise date obscured]).

Drinkard, Jim. "Casinos, Lobbying Are Winning Combination for Tribes." *USA Today,* February 12, 1998.

Drinnon, Richard. *Facing West: The Metaphysics of Indian-Hating and Empire-Building.* New York: Schocken, 1990.

Eadington, William R. "The Spread of Casinos and Their Role in Tourism Development." In Pearce and Butler, *Contemporary Issues*, 127–42.

Eisler, Kim Isaac. "Revenge of the Indians: Gambling Has Made the Once Poor Pequots Rich, and Other Tribes Are Getting In on the High-Stakes Casino Action. Double Down, Kemosabe?" *Washingtonian Magazine*, August 1993.

———. *Revenge of the Pequots: How a Small Native American Tribe Created the World's Most Profitable Casino*. New York: Simon and Schuster, 2000.

The Evans Group. *A Study of the Economic Impact of the Gaming Industry through 2005*. Evanston, Ill.: The Evans Group, 1996.

Faiman-Silva, Sandra. *Choctaws at the Crossroads: The Political Economy of Class and Culture in the Oklahoma Timber Region*. Lincoln: University of Nebraska Press, 1997.

———. "Decolonizing the Choctaw Nation: Choctaw Political Economy in the Twentieth Century." *American Indian and Culture Research Journal* 17, no. 2 (1993): 43–73.

Fanon, Frantz. *The Wretched of the Earth*. New York: Grove Press, 1968.

Farabee, Sherrie. "Creeks, Sheriff, Ink Agreement" *Atmore (Ala.) Advance*, January 28, 1987.

Field, A. Searle. Letter to the editor. *The Providence (R.I.) Journal-Bulletin*, February 9, 1997.

Field, Les, Alan Leventhal, Dolores Sanchez, and Rosemary Cambra. "A Contemporary Ohlone Tribal Revitalization Movement: A Perspective from the Muwekma Costanoan/Ohlone Tribe of the San Francisco Bay Area." *California History* 7, no. 16 (Fall 1992).

Fitzpatrick, Peter. *The Mythology of Modern Law*. New York: Routledge Press, 1992.

Fixico, Donald Lee. *Termination and Relocation: Federal Indian Policy, 1945–1960*. Albuquerque: University of New Mexico Press, 1986.

———. *The Urban Indian Experience in America*. Albuquerque : University of New Mexico Press, 2000.

Forbes, Jack. *Africans and Native Americans: The Language of Race and the Evolution of Red-Black Peoples*. Urbana: University of Illinois Press, 1983.

———. "Envelopment, Proletarianization and Inferiorization: Aspects of Colonialism's Impact upon Native Americans and Other People of Color in Eastern North America." *Journal of Ethnic Studies* 18, no. 4 (1980).

———. "The Manipulation of Race, Caste, and Identity: Classifying Afro-Americans, Native Americans and Red-Black People" *Journal of Ethnic Studies* 17, no. 4 (1990): 1–52.

———. *Native Americans and Nixon: Presidential Politics and Minority Self-Determination, 1969–1970*. Los Angeles: American Indian Studies Center, University of California, Los Angeles, 1982.

Ford, Christopher A. "Executive Prerogatives in Federal Indian Jurisprudence: The Constitutional Law of Tribal Recognition." *Denver University Law Review* 73, no. 1 (1995): 141–78.

Foreman, Grant. *Indian Removal: The Emigration of the Five Civilized Tribes of Indians.* Norman: University of Oklahoma Press, 1953.

Foster, Andrea. "Golden Hill Tribe to Wait up to Two Years for Uncle Sam's Approval." States News Service, April 7, 1994.

Friedman, Lawrence M. "Introduction: Nationalism, Identity, and Law." *Indiana Law Review* 28, no. 3 (1995): 503–11.

Fromm, Steven. "Wanted: Native Americans." *Connecticut Law Tribune* (July 7, 1997).

Fromson, Brett D. "The Pequot Uprising: How a Tiny Tribe Gambled and Won, Reclaiming the American Dream." *Washington Post,* June 21, 1998.

Gannon, Michael. "Pequot Spins Out, Eyes Fund Close." *Venture Capital Journal* (February 1, 1991).

Gibson, Mike. "Southwest Alabama Indians Have Unique Culture, Problems." *(Citronelle, Ala.) Call-News Dispatch,* November 27, 1980.

Goldberg, David Theo. *Racial Subjects: Writing on Race in America.* New York: Routledge Press, 1997

Goldberg-Ambrose, Carole. "Of Native Americans and Tribal Members: The Impact of Law on Indian Group Life." *Law & Society Review* 28 (1994).

Goldsmith, Adam. "Court Allows Pequots to Buy More Land." *Providence (R.I.) Journal-Bulletin,* September 27, 2000.

Gonzalez, Mario, and Elizabeth Cook-Lynn. *The Politics of Hallowed Ground: Wounded Knee and the Struggle for Indian Sovereignty.* Chicago: University of Illinois Press, 1999.

Gossett, Thomas F. *Race: The History of an Idea in America.* New York: Oxford University Press, 1997.

Gossman, Ginger Leigh. "Understanding Tribal Organization: How Does the Federal Recognition Process Affect a Native American Community?" Master's thesis, Department of Sociology and Anthropology, University of South Alabama, 1999.

Grabowski, Christine Tracey. "Coiled Intent: Federal Acknowledgment Policy and the Gay Head Wampanoags, Vols. 1 and 2." Ph.D. diss., City University of New York, 1994.

Green, Donald E., and Thomas V. Tonneson, eds. *American Indians: Social Justice and Public Policy Ethnicity and Public Policy, Volume 9.* Madison: University of Wisconsin Press, 1991.

Green, Michael D. *The Politics of Indian Removal: Creek Government and Society in Crisis.* Lincoln: University of Nebraska Press, 1982.

Greenbaum, Susan. "In Search of Lost Tribes: Anthropology and the Federal Acknowledgment Process." *Human Organization* 44, no. 4 (1985).

Greenfield, Lawrence K., and Steven K. Smith. *American Indians and Crime.* Washington, D.C.: GPO, February 1999.

Greenhouse, Carole J. "Constructive Approaches to Law, Culture, and Identity" *Law & Society Review* 28, no. 5 (1998): 1231–41.

Gunter, Dan. "The Technology of Tribalism: The Lemhi Indians, Federal Recognition, and the Creation of Tribal Identity." *Idaho Law Review* 35 (1998).

Hanson, Jeffery R. "Ethnicity and the Looking Glass: The Dialectics of National Indian Identity." *American Indian Quarterly* 21, no. 2 (1997).

Hardy, Jeff. "Shelby Plans to Battle For Mowa Recognition." *Mobile (Ala.) Press Register,* January 19, 1985.

Harvey, Sioux. "Two Models to Sovereignty: A Comparative History of the Mashantucket Pequot Tribal Nation and the Navajo Nation." *American Indian Culture and Research Journal* 20, no. 1 (1996): 147–94.

Hauptman, Laurence M., and James D. Wherry, eds.. *The Pequots in Southern New England: The Fall and Rise of an American Indian Nation.* Norman: University of Oklahoma Press, 1990.

Heffernan, A. E. "Creeks Stay on Warpath in Effort to Get Land Pay." *Mobile (Ala.) Press Register* (City of Mobile Archives, "Indians" vertical file, 1964 [precise date obscured]).

Henderson, Eric. "Indian Gaming: Social Consequences." *Arizona State Law Journal* 29, no. 1 (1997).

Henick, Arthur. "Tribal Nation Named Employer of the Year by Regional Chamber." *Pequot Times,* February 1999.

———. "Tribe's Economic Strategies Refined." *Pequot Times,* June 2000.

Horse, Billy Evans, and Luke E. Lassiter. "A Tribal Chair's Perspective on Inherent Sovereignty." *St. Thomas Law Review* 10 (1997): 79–86.

Hoxie, Frederick E. *A Final Promise: The Campaign to Assimilate the Indians, 1880–1920.* Cambridge: Cambridge University Press, 1989.

Jackson, Vicki C. "Seminole Tribe, the Eleventh Amendment, and the Potential Evisceration of *Ex Parte Young.*" *New York University Law Review* 72, no. 3 (June 1997).

Jaimes, M. Annette. *The State of Native America: Genocide, Colonization and Resistance.* Boston: South End Books, 1992.

Jansen, Anicca C. "American Indian Gaming Operations and Local Development." *Rural Development Perspectives* 10 (1995): 2–7.

Jansen-Verbeke, Myriam, and Els Lievois. "Heritage Resources in European Cities." In Pearce and Butler, *Contemporary Issues,* 81–107.

Jennings, Francis. "Conquest and Legal Fictions." *Oklahoma City University Law Review* 23, nos. 1, 2 (1998): 141–49.

———. *The Invasion of America: Indians, Colonialism and the Cant of Conquest.* New York: W. W. Norton, 1976.

Johansen, Bruce E. *Life and Death in Mohawk Country.* Golden, Colo.: North America Press, 1993.

———. "The Right to One's Own Home: The Seminole Chickee Sustains Despite County Codes." *Native Americas* 13, no. 3 (Fall 1996).

Johnson, Frank. "Mending a Broken Tribe." *Boston Globe,* May 30, 1989.

Johnson, Kirk. "Weicker to Veto Almost Any Expansion of Gambling." *New York Times,* February 28, 1992.

Johnson, Troy. *The Occupation of Alcatraz Island: Indian Self-Determination and the Rise of Indian Activism.* Urbana: University of Illinois Press, 1996.

Johnson, Troy, Joane Nagel, and Duane Champagne, eds. *American Activism: Alcatraz to the Longest Walk.* Chicago: University of Illinois Press, 1997.

Jolly, Brad. "The Indian Gaming Regulatory Act: The Unwavering Policy of Termination Continues."*Arizona State Law Journal* 29, no. 1 (1997).

Jones, Daniel P. "Unbroken Treaties: How a New Generation Got the Law on Its Side." *Hartford (Conn.) Courant,* May 23, 1994.

Josephy, Alvin. *Red Power: The American Indians' Fight for Freedom.* New York: American Heritage Press, 1971.

Josephy, Alvin, Joane Nagel, and Troy Johnson, eds. *Red Power: The American Indians' Fight for Freedom.* 2nd ed. Lincoln: University of Nebraska Press, 1999.

Kehoe, Alice B. "Primal Gaia: Primitivists and Plastic Medicine Men." In *The Invented Indian,* edited by James A. Clifton, 193–210. New Brunswick, N.J.: Transaction Books, 1990.

Kelly, Lawrence C. *The Assault on Assimilation: John Collier and the Origins of Indian Policy Reform.* Albuquerque: University of New Mexico Press, 1983.

Kersey, Harry A., Jr. *The Florida Seminoles and the New Deal, 1933–1934.* Boca Raton, Fla.: Atlantic University Press, 1989.

Kickingbird, Kirke, Lynn Kickingbird, Charles Chibitty, and Curtis Berkey. "Pamphlet on Self-Determination for the Indian Law Resource Center." 1977. Reprinted in Wunder, *Native American Sovereignty,* 1–65.

Kim, Jackie. "The Indian Federal Recognition Administrative Procedures Act of 1995: A Congressional Solution to an Administrative Morass." *Administrative Law Journal of the American University Washington College of Law* 9, no. 3 (1995): 899–935.

Kirksey, Hazel Jordan. "Black History Month Recalled." *(Citronelle, Ala.) Call-News Dispatch,* March 15, 1984.

Kirsch, Stuart. "Lost Tribes, Imaginary Indians, and Cultural Jurassic Parks: The Mashantucket Pequot Museum." Paper presented at the annual meeting of the American Anthropological Society, 1997 (on file with author).

Klas, James M., and Matthew S. Robinson. *Economic Benefits of Indian Gaming in the State of Minnesota.* Minneapolis: Marquette Advisors, 1997.

Krech, Shepard, III. *The Ecological Indian: Myth and History.* New York: W. W. Norton and Sons, 2000.

Kupperman, Karen Ordahl. *Settling with the Indians: The Meeting of English and Indian Cultures in America, 1580–1640.* Totowa, N.J.: Rowman and Littlefield, 1980.

Larrabee, John. "Pequots Wield the Power of Casino Wealth." *USA Today,* November 25, 1994.

LaVelle, John P. "The General Allotment Act 'Eligibility' Hoax: Distortions of Law, Policy, and History in Derogation of Indian Tribes," *Wicazo sa Review* 14, no. 1:251–302.

*(Ledyard, Conn.) Pequot Times.* "Contribution to the State," February 1999.

———. "Director Chosen For Capital Office," February 1999.

———. "National Youth Group Visits Rez," February 1999.

———. "New Police on Rez," February 1999.

———. "Reels Sworn In as Chairman," February 1999.

———. "Teens Revive Teen Council and Its Ideals, and Put Them to Work," February 1999.

———. March 2000, 12.

Letgers, Lyman, and Fremont J. Lyden, eds. *American Indian Policy: Self-Governance and Economic Development.* New York: Greenwood Press, 1994.

———. *Native Americans and Public Policy.* Pittsburgh: University of Pittsburgh Press, 1992.

Leuthold, Steven. *Indigenous Aesthetics: Native Art, Media, and Identity.* Austin: University of Texas Press, 1998.

Levitan, Sar A., and William B. Johnston. *Indian Giving: Federal Programs for Native Americans.* Baltimore: Johns Hopkins University Press, 1975.

Libby, Sam. "Tribe Seeks a Hastened Federal Status." *New York Times,* October 19, 1998, Connecticut sectional.

———. "A Tribute to the Quinnipiac Indians Who Served as Guides and Teachers." *New York Times,* January 2, 2000, Connecticut sectional.

———. "Who's an Indian? And Who Decides?" *New York Times,* January 14, 1996, Connecticut sectional.

Liberman, Ellen. "Connecticut Casino Neighbors Tell a Bleak Tale." *Providence (R.I.) Journal-Bulletin,* June 3, 1999.

Lightman, David, and Daniel P. Jones. "Day 3: Identity Crisis—When the Government Says a Tribe's Not a Tribe: Recognition; Tangled Path through Bureaucracy Can Lead Tribes to a Source of Renewal." With Hilary Waldman. *Hartford (Conn.) Courant,* May 24, 1994.

Lord, Peter B. "Six Flags Plan Moves Quietly Ahead." *Providence (R.I.) Journal-Bulletin,* September 16, 1997.

Lurie, Nancy Oestreich. "Menominee Termination from Reservation to Colony." *Human Organization* 31 (1972): 267–69.

————. "The Will-o'-the Wisp of Indian Unity." In *Currents in Anthropology: Essays in Honor of Sol Tax,* edited by Robert Hinshaw, 325–36. New York: Mouton, 1972.

Lyons, Oren. *Exiled in the Land of the Free: Democracy, Indian Nations, and the United States Constitution.* Santa Fe, N.Mex.: Clear Light, 1992.

Martin, Kaleen. "Under His Authority: Slade Gorton and the New Terminators in Congress." *Native Americas* 13, no. 4 (Winter 1996).

Mashantucket Pequot Museum and Research Center. "Discover a Nation in Southeastern Connecticut." Brochure, 1999.

————. "Museum Guide." Brochure, 1999.

————. "Our Legacy Is Yours: Mashantucket Pequot Museum and Research Center." Brochure, 1999.

Mason, W. Dale. *Indian Gaming: Tribal Sovereignty and American Politics.* Norman: University of Oklahoma Press, 2000.

Matte, Jacqueline. Fax-transmitted letter to Chief Taylor, regarding location of Choctaws for Trail of Tears marker, January 12, 1997 (provided by Chief Taylor; on file with author).

————. *Response of the Mowa Band of Choctaw Indians to the December 16, 1994 Proposed Finding.* Mt. Vernon: Mowa Choctaw, 1994.

————. *Response to the Proposed Finding against Acknowledgement of the Mowa Band of Choctaw.* Mt. Vernon: Mowa Choctaw, 1996.

Matthiessen, Peter. *In the Spirit of Crazy Horse.* New York: Viking Press, 1993.

May, Katja. *African Americans and Native Americans in the Creek and Cherokee Nations, 1830s to 1920s: Collision and Collusion.* New York: Garland, 1996.

McCool, Daniel. "Voting Behavior of American Indians in Arizona." *Social Science Journal* 19, no. 1 (1982): 1–113.

McCulloch, Anne Merline. "Issues in Identity among the Catawba." Paper presented at the annual meeting of the American Political Science Association, Marriott Wardman Park, Washington, D.C., August 31–September 3, 2000 (on file with author).

————. "The Politics of Indian Gaming: Tribe/State Relations and American Federalism." *Publius: The Journal of Federalism* 24 (Summer 1994).

McCulloch, Anne Merline, and David E. Wilkins. "Constructing Nations within States: The Quest for Federal Recognition by the Catawba and Lumbee Tribes." *American Indian Quarterly* 19, no. 3 (1995).

McDonnell, Janet. *The Dispossession of the American Indian, 1887–1934.* Bloomington: Indiana University Press, 1991.

McKee, Jesse O. "The Choctaw: Self-Determination and Socioeconomic Development." In *A Cultural Geography of North American Indians,* edited by Thomas E. Ross and Tyrel G. Moore, 173–90. Boulder, Colo: Westview Press, 1987.

McNickle, D'Arcy. *Native American Tribalism: Indian Survivals and Renewals.* New York: Oxford University Press, 1973.

Medcalf, Linda. *Law and Identity: Lawyers, Native Americans, and Legal Practices.* Beverly Hills: Sage, 1978

Medicine, Bea. "Native American Resistance to Integration: Contemporary Confrontations and Religious Revitalization." *Plains Anthropologist* (1981): 26–94.

Michel, Karen Lincoln. "Fielding New Clout: Indian Power and Party Politics" *Native Americas* 15, no. 3 (1998): 3–21.

Miller, Bruce. "After the F.A.P.: Tribal Reorganization after Federal Recognition." *Journal of Ethnic Studies* 17, no. 2 (1990).

*Minneapolis Star Tribune.* "Government Recognizes Tribe That Welcomed Lewis and Clark," January 4, 2001.

*Mobile (Ala.) Press Register.* "Shards of Choctaw," Four-part ser., November 26–December 25, 1984.

Mobile-Washington County Band of Choctaw Indians of South Alabama. "The Chata: Mowa Choctaw Newsletter." Mt. Vernon: Mowa Band of Choctaws, 1999–2000 ed.

————. *Response of the Mowa Band of Choctaw Indians to the December 16, 1994 Proposed Finding.* Mt. Vernon: Mowa Band of Choctaws, 1996.

Mohanty, Chandra Talpade. "Under Western Eyes: Feminist Scholarship and Colonial Discourses." *Feminist Review* 30 (Fall 1988): 65–88.

Montana, Cate. "Indian Community Opposes Washington State Republican Senator." *Indian Country Today,* December 24, 2000.

Morgan, Ted. *Wilderness at Dawn: The Settling of the North American Continent.* New York: Simon and Schuster, 1993.

Morris, Patrick C. "Termination by Accountants: The Reagan Indian Policy." In Letgers and Lyden, *Native Americans and Public Policy,* 63–84.

Murphy, Kim. "Campaign 2000: Native Americans Get in the Spirit of Political Empowerment; Elections: Tribes Nationwide Are Launching Get-Out-the-Vote Drives, Seeking to Raise Their Voice over Environmental and Other Issues Affecting Them." *Los Angeles Times,* November 21, 2000.

Murphy, Sean P. "Decision Day a Bust for Nipmuc Indians." *Boston Globe,* November 15, 2000.

Nagel, Joane. *American Indian Ethnic Renewal: Red Power and the Resurgence of Identity and Culture.* New York: Oxford University Press, 1996.

National Indian Gaming Association. *Fact Sheets and Folder.* Washington, D.C.: National Indian Gaming Association, 1999.

————. *Sharing in Community: 1999 Annual Report.* Washington, D.C.: National Indian Gaming Association, 2000.

Nelson, Dennis J., Howard L. Erickson, and Robert J. Langan. *Indian Gaming and Its Impact on Law Enforcement in Wisconsin.* Madison, Wis.: Attorney's Process and Investigation Services, 1996.

*New York Times.* "New Means for Recognizing Tribes Split Indians," July 29, 1992.

————. "Surprises in a Study of Life Expectancies," December 4, 1997.

Nolin, Robert. "Indian Tribe Waiting to Cash In on Land Tract." *Fort Lauderdale Sun-Sentinel,* January 4, 1996.

Norgren, Jill. *The Cherokee Cases: The Confrontation of Law and Politics.* New York: McGraw-Hill, 1996.

Novack, Steven J. "The Real Takeover of the BIA: The Preferential Hiring of Indians." *Journal of Economic History* 50, no. 3 (1991): 639–54.

Novak, Viveca, and Mark Thompson. "The Lost Tribe?" *Time* 155, no. 9 (May 6, 2000).

O'Brien, Sharon. *American Indian Tribal Governments.* Norman: University of Oklahoma Press, 1989.

————. "The Concept of Sovereignty." In Green and Tonneson, *American Indians,* 44–82.

Officer, James. "Termination as Federal Policy: An Overview." In *Indian Self-Rule: First-Hand Accounts of Indian-White Relations from Roosevelt to Reagan,* edited by Kenneth R. Philp, 114–28. Salt Lake City, Utah: Howe Brothers, 1986.

Ortiz, Alfonso. "Half a Century of Indian Administration: An Overview." In *American Indian Policy and Cultural Values: Conflict and Accommodation,* edited by Jennie R. Joe, 7–24. Los Angeles: American Indian Studies Center, University of California, Los Angeles, 1986.

Ortiz, Roxanne Dunbar. *Development in American Indian Reservations.* Native American Studies. Albuquerque: University of New Mexico Press, 1979.

————. *Indians and the Americas: Human Rights and Self-Determination.* New York: Praeger, 1984.

————. "Wounded Knee 1890 to Wounded Knee 1973: A Study in United States' Colonialism." *Journal of Ethnic Studies* 8, no. 2 (1980).

Owens, Louis. *Mixedblood Messages: Literature, Film, Family, Place.* Norman: University of Oklahoma Press, 1998.

Paredes, J. Anthony. "Federal Recognition and the Poarch Creek Indians." In *Indians of the Southeastern United States in the Late Twentieth Century,* edited by J. Anthony Paredes, 120–39. Tuscaloosa: University of Alabama Press, 1992.

————. "In Defense of NPS and BIA." *St. Thomas Law Review* 10, no. 1 (1996).

Paredes, J. Anthony, and Sandra K. Joos. "Economics, Optimism, and Community History: A Comparison of Rural Minnesotans and Eastern Creek Indians." *Human Organization* 39, no. 2 (1980).

Parloff, Roger. "Pequot Counsel Hits Jackpot." *American Lawyer* (June 1991).

Paschal, Rachael. "The Imprimatur of Recognition: American Indian Tribes and the Federal Acknowledgment Process." *Washington Law Review* 66, no. 1, (January 1991).

Patriquin, Ronni. "Firm Wants to 'Mess Up' Poarch Casino Plans." *Mobile (Ala.) Press Register,* May 10, 1994

Patton, Joe. "Another Celebration for the Poarch." *Atmore (Ala.) Advance,* October 15, 1982.

———. "Bingo Attracts Big Crowd." *Atmore (Ala.) Advance,* December 9, 1985.

———. "Creeks Building More." *Atmore (Ala.) Advance,* December 30, 1985.

———. "Creeks Forming Tribal Police Force, Drafting Codes for Lower Court System." *Atmore (Ala.) Advance,* July 17, 1985.

———. "Creeks Take Over Motel and Restaurant as New Tribal Enterprises Wednesday." *Atmore (Ala.) Advance,* December 30, 1985.

———. "Poarch Pow Wow."*Atmore (Ala.) Advance,* October 11, 1981.

Pavlik, Steve. *A Good Cherokee, a Good Anthropologist: Papers in Honor of Robert K. Thomas.* Los Angeles: American Indian Studies Center, University of California, Los Angeles, 1998.

Pearce, Douglas G., and Richard W. Butler. *Contemporary Issues in Tourism Development.* London: Routledge Press, 1999.

Peroff, Nicholas C. *Menominee DRUMS: Tribal Termination and Restoration, 1954–1974.* Norman: University of Oklahoma Press, 1982.

Perry, Richard J. *From Time Immemorial: Indigenous Peoples and the State Systems.* Austin: University of Texas Press, 1996.

Perry, Richard Warren. "The Logic of the Modern Nation-Sate and the Legal Construction of Native American Tribal Identity." *Indiana Law Review* 28, no. 3 (1995): 547–75.

Peterson, Geoff. "Native American Turnout in the 1990 and 1992 Elections." *American Indian Quarterly* 21, no. 2 (1997): 321–31.

Peterson, Paul E. *Classifying by Race.* Princeton: Princeton University Press, 1995.

Philp, Kenneth R. *Termination Revisited: American Indians on the Trail to Self-Determination, 1933–1953.* Lincoln: University of Nebraska Press, 1999.

Plane, Ann Marie. "Legitimacies, Indian Identities, and the Law: The Politics of Sex and the Creation of History in Colonial New England." *Law and Social Inquiry* 23 (1998): 55–75.

Pommersheim, Frank. *Braid of Feathers: American Indian Law and Contemporary Tribal Life.* Berkeley: University of California Press, 1995.

Porter, Frank W., III. "In Search of Recognition: Federal Indian Policy and the Landless Tribes of Western Washington." *American Indian Quarterly* 14, no. 2 (1990): 113–32.

———. "Without Reservations: Federal Indian Policy and the Landless Tribes of Washington." In Castile and Bee, *State and Reservation,* 110–36.

Porter, Robert. "Akwe:kon Forum: In Troubled Times a Vision of Nation Building." *Native Americas* 13, no. 4 (Winter 1996).

———. "The Demise of Ongwehoweh and the Rise of the Native Americans: Redressing the Genocidal Act of Forcing American Citizenship upon Indigenous Peoples." *Harvard Law Review* 15 (1999): 108–83.

Preston, Douglas. "The Lost Man." *New Yorker,* June 16, 1997.

Prucha, Francis Paul. *American Indian Policy in the Formative Years: The Indian Trade and Intercourse Acts, 1790–1834.* Cambridge, Mass: Harvard University Press, 1962.

———. *Documents of United States Indian Policy.* 3rd ed. Lincoln: University of Nebraska Press, 2000.

———. *The Great Father: The United States and the American Indians.* Lincoln: University of Nebraska Press, 1984.

Quinn, William W. "Federal Acknowledgment of American Indian Tribes: The Historical Development of a Legal Concept." *American Journal of Legal History* 34 (1990).

———. "The Southeast Syndrome: Notes on Indian Descendant Recruitment Organizations and Their Perceptions of Native American Culture." *American Indian Quarterly* 14, no. 2 (1990).

Radalet, Ana. "Congressmen Renew Push to Block Wetumpka Casino." *Montgomery (Ala.) Advertiser,* January 26, 2001.

Reed, Jewel. "Open Letter." *(Citronelle, Ala.) Call-News Dispatch,* February 20, 1986.

———. "The People Whom Time Forgot: A History of the Choctaws." Pts. 1–3. *(Citronelle, Ala.) Call-News Dispatch,* January 16, 1986; January 23, 1986; and January 30, 1986.

Reid, John Philip. *Law for the Elephant: Property and Social Behavior in the Overland Trail.* Santa Monica, Calif.: Huntington Library, 1980.

Resnik, Judith. "Dependent Sovereigns: Indian Tribes, States, and the Federal Courts." *University of Chicago Law Review* 56, no. 671(1989): 711–19.

Richter, Linda K. "Politics of Heritage Tourism Development." In Pearce and Butler, *Contemporary Issues,* 108–26.

Robbins, Rebecca L. "Self-Determination and Subordination: The Past, Present, and Future of American Indian Governance." In Wunder, *Native American Sovereignty,* 287–322.

Rollins, Peter C., and John E. O'Connor, eds. *Hollywood's Indian: The Portrayal of the Native American in Film.* Lexington: University Press of Kentucky, 1998.

Rosier, Paul C. "The Old System Is No Success: The Blackfeet Nation's Decision to Adopt the Indian Reorganization Act of 1934." *American Indian Culture and Research Journal* 23, no. 1(1999): 1–37.

Roth, George. "Overview of the Southeastern Tribes Today." In *Indians of the Southeastern United States in the Late Twentieth Century,* edited by J. Anthony Paredes. Tuscaloosa: University of Alabama Press, 1992.

Rountree, Helen C. "Ethnicity among the 'Citizen' Indians of Tidewater Virginia, 1800–1930." In Paredes, *Indians Of the Southeastern United States,* 9–28.

Rusco, Elmer R. *A Fateful Time: The Background andd Legislative History of the Indian Reorganization Act.* Reno, Nev.: University of Nevada Press, 2000.

Russell, Howard S. *Indian New England Before the Mayflower.* Hanover, N.H.: University Press of New England, 1980.

Sack, Kevin. "As Legalized Gambling Spreads, So Does Its Influence." *Austin (Tex.) American-Statesman,* December 21, 1995.

Sandefur, Gary D. "Economic Development and Employment Opportunities for American Indians." In Green and Tonneson, *American Indians,* 208–22.

Sands, David R. "Blue-Collar Votes Went Republican." *Washington Times,* April 18, 1999.

Scheffey, Thomas. "In House with the Indians." *Connecticut Law Tribune,* December 27, 1993.

Scogin, Johanna. "Accounting Department Sees Dramatic Growth." *Atmore (Ala.) Advance,* February 25, 1995.

———. "Creek Bingo Palace Brings 1000s from Southeast." *Atmore (Ala.) Advance,* January 25, 1985.

———. "Dancers Revive Creek Culture." *Atmore (Ala.) Advance,* February 25, 1990.

———. "Mushrooms Low-Cost, High-Yield Product." *Atmore (Ala.) Advance,* Feburary 25, 1990.

———. "Years of Work Pay Off for Poarch Creeks." *Atmore (Ala.) Advance,* February 25, 1990.

Scogin, Mike. "Atmore, Authority Recognized in Profiles in Rural Economic Development Report." *Atmore (Ala.) Advance,* May 4, 1988.

———. "Atmore, Escambia County Launch Advertising Campaign." *Atmore (Ala.) Advance,* October 4, 1987.

———. "Callahan Praises County." *Atmore (Ala.)Advance,* January 10, 1988.

———. "City's Financial Condition Improves." *Atmore (Ala.) Advance,* September 17, 1989.

———. "Court Ruling Favors Creek Indian Bingo." *Atmore (Ala.) Advance,* March 1, 1987.

———. "Creek Project in Planning Stage." *Atmore (Ala.) Advance,* February 13, 1987.

———. "Creeks Dedicate 1 Million Dollar Factory." *Atmore (Ala.) Advance,* April 5, 1987.

———. "Poarch Creeks to Open Tribal Complex Friday." *Atmore (Ala.) Advance,* April 1, 1987.

———. "The Top 10 of 1987." *Atmore (Ala.) Advance,* December 30, 1987.

———. "Tullis, Creeks Watch Gambling Legislation." *Atmore (Ala.) Advance,* February 13, 1987.

Shattuck, George C. *The Oneida Land Claims.* Syracuse, N.Y.: Syracuse University Press, 1991.

Sheffield, Gail K. *The Arbitrary Indian: The Indian Arts and Crafts Act of 1990.* Norman: University of Oklahoma Press, 1997.

Sider, Gerald. *Lumbee Indian Histories: Race, Ethnicity and Indian Identity in the Southern United States.* New York: Cambridge University Press, 1993.

———. "When Parrots Learn to Talk, and Why They Can't: Domination, Deception, and Self-Deception in Indian-White Relations." *Comparative Studies in Society and History* 29, no. 1 (January 1987).

Slagle, Allogan. "The Native American Tradition and Legal Status: Tolowa Tales and Tolowa Places." *Cultural Critique: Special Issue on the Nature and Context of Minority Discourse* 2, no. 7 (Fall 1987).

———. "Unfinished Justice: Completing the Restoration and Acknowledgment of California Indian Tribes." *American Indian Quarterly* 13, no. 4 (1989).

Snipp, Matthew. "Who Are Native Americans?" *Population Research and Policy Review* 5 (1986): 237–52.

Snyder, David. "Repeal Won't Halt All Casinos." *(New Orleans) Times-Picayune,* January 26, 1996.

Song, Elaine. "Into the Legal Wilderness." *Connecticut Law Tribune,* May 15, 1995.

———. "Limited Sovereignty." *Connecticut Law Tribune,* June 24, 1995.

Spilde, Katherine A. "Grassroots Support Gives Tribes Growing Political Clout." *International Gaming and Wagering Business* (April 2000): 12–13.

———. "Rich Indian Racism—Direct Attack on Tribal Sovereignty." *Hocak Worak* 5 (1999).

Starna, William. "The Southeast Syndrome: The Prior Restraint of a Non-Event." *American Indian Quarterly* 15, no. 1 (1991): 493–502.

State of Alabama. "Where Alabama Began: Washington County; First County in Alabama." Brochure, 1998.

Stewart, James Brewer. "The Emergence of Racial Modernity and the Rise of the White North, 1790–1840." *Journal of the Early Republic Spring* 18 (1998): 181–236.

Stuart, Paul H. "Financing Self-Determination: Federal Indian Expenditures, 1975–1988." *American Indian Culture and Research Journal* 14, no. 2 (1990): 1–18.

Sturtevant, William C. "Tribe and State in the Sixteenth and Twentieth Centuries." In *The Development of Political Organization in Native North America: The 1979 Proceedings of the American Ethnological Society,* edited by Elisabeth Tooker, 3–16. Washington, D.C.: American Ethnological Society, 1983.

Sullivan, Mark T. "After the Claims." *Yankee* 59 (July 1995): 46–57.

Sutton, Imre. *Irredeemable America: The Indians' Estate and Land Claims*. Albuquerque: University of New Mexico Press, 1985.

Taylor, Graham D. *The New Deal and American Indian Tribalism: The Administration of the Indian Reorganization Act, 1934–1945*. Lincoln: University of Nebraska Press, 1980.

Taylor, William B., and Franklin Pease, eds. *Violence, Resistance, and Survival in the Americas: Native Americans and the Legacy of Conquest*. Washington, D.C.: Smithsonian Institution Press, 1994.

Tomas, Lois. "A Look at Wannabe-ism." *Red Sticks Press* 1, no. 1 (June 30, 1994): 12.

Trennert, Robert A. *Alternative to Extinction: Federal Indian Policy and the Beginnings of the Reservation System, 1846–1851*. Philadelphia: Temple University Press, 1975.

Tsosie, Rebecca. "Negotiating Economic Survival: The Consent Principle and Tribal-State Compacts under the Indian Gaming Regulatory Act." *Arizona State Law Journal* 29, no. 25 (1997).

Utley, Robert M. *The Indian Frontier of the American West, 1846–1890*. Albuquerque: University of New Mexico Press, 1984.

Vest, Jason, and Ken Silverstien. "Trumps Gamble for Indian Wampum: The Self-Proclaimed 'Biggest Enemy of Indian Gambling' Has Suddenly Backed a Plan to Build Casinos on Seminole Land." *Village Voice*, July 7, 1998.

Vizenor, Gerald. *Cross Bloods: Bone Courts, Bingo, and Other Reports*. Minneapolis: University of Minnesota Press, 1990.

Waldman, Hilary. "New Life for a Forgotten People." *Hartford (Conn.) Courant*, May 22, 1994.

Walker, James C. Letter to the editor. *Atmore (Ala.) Advance*, March 13, 1991.

————. Letter to the editor. *Atmore (Ala.) Advance*, March 27, 1991.

Washburn, Wilcomb E. *The Assault on Tribalism: The General Allotment Law (Dawes Act) of 1887*. Philadelphia: Lippincott, 1975.

————, ed. *Handbook of North American Indians, Volume 4: History of Indian-White Relations*. Washington, D.C.: Smithsonian Institution Press, 1988.

Wearne, Philip. *Return of the Indian: Conquest and Revival in the Americas*. Philadelphia: Temple University Press, 1996.

Weeks, Philip. *Farewell My Nation: The American Indian and the United States, 1820–1890*. Arlington Heights, Ill.: H. Davidson, 1990.

Weibel-Orlando, Joan. *Indian Country, L.A.: Maintaining Ethnic Community in Complex Society*. Chicago: University of Illinois Press, 1991.

Weyler, Rex. *Blood of the Land: The Government and Corporate War against the American Indian Movement*. New York: Random House, 1982.

Wilkins, David E. *American Indian Sovereignty and the U.S. Supreme Court: The Masking of Justice*. Austin: University of Texas Press, 1997.

————."Breaking Into the Intergovernmental Matrix: The Lumbee Tribe's Efforts to Secure Federal Acknowledgment." *Publius: The Journal of Federalism* 23, no. 4 (1993): 123–43.

————. "Convoluted Essence: Indian Rights and the Federal Trust Doctrine." *Native Americas* 14, no. 1 (1997): 24–31.

————. "Reconsidering the Tribal-State Compact Process." *Policy Studies Journal* 22, no. 4 (1994): 474–88.

Wilkins, David E., and K. Tsianina Lomawaima. "Tribal-State Affairs: American States as 'Disclaiming' Sovereigns." *Publius: The Journal of Federalism* 28, no. 4 (1998): 55–77.

————. *Uneven Ground: American Indian Sovereignty and Federal Law.* Norman: University of Oklahoma Press, 2001.

Wilkinson, Charles F. *American Indians, Time, and the Law: Native Societies in a Modern Constitutional Democracy.* New Haven, Conn.: Yale University Press, 1987.

Williams, Robert A. *The American Indian in Western Legal Thought: The Discourses of Conquest.* New York: Oxford University Press, 1990.

Wunder, John R. *Native American Law and Colonialism, before 1776 to 1903.* New York: Garland, 1996.

————, ed. *Native American Sovereignty.* New York: Garland, 1996.

————. "No More Treaties: The Resolution of 1871 and the Alteration of Indian Rights to Their Homeland." In Wunder, *Native American Law,* 195–212.

————, ed. *Recent Legal Issues for American Indians, 1968–Present.* New York: Garland, 1996.

————. *Retained by the People: A History of American Indians and the Bill of Rights.* New York: Garland, 1994.

Zielbauer, Paul. "Study Finds Pequot Businesses Lift Economy." *New York Times,* November 28, 2000.

Zuckman, Jill. "House Drops Bid to Tax Indian Casino Profits." *Boston Globe,* June 14, 1997.

# Index